UNDER ARREST

Canadian Laws You Won't Believe

Bob Tarantino

Illustrations by Julia Bell

DUNDURN PRESS
TORONTO

Editor: Michael Carroll
Copyeditor: Jennifer Gallant
Design: Jennifer Scott
Printer: Webcom

Library and Archives Canada Cataloguing in Publication

Tarantino, Bob
        Under arrest : Canadian laws you won't believe / by Bob Tarantino.

Includes bibliographical references.
ISBN 978-1-55002-703-7

        1. Law—Canada—Miscellanea. 2. Law—Canada—History—Miscellanea. 3. Law—Social aspects—Canada—History—Miscellanea. 4. Law—Canada—Popular works. I. Title.

K184.7.C2T37 2007   349.7102   C2007-902049-6

1   2   3   4   5   11   10   09   08   07

Conseil des Arts
du Canada

Canada Council
for the Arts

ONTARIO ARTS COUNCIL
CONSEIL DES ARTS DE L'ONTARIO
an Ontario Government Agency | un organisme du gouvernement de l'Ontario

Canada

We acknowledge the support of the **Canada Council for the Arts** and the **Ontario Arts Council** for our publishing program. We also acknowledge the financial support of the **Government of Canada** through the **Book Publishing Industry Development Program** and **The Association for the Export of Canadian Books**, and the **Government of Ontario** through the **Ontario Book Publishers Tax Credit program**, and the **Ontario Media Development Corporation**.

Care has been taken to trace the ownership of copyright material used in this book. The author and the publisher welcome any information enabling them to rectify any references or credits in subsequent editions.

                                                                        J. Kirk Howard, President

Printed and bound in Canada.
Printed on recycled paper.

www.dundurn.com

Dundurn Press
3 Church Street, Suite 500
Toronto, Ontario, Canada
M5E 1M2

Gazelle Book Services Limited
White Cross Mills
High Town, Lancaster, England
LA1 4XS

Dundurn Press
2250 Military Road
Tonawanda, NY
U.S.A. 14150

UNDER ARREST

To my mother (for inspiration),
my sister (for guidance),
and my wife (for everything)

CONTENTS

ACKNOWLEDGEMENTS

There are a number of people without whom it can be said that the publication of this book would not have happened. In that regard, I wish to thank Jonathan Kay of the *National Post* for seeing the potential in the original *lex cetera* series of newspaper columns that formed the kernel of this book; James Bow for his encouragement and strategic indispensability in making contact with a publisher; Mike Filey for opening a door at The Dundurn Group; and Michael Carroll and Jennifer Gallant at Dundurn for their enthusiasm for the project and for their deft editorial hands. Large portions of this book would not have been possible without the dogged research abilities of Yvonne Parkhill — many of the sources relied on were obtained only with her assistance. Endless gratitude is owed to my spectacular wife, Heather, whose unflagging support for me and for this project was absolutely critical in its realization — neither piles of books, articles, and case decisions taking over the dining room nor my editing of draft chapters during our honeymoon managed to dissuade her, and for that I will remain eternally grateful.

INTRODUCTION

Did you know that it is illegal in Canada to sell a comic book that depicts the commission of a crime? That for decades it was illegal in some provinces for Chinese business owners to hire white females as employees? That sleepwalking can be a defence to murder? Or that putting a picture of a poppy on your website can get you in trouble with the Royal Canadian Legion? Many more somewhat startling aspects of Canadian law and legal history will be recounted by the end of this book. From criminal law to corporate cases and from copyright to comics, Canadians are blessed with a rich past and present of quirky statutes, odd (and sometimes harrowing) laws, as well as snicker- and cringe-inducing cases. What you hold in your hands is an attempt to cover some of the highlights.

Each chapter covers a discrete law or set of related laws (save for Chapter 5, which concerns laws so obscure that very little connects them other than the fact that they exist). While each chapter can be enjoyed on its own, the journey through the entire book will hopefully reveal certain recurring themes: the manner in which what we deem to be a crime punishable by law changes; the similarities in our efforts to grapple with changing social behaviour; the necessity for the law to respond to changing technology; and, above all, the intertwining strands of gravity and humour that permeate one of our society's most profound constructions — the law, with all its faults, foibles, and grandeur. Fundamentally, our criminal laws are an expression of what we determine to be the outer boundaries of permissible conduct, as well as a mechanism for maintaining control over mercurial human behaviour and managing emerging social phenomena. Not all, perhaps not even most, of the laws and legal history recounted in this book are especially humorous (wrenching chuckles out of the laws on murder or military tribunals is as difficult as it sounds), but everything has been selected with the goal of providing readers with access to parts of our legal tradition that they might not otherwise encounter.

Having used up your time explaining what this book *is*, I should point out in some detail what it is *not*. This is not a legal text, and none of the information contained herein should be construed as legal advice. Readers who find themselves in a situation (through whatever no doubt fascinating set of circumstances that would be required) involving the potential application of any of the laws or cases discussed in this book should consult a lawyer. The chapters that make up this book are also not intended to be definitive histories or comprehensive treatments of the subjects or themes; while a concern for accuracy has been paramount, considerations of space and reader interest have meant that some nuance has been glossed over. There are materials in the Recommended Further Reading section that will hopefully serve the purpose for readers desiring more comprehensive treatments of, say, the Canadian comic book industry between 1940 and 1960, or the Winnipeg General Strike of 1919. The surveys herein are meant to inform, entertain, and illuminate, not only by highlighting underappreciated aspects of our common social and legal history, but also by enabling readers to appreciate current events in a new light. Understanding the past remains the best guide for assessing the present — a maxim that applies to the law with perhaps even more relevance than to other aspects of our lives. An effort has been made to avoid the sometimes dry and plodding language of legal treatises and historical tomes — I remain convinced that both our history and our laws are fascinating, and this book aims to present stories and information in a manner that readers will enjoy.

Moving on from the pedantic disclaimers, a further bit of explanation may be required. Sometimes when I'm speaking to people about some of the more obscure laws discussed in this book the question arises: why don't they just change the law? We probably no longer *need* a law against practising witchcraft, so why not just get rid of it? Two concerns are inherent in the question being posed. The first relates to the danger, if any, of retaining obsolete laws on the books. Under the Canadian criminal justice system, considerable discretion is accorded

to police and Crown prosecutors in deciding which circumstances require police intervention and which offences require the laying of charges. In the vast majority of cases, this discretion is wisely exercised, with the finite resources of police officers and court time devoted to crimes that cause harm to innocent persons. But we must also construct laws with an eye towards ensuring that the unscrupulous or power-hungry cannot abuse the power to arrest, charge, and bring to trial to the detriment of the innocent. Changing political circumstances also mean that seemingly harmless provisions can suddenly take on a new (and dangerous) aspect. No one should ever be forced to face the psychological, emotional, and economic stress of being charged with "blasphemy," for example, even though a charge laid under such an archaic provision of the Criminal Code is unlikely to withstand the scrutiny of a judge under the Charter of Rights and Freedoms. With respect to some of the "crimes" discussed in this book, most reasonable people will probably agree that it shouldn't even be an *option* for you to be arrested or charged.

Which brings us to the second concern alluded to above: how do we go about actually *eliminating* some of these provisions and cleaning up our Criminal Code? The reason these crimes remain in the code decades after they have faded into anachronism is a function of the way our legislative system works. An act of Parliament must be passed in order to definitively remove these crimes from the Criminal Code and, frankly, the legislature probably has better things to do than to worry about crimes that haven't been prosecuted with any vigour since before television became widely available. (Of course, sometimes our honourable Members of Parliament will surprise us with exactly what they *do* think is worthy of their time.) Until a comprehensive modernization of the Criminal Code (or some of the other laws referred to herein) occurs, it is unlikely in the extreme that any of these provisions will be modified. There remains one other mechanism that could potentially be used to purge the code of unnecessary laws: a court decision ruling that the law in question is impermissible pursuant to the Charter of Rights and Freedoms, as happened in 1988 when the Supreme Court of Canada ruled that Section 287 of the Criminal Code, which made it a crime to perform an abortion, violated Section 7 of the Charter of Rights and Freedoms, and the law was declared to be of no force and effort across Canada.[1] The problem with relying on this approach was alluded to above: it requires someone to be the sacrificial lamb, if you will, who will endure the ignominy and headaches of being charged and standing trial, all in reliance on the hope that their lawyer properly raises and argues the Charter in their defence and that the judge will find in their favour. No one should have to go through that, nor should our police, prosecutors, and courts be bothered with the spectacle, all to do away with laws that no longer make sense in our current social and cultural context.

So until either of those eventualities occurs, we retain the laws in question. Of course, even were they to be discarded in the future, we would still have the pleasure of being able to reflect on the fact that they, and the cases that they spawned, are woven into the tapestry of our shared Canadian experience. It is sometimes the quirky thread in the tapestry that catches our eye and lends the piece its particular flair and originality: the following nine chapters trace some of the more eccentric strands that make up our past. Please enjoy.

1

Psst, Wanna Buy a Comic Book?

*T*he stark white beam of Bill's flashlight fitfully plays across the ceiling of the attic, showing the jumbled boxes and odds and ends that have accumulated over the years. He licks his lips. Where is the locked chest containing his stash? An excruciating creak echoes with his next step, and he freezes, feeling the sweat trickle down his spine — Bill can't let anyone know about what he has hidden away up here, and he prays his family hasn't been woken from their slumber. Not even Bill's wife knows about what he keeps up here, to say nothing of the kids or neighbours. How can he risk telling anyone? The punishment that potentially awaits someone who tries to sell what is in the chest is more than a law-abiding citizen like Bill can stomach: up to two years' imprisonment.

Finally, there it is! Under that old knitted blanket with the sunflowers that has been exiled up here by his wife. A jumble of shaking fingers, clanking keys, and rusty locks finally yield, and Bill slowly opens the heavy lid. He rests back onto his heels, eyes opening wide at the lurid images and words before him ... the four-colour covers of issues of Crime Reporter, The Vault of Horror, *and* Shock SuspenStories.

Crime comics. Illegal in Canada.

Sound far-fetched? Perhaps not as much as you might think. Section 163 of the Criminal Code[1] reads as follows:

163. (1)   Every one commits an offence who …

(b)   makes, prints, publishes, distributes, sells or has in his possession for the purpose of publication, distribution or circulation a crime comic.

(7)   In this section, "crime comic" means a magazine, periodical or book that exclusively or substantially comprises matter depicting pictorially

(a)   the commission of crimes, real or fictitious; or

(b)   events connected with the commission of crimes, real or fictitious, whether occurring before or after the commission of the crime.

These provisions, some of the last remaining artifacts of a post–Second World War concern with rising juvenile delinquency, were first enacted in the late 1940s and continued to draw parliamentary attention throughout the 1950s. Those familiar with Eisenhower-era American efforts to stamp out the scourge of "crime comics," which reached their apogee with hearings of the United States Senate in 1955 following the 1954 publication of Dr. Fredric Wertham's (in)famous book *Seduction of the Innocent,* may be surprised to learn that Canada was well in the vanguard when it came to dealing with crime comics: what would become known as the Fulton Bill was passed in Canada late in 1949, more than five years before our American neighbours began to act in earnest.

The crime comics provisions referenced above are found in a subsection of Part V of the Criminal Code entitled "Offences Tending to Corrupt Morals," which includes other crimes such as making child pornography and luring a child over the Internet. As North American society sought to reorient itself after the bloodshed and misery of the Second World War, parents, police, pundits, and legislators were alarmed by an increase in juvenile criminal activity.[2] Attempting to identify the catalyst for this rash of juvenile assaults, robberies, and murders, more and more they came to blame a series of publications that some regarded as virtual "how-to" manuals for delinquency. The title of Wertham's book evokes the prevailing belief of adult policymakers: impressionable and blameless young minds were being malignantly corrupted by exposure to compelling images of criminal exploits. Any question as to how to respond virtually answered itself: get the comics away from the children by throwing retailers and publishers in jail if necessary.

Of course, those concerned parents and educators who flipped through the five- and ten-cent illustrated periodicals that could be found clutched in seemingly every pair of preteen and teen hands could hardly be blamed for being shocked. Some of the publications, though consisting of panels of coloured figures, word balloons, and exaggerated sound effects, could hardly be described as innocently cartoonish: "In other pictures a woman is having her eye put out with a needle; a man having his face crashed in with a nailed boot; girls are about to be raped, in one case with a red-hot poker ... [a] page is devoted to a chart showing how a man can best be hurt by having his eyes gouged out, his temple or stomach kicked, his throat or nose smashed with suitable blows...."[3] The amiable and uplifting exploits of Superboy and his dog Krypto these were not.

By the late 1940s a concerted effort was underway by parents and educators (parent-teacher associations were particularly active proponents of the notion that something needed to be done by the government), and by 1948 their efforts had reached E. Davie Fulton, Progessive Conservative Member of Parliament for Kamloops, British Columbia (and one day to become minister of justice in John Diefenbaker's 1957 and 1958 cabinets). Fulton championed the cause, carrying it all the way to enactment by Parliament of amendments to the Criminal Code. The postwar reaction to comic books offers us one of the first, but certainly not the only, episodes of Canadian lawmakers attempting to come to grips with the social impact of a youth culture phenomenon.

Today the North American comic book industry (at least the dominant "mainstream" commercial aspects) is largely an American enterprise. The largest publishers, Marvel Comics, DC Comics, and Image, are centred in the United States, and though the books themselves are often printed in Canada, the corporate head offices and the artists and writers themselves are concentrated south of the border. In the middle of the past century, however, there existed a vibrant Canadian comic book industry that published dozens of titles and sold hundreds of thousands of copies a month.[4] The Canadian industry had blossomed largely as a result of a wartime ban on the importing of comics from the United States imposed in 1940. The government had instituted a ban on the importation of non-essential goods from the United States in an effort to combat the growing trade deficit with the Americans and conserve precious U.S. dollars, which were needed to purchase war *matériel*; because the import restrictions extended to "fiction periodicals," comics were caught behind the wall.[5] When the import ban was lifted shortly after the end of the war, the marketplace was flooded with American titles, the most popular of which contained the stories that were cited by the campaigners against crime comics. Canadian publishers, while largely content to import or reprint American content, also created titles that would qualify as crime comics, but the general consensus appears to be that, for Canadian boys and girls seeking the most thrilling and illicit tales of criminal depravity, it was to American publishers such as William M. Gaines's EC Comics that they turned.[6]

The public campaign that blossomed against crime comics was relatively widespread (voluntary associations to lobby the Canadian government were formed in various provinces, including British Columbia and Alberta), well-organized, and genuine in the concerns expressed about the deleterious effects that crime comics were having on youth.[7] The British Columbia Parent-Teacher Association began a mail campaign against the plague of crime comics that struck a chord with constituents of Davie Fulton, who in turn contacted their Member of Parliament. On June 3, 1948, Fulton, then sitting on the Opposition benches, challenged Minister of Justice James L. Ilsley on what the government proposed to do in light of the fact that in the city of Kamloops (population twelve thousand), nearly fifteen thousand copies of "crime comics" were being sold each month.[8] Reluctant to countenance a purported need to enact a new law, and troubled by how any such law could be properly worded so as to avoid undue censorship, Ilsley responded that existing laws could be relied on to prosecute those who published materials that "contribute[d] to juvenile delinquency."[9] Despite Ilsley's reluctance, however, even he was troubled by the comics in question: he concurred that crime comics constituted "a shocking instance of the abuse of freedom of the press."[10]

Within weeks, Fulton proposed an amendment to the Criminal Code that would make it an offence to publish or sell any magazine or periodical that exclusively or substantially consisted of material depicting the commission of a crime; Fulton's proposed language also added a qualification requiring that the material in question be "tending or likely to induce or influence youthful persons to violate the law or to corrupt the morals of such persons." Ilsley, as minister of justice, read the draft in Parliament but indicated that he had no intention of passing any such law. It was too vague, Ilsley argued, and he still hadn't been provided with any hard evidence that comic books were leading to an increase in criminal activity among the young. To the contrary, Ilsley indicated that he had communicated with mental health professionals, judges, and police officers who had stated that the comics were no more than vulgar trash, and certainly not the proximate cause of crimes.[11] Fulton countered with his own recollections of discussions with people who had experience in dealing with juvenile delinquents, and allowed that it was their considered opinion that the comics, with attractive pictures and easily understood prose captions, were purposely designed to "make the maximum impression on juvenile minds."[12] Ilsley protested that in the absence of evidence it would be imprudent to enact a new law that could circumscribe free speech — the mere theory that the comics in question may do some harm was insufficiently compelling to warrant restricting free expression.

Fulton persevered, however, and eventually his cause and the amendments he proposed became so identified with him that they were called the "Fulton Bill." Though the parliamentary sessions of 1948 concluded without his proposed amendment being enacted, Fulton spent the time between sittings of the legislature gathering evidence and rallying others to his banner. As 1948 turned to 1949, the Liberal political dynasty continued with the election of the government of Louis St. Laurent; Fulton remained consigned to the Opposition. Undaunted, Fulton forged on. In September of that year the amendment was reintroduced into Parliament and debates began in earnest, with members of all parties lending their efforts to the cause. The campaign in favour of the crime comic ban was in full swing: a number of newly elected MPs felt strongly enough about the issue (and were sufficiently convinced that doing so could reap rewards with their constituents back home) that they chose crime comics as the subject of their initial speech in the legislature.

An odd change in the dynamic of the debate had occurred since Fulton's first introduction of the amendment the prior year. The failure to meet the justice minister's demands for concrete evidence of the link between comics and crime had somehow transformed into a conviction on the part of many of the Fulton Bill's advocates that the link was so obvious it didn't need to be substantiated. As H.P. Cavers, Liberal

Member of Parliament for the Ontario riding of Lincoln, stated, "I think we can start with the premise that crime comics are detrimental to youth and have a bad influence [on their morals]."[13] The issue of causation was trumped by a compelling narrative of correlation: as Fulton had earlier stated in the legislature, while it was "difficult to prove that these magazines do actually increase juvenile delinquency ... one can say at least that ... there is an increase in juvenile delinquency and an increase in the circulation of this type of magazine in Canada."[14] Not much more was needed, apparently. Nevertheless, a litany of horrendous cases was cited as evidence of the onrushing wave of comic-fuelled crime: an eleven-year-old and a thirteen-year-old had been tried for murdering a man in Dawson Creek, British Columbia; in Montreal, a twelve-year-old had beaten his mother to death with a bat; in Philadelphia, a sixteen-year-old had murdered a friend with scissors; in Los Angeles, a fourteen-year-old had poisoned a fifty-year-old woman.[15] The common element in each case? The boys in question were avid readers of crime comics (up to fifty a week in the case of one of the Dawson Creek murderers) and had stated that they had derived inspiration for their homicidal impulses (and, in the case of the Los Angeles killing, even acquired the recipe for the poison) from their reading material.

The emotional appeal and rhetorical effectiveness of the anti-crime comic campaign proved decisive, and despite the initial reluctance of Minister of Justice Ilsley in 1948, under new Minister of Justice Stuart Garson the Fulton Bill passed third and final reading on December 5, 1949. Parliamentarians, perhaps in an attempt to forestall any potential criticism that they were inattentive to the problem of juvenile crime, voted unanimously in favour of the bill;[16] and so, with royal assent following shortly thereafter, what is now Section 163 of the Criminal Code became law.[17]

The Fulton Bill as enacted late in 1949 contained somewhat different language than what had originally been proposed in 1948. Most important, the qualifying language (which would have required that the comics in question be shown to be "likely to induce or influence youthful persons to violate the law") had been deleted. The effect of the deletion was to remove any need for inquiry into whether the comic book in question actually had (or even could have had) the purported effect of causing youth to commit crimes: all that was required to ground a charge was evidence that the comic book in question contained pictures depicting "the commission of crimes, real or fictitious." The language describing the crime was dictated by the realities of the market in which comic books were being sold and purchased in Canada. It was not a crime to *buy* a crime comic (presumably no one had the stomach for hauling nine-year-olds before magistrates for spending ten cents on the funnies); rather, it became a crime to publish or possess for the purposes of *distribution*. The intent was to cut off the supply of comic books at the source: namely, the publishers, distributors, and retailers. The law prohibiting the publication and sale of crime comics is an effort to prevent the decadent world of adult morals from infecting the innocent (if receptive) minds of the young.

Because the primary source for crime comics, namely American publishers, was effectively beyond the reach of Canadian laws, the focus of the law and subsequent prosecutions was going to rest with the businesses that sought, even in the absence of malevolent intentions, to bring the contraband materials to the nation's youth. Given the ulti-

mate source of the comic books, there was also a whiff, however faint, of cultural chauvinism at play: one Member of Parliament justified his support for the ban on the grounds that the American crime comics were un-Canadian and an impediment to the development of an indigenous Canadian culture.[18]

With the passing into law of the Fulton Bill, it became time for the identity of those patrolling the front line in the battle against corrupting influences to change from lobbyists and legislators to police and courts. In turning our attention to how the justice system viewed the matter, time should be taken for a brief description of how the decisions of judges are reported, a matter that will be relevant for many of the topics discussed in this book. The decisions handed down by judges in a large number (and prior to the advent of digital databases certainly the vast majority) of cases decided in Canada are not reported anywhere outside of the records maintained by the court. However, because the principle of *stare decisis* (i.e., that cases with similar facts should be decided in a similar manner; in other words, that the decisions in previous cases that are similar to yours should serve as a *precedent* for the decision in your case) is an integral part of our common law system, it is critical for lawyers and judges to have access to, if not all decisions, at least those decisions that serve as precedents or are considered important because, for example, they clarify a confusing area of law or enunciate a clear principle by which future cases should be decided. It is in order to provide the legal profession with a repository of important cases that case "reporters" are published: collections of written decisions, usually in bound journal format, often supplemented by various "key word" indexes to allow easy cataloguing and quick reference. Courts, professional societies, and various private enterprises have taken it upon themselves to cull the multitude of decisions issued by courts for those decisions that may prove of precedential worth; the shelves of the libraries in law schools and law firms groan with the weight of these collected volumes. It is to these reporters that we must turn to recall how the courts dealt with those who fell afoul of the crime comics ban. Because of the nature of the case reporting process it is not clear whether every case that dealt with crime comics is available to us — the records of some (or many) decisions may be languishing in courthouse archives. What *is* present in the reports and in the academic writings (especially the comprehensive work of Dr.

Janice Dickin McGinnis on the topic), however, provides a glimpse of how the Fulton Bill impacted Canada in the 1950s.

It is clear from the handful of reported decisions that the courts were somewhat ambivalent about punishing violations of the Fulton Bill. Though some cases made it all the way to the court of appeal, and prompted at least one chief justice to state that efforts to prosecute those who broke the law were a "matter of considerable importance to the citizens of this country,"[19] other cases were thrown out of court for technical improprieties on the part of the prosecutors.[20] Nevertheless, the federal government did not simply let the Fulton Bill fade into obscurity after 1949. As will be seen, the government responded forth-with throughout the 1950s to court decisions that either encouraged Parliament to expand the language of the ban or had the effect of mak-ing prosecutions more difficult.

Alberta News Ltd. found itself in court in July 1951,[21] charged for having "in its possession for distribution to news vendors a large quan-tity of magazines entitled 'Underworld Detective.'" The court observed that the magazine in question could be described as "lurid" and "sen-sational" and that it contained pictures "of persons involved in crime, suspects, prisoners, victims, corpses, witnesses and enforcement offi-cers." This first reported decision under the Fulton Bill encountered, however, a troubling definitional issue. Although the history of the Fulton Bill and the public campaign surrounding it were predicated upon protecting children from the influence of harmful images, the language of the Criminal Code provision made no distinction between magazines intended for children and magazines intended for adults. In fact, no mention whatsoever was made of children: it was just as much a crime to sell a magazine "depicting pictorially the commission of crimes" to a forty-two-year-old adult as to an eight-year-old child. The Calgary Police Court in Alberta News Ltd. was decidedly uncomfort-able with the case before it, because Underworld Detective, with its text-heavy layout and higher price (twenty-five cents), was "obviously pub-lished for adult consumption and not for children of tender age"; when dealing with comics, the court expected to be confronted with "Bugs Bunny, Roy Rogers [or] Buck Rogers" — not a magazine that contained "the same type of illustration ... often seen in reputable newspapers." The language of the Fulton Bill permitted no such fine distinctions, however. Obviously reluctant to sentence someone for selling a magazine clearly aimed at adults, the court rather creatively managed to side with its conscience. The original wording of the Fulton Bill stipulated that a "crime comic" was one that depicted "the commission of crimes, real or fictitious." But *Underworld Detective* didn't depict the actual *commission* of crimes; it only showed the *aftermath* or *investigation* of the crime. Charge dismissed.

Not to be outdone by clever defence lawyers relying on the precedent set by the *Alberta News Ltd.* decision, Parliament eventually amended the Criminal Code to add what is now subsection 163(7)(*b*), expanding the definition of "crime comic" to include the pictorial representations of "events connected with the commission of crimes, real or fictitious, *whether occurring before or after the commission of the crime.*" In the future, it would take more than merely shoving the *coup de grâce* off-panel to get away from the long arm of the law.

The Manitoba Court of Appeal, in the 1953 *R. v Roher* decision,[22] was decidedly more stern — the court noted that the matter before it was "definitely harmful to the children of this country," and Chief Justice McPherson hoped to assist other police magistrates and courts by clearly enunciating what constituted the basics of the crime comics offence. The broad wording of the Fulton Bill that had resulted in the adverse decision in *Alberta News Ltd.* resulted in some other odd cases ending up before the courts: even comics that ostensibly portrayed the virtues of obeying the law and sought to cast criminals in as unflattering a light as possible and that included traditional story resolutions showing the ultimate triumph of law and order over evil (by ending with the criminal enterprises shattered and the bad guys themselves dead or carted off to prison) could not pass muster under the legislation. In *Roher*, it was the venerable *Dick Tracy* title, describing the exploits of the relentless and upstanding police officer, which resulted in charges being laid. On appeal, after describing the comic in question virtually panel by panel ("the illustrations then revert to the previous murder and devote 5 panels to it"), the court upheld the conviction as well as the punishment of $5 or five days in jail — though the chief justice did add his "personal opinion" that fines were not the appropriate sentence for crimes of a commercial nature, since the fine would merely be passed along to consumers as a cost of doing business. More "just, appropriate and effective" would be "a term in gaol or penitentiary."

The *Roher* court also made mention of rumours that had reached its ears of a troubling development in the comics industry: tied selling, whereby distributors would refuse to provide *any* magazines to a retailer unless the retailer also accepted titles (including illicit crime comics) designated by the distributor. By this bit of strong-arming, even retailers who wanted to remain on the right side of the law by only stocking comics that were (in the court's words) "clean and proper" would be forced to be complicit in the ongoing corruption of the nation's youth. Parliament was listening and reacted to the difficulties in prosecution and the changing circumstances of the market. By 1959 a prohibition on tied selling had been added to the Criminal Code. By the beginning of the 1960s, the language describing the crime had stabilized to the form currently found in Section 163. Though some prosecutions in Ontario had been overturned on appeal on technical grounds,[23] stiff sentences were handed out in Quebec: three distributors were fined $1,000 each.[24]

Davie Fulton's efforts and the prosecutions under the new provisions of the Criminal Code didn't occur in a vacuum, of course. The late 1940s and early 1950s witnessed the enactment of a number of laws in various U.S. states, including Washington and California. (Each American state is empowered to enact its own criminal law, unlike in Canada, where legislating in respect of what constitutes a crime is a power reserved exclusively for the federal government.[25]) A number of appeal decisions in the United States resulted in the laws being overturned on constitutional grounds. But, in a theme that recurs throughout the histories examined in this book, the law and its enforcement are often simply a reflection of the currents and concerns reverberating through a society at a given time. The determined campaigns on both sides of the border led the comic book publishing industry to take proactive steps in an effort to avoid government regulation. A group of publishers banded together in 1948 to form the Association of Comics Magazine Publishers, which promulgated a voluntary "Comics Code" by which member publishers agreed to be bound; the code included prohibitions against depicting crimes in a manner that inspired "the desire for imitation" and forbade the representation of police, judges, government officials, and social institutions so as to "weaken respect for established authority."[26] However, the association would disband a few years later, with crime comics still largely flourishing.

A subtle shift in content was underway. Pure "crime" comics were being supplemented (though not supplanted) by "horror" comics, which included supernatural elements (such as werewolves and zombies) to amplify the tales of murder, kidnapping, and torture. Nor was the cultural concern limited to this side of the Atlantic: England enacted a ban on the publication of horror comics in 1955.[27] It wasn't until 1954, five years after Canada first enacted the prohibitions on crime comics, that the legislative and social efforts to ban crime comics truly began to bear fruit in the United States. The U.S. Senate Subcommittee to Investigate Juvenile Delinquency undertook a series of hearings (which included an appearance by E. Davie Fulton), and Fredric Wertham's *Seduction of the Innocent*, published the prior year, prompted a public outcry. Perhaps seeing the proverbial writing on the wall, the comics industry reconvened in the form of the Comics Magazine Association of America and set out a revised Comics Code to be policed by the Comics Code Authority, which highly circumscribed the manner in which "crime" and "horror" could be depicted.[28] The code proscribed such things as presenting the "details and methods of a crime," "unique or unusual methods of concealing weapons," and "scenes of brutal torture … [or] physical agony." "Sex perversion" or any inference thereof was strictly prohibited, and "in no case shall evil be presented alluringly." Even use of the word *crime* on the covers of comics was restricted.

More legal prohibitions were enacted in various U.S. states, and Canadian efforts to update and revise the Criminal Code language in order to react to unfavourable court decisions and the changing circumstances of the industry, as described above, continued apace. Regardless of the relatively small number of reported cases, we have an opportunity to assess the effectiveness of the legislative crime comic ban, which was simply one component of a battle waged on multiple fronts. Changes in cultural attitudes occurred, and faced with a rising tide of outrage, and doubtlessly "encouraged" by the passing of laws, publishers moderated the content of their output. As the calendar pages were turned from the 1950s to the 1960s, crime and horror comics, especially as compared to the dominance they had enjoyed over shelf racks in the early years of the decade, had effectively ceased to be published.

With the onset of the 1960s, prosecutions under the crime comics section appear to have entered into a fallow period. This was not, however, simply because the materials in question were no longer available, nor because the problem of juvenile crime had abated in the absence of the fell example offered by *Crime SuspenStories*. Alan Walker, later executive editor of *Maclean's*, commented that a popular publication that he edited in 1971, *The Great Canadian Comic Books*, contained "many scenes in flagrant violation of the Fulton law," and yet no one came knocking at the door of the publisher.[29] A number of other retrospective books were made widely available throughout the 1970s that reprinted in whole or in part selections from the very same crime comics that a decade or so earlier had prompted such consternation and even criminal convictions; no charges were laid in respect of these later books.

The threat alluded to in the introduction, that these nearly forgotten provisions of the Criminal Code could be exhumed and result in charges being laid in the modern era, was realized in the late 1980s in Calgary. In September 1987, ninety-two comics were seized from the Calgary store Comic Legends, and crime comics charges were laid.[30] Because the materials were sexually explicit, the charges were eventually changed to the distribution of obscene materials, and the store owner was convicted and fined.[31] The shift in public concern and lack of official sanction is indicative of the underlying societal currents at play.

We should avoid the temptation to view the Fulton Bill as an aberration. The concern over crime comics was neither a mania (the public campaign, the efforts to pass the legislation, and the subsequent prosecutions and appeals occupied the better part of a decade) nor the preserve of the unbalanced (attention and energy were given to the matter by some of the most learned and respected members of society, from teachers and police to judges and senators). Most salient is the fact that the same cycle of public outcry, legislation, and industry self-regulation echoes through to the present day. The parental impulse to protect children from harmful materials and activities is translated into a societal imperative, which is why we have laws that seek to protect the underaged from influences that may corrupt their morals. As a society, we have recognized that children are vulnerable and impressionable in a fashion that adults (generally) are not. The goals of protecting and shielding the young from adverse images did not end with the Fulton Bill, of course, and in addition to the retention of Section 163 of the Criminal Code, other devices have been put into place in an effort to protect children. The need for other devices has been driven by technological change: with all due respect to the comic book industry, a large part of the reason that few people today are concerned about the content of comic books is that so few children read them, certainly as compared to the cultural dominance they enjoyed decades ago. As other media have occupied the attention span of young people, the impulses that informed the Fulton Bill have resulted in other legislation and "content codes" that inform what is made available and easily accessible to children.

Television was the next mass medium to be made subject to the same dynamic that chased crime comics from magazine racks. The technological advances that resulted in the expansion of the television universe from a handful of broadcast networks to a plethora of over-the-air, cable, and pay-per-view channels also resulted in a multitude of programming options to fill the newly available broadcast real estate. With more time to fill, and with eyeballs now empowered to roam ever farther up the dial, a growing emphasis was placed on raunchier spectacle in an effort to attract and retain viewers. Concerns about violence and sexual content being available to children prompted public murmurings, and the television industry, perhaps hoping to pre-empt the matter from being ridden by politicians into a less-than-palatable legislative result, acting through the Canadian Association of Broadcasters (CAB), developed the Voluntary Code Regarding Violence in Television Programming (more commonly referred to as the CAB Violence Code), first adopted in 1987.[32] In the absence of industry self-regulation, broadcasters faced potential sanction from the Canadian Radio-television and Telecommunications Commission (CRTC), the independent government agency charged with oversight of the nation's airwaves. The CRTC has essentially delegated the policing of violent content to the Canadian Broadcast Standards Council, an arm of the CAB, which administers, among other things, complaints about violations of the Violence Code. Some of the language in the Violence Code would be familiar to those who argued in favour of the passage and enforcement of the Fulton Bill a generation earlier. The section dealing with "Children's Programming" (meant to apply to those under the age of twelve) stresses the need to avoid images that can "invite children to imitate acts which they see on screen." Programming that "glamourizes" violence is also strictly prohibited, and scenes of violence intended for adults are restricted to broadcast after nine o'clock in the evening. The faintest whiff of the didactic unease that animated the Fulton Bill can be detected: if the kids weren't being exposed to this stuff in their leisure activities, they wouldn't be committing crimes on the streets.

Nearly twenty years after the CAB Violence Code was adopted, the recreation habits of children evolved yet again, and an even more exact parallel with the crime comics era unfolded.

It is a peculiarly grim scene: armed with high-calibre weapons, an apparent sociopath has blasted his way through a suburban neighbourhood, leaving in his bloody wake a trail of broken bodies — men, women, the elderly, police officers…. The smoking ruins of exploded cars lie in the distance, and the air echoes with the hollow clacks of guns being reloaded.

But as you survey the wreckage, some things seem out of place: in the background plays an omnipresent soundtrack of heavy metal riffs and techno drumbeats, and everything you see seems oddly … pixelated.

Because you're looking at a video game.

And, if you are under the age of eighteen, the person who sold or rented that game to you may have committed a crime.

In the early years of the new millennium, the governments of Ontario, Nova Scotia, and Manitoba responded to a public outcry over the shocking images found in unapologetically hyper-violent and realistic video games such as *Grand Theft Auto* and *Manhunt*.[33] Ontario's Film Classification Act, 2005, contains regulations that make it a crime to sell, rent, or even exhibit certain video games to persons under eighteen years of age.[34] The video game industry, having learned its lessons from its entertainment industry forebears, had created the Entertainment Software Rating Board (ESRB), which administers a classification system somewhat similar to that for motion pictures, indicating age suitability and content descriptors that give more detail about the product in terms of violence, sexual themes, and strong language. Under the legislation, the Ontario Film Review Board reserves the power to classify titles made by publishers whose games are not reviewed by the ESRB. Like the Fulton Bill, the Film Classification Act places legal responsibility with the retailers: video games that are classified as "Mature" may not be sold, rented, or exhibited to a person under the age of seventeen, and video games that are classified as "Adults Only" may not be sold, rented, or exhibited to a person under the age of eighteen. What is listed among the characteristics that will cause a video game to be classified in one of the two restricted categories? The "graphic depiction of violence involving … criminal activity."

The history of the crime comics ban traces a narrative arc that is instructive on a number of levels, but one facet that should be stressed is that our laws should not be simplistically viewed as pillars that define the parameters of acceptable conduct in our society. Rather, "the law" is profitably viewed as one vector of the expression of our society and our culture: what the law means and what the law consists of is constantly in flux, and "the law," being entirely a construction of human activity, is a reflection of the concerns and passions that animate a particular moment in time. Only the postwar era of the 1940s and 1950s, with its dominant print-based mass media, the emergence of the leading wave of the baby boom generation, and the need to reassert and rely on central moral authority after the privation of the war years, could have produced the crime comics ban. But that should not be taken as the passing of judgment on the initiative, or at least we cannot do so on the basis that we have moved beyond the expression of simple pieties. As the regulations that back up the authority of the ESRB show, we haven't lost any of our desire or need to regulate what our children consume. The Fulton Bill didn't end crime comics, any more than the Film Classification Act will end violent video games: the manifold pressures of parental concern, legal sanction, technological change, shifting cultural tastes, and the exhaustion of an artistic form all did and will play their part. Youth violence and the resultant efforts to combat it aren't new, but what has changed is the media through which popular youth culture is disseminated, and this in turn informs the legal response. None of which is to say that these are matters to be treated lightly, but one can hope that the efficacy (or lack thereof) of previous efforts to address the source of the problem — be they "funny books," mid-afternoon movies, or kinetic first-person shoot 'em ups — will inform future efforts.

2

A Gun Fight at High Noon?
Too Uncivilized

The Duel

In the summer of 2005, many people bopped along to Gwen Stefani's hit song "Hollaback Girl." Many more listeners pondered, "Just what is that song *about?*" While the tune is propulsively catchy, the lyrics can be, at best, oblique (the chorus consists largely of Stefani chanting "I ain't no hollaback girl"). Peter Wood, writing at *National Review Online*, offered one of the better explanations: to deny being a "hollaback girl" is to say "I don't just return insults with words. I step it up."

In short, wrote Wood: "Pistols at dawn."

In its goofily charming way, perhaps Stefani's anthem is meant to provide the braggadocio-drenched soundtrack to that after-school ritual also beloved of nineteenth-century petty nobility: the duel. Those prompted to unleash their inner gladiator may wish to restrain themselves. Everyone should know that fighting is against the law, but few appreciate just how comprehensive the legal prohibition is: excluding licensed sporting events that require official sanction, even mutually agreed-upon fights are prohibited.

Section 71 of the Criminal Code reads as follows:

> 71.   Every one who
>
> (*a*) challenges or attempts by any means to provoke another person to fight a duel,
>
> (*b*) attempts to provoke a person to challenge another person to fight a duel, or

(*c*) accepts a challenge to fight a duel, is guilty
of an indictable offence and liable to imprisonment for a term not exceeding two years.

The language prohibits most aspects of duelling: you are not permitted to challenge someone to duel, nor to accept a challenge, nor
even to attempt to provoke someone into challenging a third person
to a duel. So broad is the prohibition that no duel actually needs to
take place in order for a crime to have occurred. Interestingly, the duel
itself is not a crime; it is only the events leading up to the duel that are
prohibited. It should also be noted that the section is worded in a manner that in later years and in a different context would be referred to as
"technology neutral": the *substance* of the proposed duel doesn't matter,
whether conducted with guns, knives, baseball bats, or fists — what is
deemed unacceptable is the *form* of agreeing to engage in premeditated

violence. Though we have been conditioned to view the artifice of the formal duel (the challenge issued by men wearing starched waist-coats for a perceived insult to honour; the early-morning meeting with long-barrelled pistols of an antique vintage; stiff back to stiff back as the combatants begin to walk their allotted twenty paces) as a quaint anachronism, the presence of Section 71 in the Criminal Code reflects the fact that duelling was once a matter of (deadly) serious concern.

At least a dozen Canadians were killed in formal duels.[1] Hugh A. Halliday, in his definitive history of Canadian duels,[2] describes them as an affectation adopted by provincial elites, far from the centres of imperial power, in an effort to assert their primacy in the face of official prohibition. While the fights of less-moneyed individuals usually brought punishment by the criminal justice apparatus, duel participants often escaped meaningful sanction, largely because of their elevated social standing in the community. To heighten the irony, lawyers were disproportionately represented among duellists: not only did a treasurer of the Law Society of Upper Canada (i.e., the most senior officer of the body that governs lawyers in what is now Ontario) fight a duel with the attorney general of the province, the first attorney general of Upper Canada had been killed in an earlier duel (by the clerk of the Executive Council, no less).[3]

A number of historically prominent Canadians were involved in duels, and their stories offer some insight into the sort of squabble or affront to honour that could quickly turn deadly. George-Étienne Cartier, later to be a Father of Confederation, was involved in the Rebellion of 1837, more particularly in the initial skirmish of that episode at St. Denis, Quebec.[4] Cartier and his fellows, armed only with firearms, had managed to successfully hold off and then overcome British forces armed with cannon. Eleven years later, a newspaper published by political opponents of Cartier printed a letter that accused him of absconding from the scene of the fighting at St. Denis. Telling his comrades he was going to retrieve ammunition, Cartier had supposedly escaped the heat of battle, returning only once the firing had stopped and the British had been repulsed. In other words, he had acted with cowardice on the battlefield.

Enraged, Cartier challenged the twenty-three-year-old editor of the newspaper to a duel, which was scheduled to take place on Mount Royal. In accordance with custom, both men were accompanied by seconds and made preparations to duel with pistols. Cartier's brother, however, had notified the constabulary, who interrupted the men before shots could be fired. The two would-be combatants were charged with disturbing the peace and tried before a magistrate but let off with a warning. Evidently not having learned that the wrath of George-Étienne was not to be taken lightly, the editor and his friends shortly thereafter planted stories that Cartier himself had arranged for the interruption to the duel, perhaps concerned that the younger man would better him. A new duel was scheduled — this time shots were fired, but both missed the other. After a second round of gunfire and still no casualties, the seconds put an end to the affair. Left unsatisfied, Cartier and the editor remained enemies, though no further clashes occurred.[5]

The Jarvis family, a prominent early Canadian family after whom Toronto's Jarvis Street is named, also had a history punctuated by duels. William Jarvis challenged no less than four men to duels in 1795 in response to accusations that William had written a scandalous satire of some prominent Upper Canadian families. Evidently, only one of the challenges resulted in a duel, but no report of injuries survives. A little over twenty years later, William's son, Samuel Peters, would be involved in a deadly duel of his own. A bitter feud had sprung up between the Jarvis and Ridout families, each allied to different political factions — though the immediate cause of the feud was rumours spread by the Ridouts that the Jarvises were unreliable debtors. In the event, a Ridout brother had been hired by a Jarvis creditor, which eventually led to a confrontation between Samuel Peters Jarvis and John Ridout. Fisticuffs occurred, followed by the issuance of a formal challenge by Ridout to meet with pistols at dawn on July 12, 1817. The two met at the appointed time with their seconds and discussed the formalities: each was to stride eight yards from the starting point and fire upon a count of "one, two, three, fire."

After taking their positions, Ridout fired on "two," missing Jarvis.

A discussion ensued as to the proper protocol in the face of such a violation of the rules by Ridout. It was eventually settled that Jarvis was entitled to take his own shot at Ridout, who was obliged to remain still as Jarvis was afforded his opportunity. Jarvis did so, and Ridout was killed.[6] Jarvis surrendered to the authorities and was charged with manslaughter (a specific prohibition on duelling not yet having been enacted into law), imprisoned awaiting trial, and finally acquitted by a jury.

The distinction of the Cartier and Jarvis names hints at the origin of the duel in pre-Confederation Canadian society: it was largely an importation by transplanted aristocrats from the colonial homelands of England and France. The Europeans took their duels seriously: the French duelling code consisted of eighty-four clauses, while the apparently widely followed "Irish Code" contained twenty-six, which spelled out the types of insults for which satisfaction could be sought by duel (Irish Code, clause X: "any insult to a lady under a gentleman's care or protection to be considered as by one degree a greater offence than if given to the gentleman personally"), the proper role of the participants' seconds (Irish Code, clauses XIII and XX: "Seconds to be of equal rank in society with the principals they attend.... Seconds are bound to attempt a reconciliation before the meeting takes place, or after sufficient firing or hits, as specified"), and the selection of weapons (Irish Code, clause XV: "The challenged has the right to choose his own weapons ...").[7] Of course, both codes were extra-legal, as duelling was frowned upon by the Crown and government — a recognition that it served little purpose to have members of the most educated and wealthiest class of society attempting to kill each other for perceived insults, regardless of the gloss of respectability they tried to put on the practice. While the duelling codes evolved as an attempt to give structure to what was otherwise just a brawl, the obviating of the most apparent brutality wasn't much more than putting lipstick on a pig.

The authorities often sought to bring participants in duels before the courts, but successful prosecutions were relatively rare, as juries often returned verdicts of acquittal. In the case of the lethal Samuel Peters Jarvis duel described above, eleven years after the duel took place (with Jarvis securing an acquittal), both seconds to the duel, who were lawyers, were arrested while they were actually arguing a case in court and charged as accessories to the murder; the juries declined to convict. It should be noted that the social context in which authorities and juries were operating was at times ambivalent about their duty to prosecute for murders taking place in the context of a duel. Writing a history of Ontario duels in 1915, one judge described "the 'unwritten law' that if the duel was fair in all respects, the survivor and the seconds should not be convicted. Accordingly ... the Crown Counsel ... never pressed for a conviction; and the jury knew what was expected of them."[8] That convention helps explain, despite the formal prohibitions against homicide, the quick acquittals accorded to both Jarvis and the seconds involved in his duel.

Just as the social ritual of the duel originated in the overseas seat of the empire, the process of abolishing the duel began in England and migrated to Canada. As a formal matter, English criminal law had long prohibited duelling. The earliest commentaries on English law confirm that a killing that occurred in the course of a duel was properly regarded as murder and that the appropriate punishment for such a crime was death (for both the combatant and his second).[9] As noted above, though, the prevailing social convention meant that judges, prosecutors, and juries were reluctant to convict members of the upper classes of the crime. By the middle of the 1800s, concerns about the senseless waste involved in duelling had reached the highest levels of English society. The English Mutiny Act had once provided that military officers could be dishonourably discharged for *failing* to defend their impugned honour by duel. In 1844, Queen Victoria prompted a change in the law that provided for the court-martial of any officer who participated in a duel or failed to stop an incipient one.[10] As sometimes happens in the history of criminal conduct, perhaps the most effective deterrent was not a change to the criminal law but legislation that enabled injured parties to bring civil lawsuits against duel participants. Prior to the middle of the nineteenth century, the only potential punishment that a duellist faced was a potential criminal charge, but because a conviction was so unlikely to be brought to bear against someone who had killed another in a duel, the sanction of the criminal law was an ineffective deterrent. In 1847, the English Parliament passed a law that enabled the survivors of a person killed in a duel (i.e., his wife, children, or parents) to sue the duellist (and his second) who had murdered their loved one for monetary damages arising from a wrongful death. As one legal historian dryly notes, the threat of losing significant amounts of money "took the fun out of duelling."[11] When Canada's first Criminal Code was introduced in 1892, the prohibition on duelling, inherited from the English criminal law, was present, though the last report of a serious duel had passed a couple of decades earlier. Nonetheless, Section 71 remains on the books to the present day.

As the legal framework transformed along with the social context surrounding duelling, the concept passed from societal blight to historical curiosity and, eventually, to kitsch. The town of Perth, Ontario, proudly claims the mantle of having hosted the last fatal duel — though whether the title extends only to Ontario or across Canada is a matter of some dispute. The historic plaque placed on the site to commemorate the June 13, 1833, duel between two law students, John Wilson and Robert Lyon, which resulted in Lyon's death (and Wilson's subsequent acquittal on murder charges), states that the event marked the last fatal duel in the province. The tourist literature and souvenirs (including the town's website), however, allege that the fatality was the last one in the country.[12] Though it seems an odd honorific over which to quibble, at least one subsequent fatal duel has been documented: in 1838 Major John Henry Warde was killed by Robert Sweeney in a duel that took place near the racetrack in Verdun, Quebec. The coroner's jury investigating the matter acknowledged that a death had taken place but declined to identify Sweeney as the culprit, setting off a storm of controversy over the efforts to protect a member of the "gentleman" caste (Sweeney was a lawyer and militia officer).[13] In any event, the town of Perth appears much more willing to trade on the notoriety of its fatal confrontation, hosting the occasional (non-fatal) re-enactment and even naming its twenty-seven-acre recreational area Last Duel Park.

Reflecting the farcical notion to which the duel has been reduced, the most recent potential duel that garnered significant public attention occurred in Ottawa in 1948, when the consul general of the Dominican Republic issued a public challenge to Argentina's ambassador.[14] The dispute followed the mysterious death of two dogs at the Argentine embassy. During a reception, the Dominican consul general made a light remark about the dogs to the Argentine ambassador's wife; she responded by associating his country with a racial epithet (it rhymes with "trigger"). The insult was compounded by the lack of an invitation to a subsequent party hosted by the Argentine diplomat. Incensed, the Dominican consul general demanded that the ambassador afford him an opportunity to defend the honour of his republic by means of the martial contest, with either swords or pistols.

The dispute quickly became public, the feud being reported on the front pages of Ottawa newpapers; one mockingly suggested that the two don boxing gloves rather than use weapons, with Canadian diplomats playing the role of referee. While the Dominican consul general was prepared to fight, his Argentine counterpart refused to countenance the spectacle. The ambassador was eventually recalled to Argentina, and the duel never took place. Concerns about the duel being contrary to Canadian law had been addressed by the Dominican consul general's offer to duel the ambassador on the grounds of the Argentine embassy itself, where the writ of Canadian law didn't run.

While the formal prohibition on duelling remains firmly ensconced, there have been no reported convictions of the crime for decades. Because the formal requirements for duels (which included a public challenge and the participation of assistants called "seconds") are no longer observed, it would be rare for the police to even be aware of a duel until it had actually occurred — at which point the standard charges of assault or murder could be relied on.[15] In the meantime, the courts themselves are somewhat split on how to view the crime of duelling. While the Supreme Court of Canada, in a reference to Section 71, called the prohibition on duelling "integral to our ideas of civilized society,"[16] the Alberta Court of Appeal, in determining what sorts of crimes warranted extradition, thought it "bursts the seams of credulity" to think that "duelling" was sufficiently serious.[17]

Prizefights

Duels offer a convenient vantage onto our splintered view of fights between consenting adults. One of the fundamental prohibitions in the Criminal Code is that against assault: Section 265 describes assault as the intentional application of force to another person without that person's consent. One of the slipperiest elements of the crime of assault is the requirement that the application of force take place *in the absence of consent*. What about situations where the individuals involved agreed to engage in a fight? The courts have erected a number of guidelines where the concepts of assault and consent intercept. The Supreme Court of Canada had occasion to consider the matter in the 1991 *Jobidon* case,[18] which found that "the consent of an opponent is no defence [to a charge of assault] when an adult intentionally inflicts bodily harm during a brawl or fistfight; in cases involving contact during worthwhile, rough sports, the central issue is the scope of players' implied consent."[19] So, for example, individuals can consent to engage in a fistfight and no criminal conviction will result — unless serious hurt or "non-trivial" bodily harm occurs, in which case the consent that was previously given is obviated, on the theory that you cannot consent to have serious damage inflicted on you. (The crime of "aggravated assault," which involves the wounding, maiming, disfiguring, or endangering of the life of the victim, is a separate crime, described in Section 268, and consent cannot be used as a defence.) It has been held that adults can engage in consensual fistfights, where the fighting is fair.[20] But where one combatant ceases to consent (e.g., because he or she is unconscious) or the actions of one combatant exceed what the other combatant thought they were agreeing to (e.g., using a weapon), consent cannot be raised as a defence.

We already know that a duel, which is presumably intended to result in the lethal use of force, is the subject of an outright prohibition. Stepping back from the presumptive lethality of the duel, yet not going quite so far as the rather unrewarding nature of the common street brawl, there exists a third general type of consensual fight with which the law has attempted to grapple: the prizefight. A curious adaptation of the duelling prohibition in the Criminal Code states:

> **83.** (1) Every one who
> (a) engages as a principal in a prize fight,
> (b) advises, encourages or promotes a prize fight, or
> (c) is present at a prize fight as an aid, second, surgeon, umpire, backer or reporter,
> is guilty of an offence punishable on summary conviction.

The potential punishment for violating Section 83 is a fine of not more than $2,000 or imprisonment for up to six months, or both. It is noteworthy that while the potential punishment for duelling is more serious (up to two years' imprisonment), the scope of the prizefight prohibition is much broader: it applies not only to the combatants but also to any advisers, promoters, or even *reporters* who are present. Though the formal duelling codes required the presence of seconds, their attendance at an actual duel is not expressly prohibited by the Criminal Code. Only in the case of prizefights, which are presumably less inherently lethal than duels, is the presence of individuals other than the combatants outlawed. Despite the obvious connotation of the name of the offence, it doesn't appear to be a requirement that the fight be arranged for any prize whatsoever, be it monetary or otherwise — Section 83(2) defines a prizefight as "an encounter or fight with fists or hands between two persons who have met for that purpose by previous arrangement made by or for them." This offers the only obvious distinction between the prize-fight and the duel: where the "encounter or fight" is held with something other than "fists or hands" (i.e., weapons), the activity is a duel and not a prizefight. On such fine distinctions are legal histories written.

Not all prearranged fistfights are prohibited under the current legislation. There are two categories of fights carved out in Section 83(2): any boxing contest that is held under the auspices of a provincially authorized athletic board or commission or any amateur boxing contest where the contestants wear "boxing gloves of not less than one hundred and forty grams each in mass" is deemed not to be a prizefight. Those two categories offer their own food for thought. Untrained amateurs who wear really big boxing gloves need not obtain the sanction of a boxing commission and can fight without fear of being charged; professional boxers, however, wearing gloves of any sort, need to get permission from the government. Perhaps there is some sort of glove cushion to injury ratio that militates in favour of the distinction. In any event, this constitutes further recognition that a complete ban on consensual fighting is unenforceable: there will always be those who are happy to participate in and witness fisticuffs.

Prizefighting was once a crime warranting significant attention from the authorities. The first legislation addressing the conduct in Canada was "An Act respecting prize-fights," introduced in 1881.[21] When Canada passed its first comprehensive Criminal Code in 1892, the code incorporated the earlier prohibitions on prizefighting, which extended so broadly that it was actually a crime to leave the country to engage in a prizefight.[22] The legislative prohibition on prizefighting had emerged from a common law prohibition, which itself had stemmed from two concerns: injury to the participants and a perception on the part of the authorities that there was a general degradation of the public condition when prizefights were allowed to occur. As one English judge described the matter in 1881: "the injuries given and received in prize-fights are injurious to the public, both because it is against the public interest that the lives and the health of the combatants should be endangered by blows and because prize-fights are disorderly exhibitions, mischievous on many obvious grounds."[23]

The "many obvious grounds" referred to were somewhat less than evident. An early legal treatise on crimes explained, somewhat paradoxically, that prizefights tended to "encourage idleness by drawing together a number of disorderly people"; the more obvious concern, also cited in the same treatise, was the unruliness of crowds: "meetings of this kind have also a strong tendency to cause a breach of the peace."[24] The matter was treated with such gravity that the first Canadian legislation to address the topic contained provisions imposing special duties on law-enforcement officers to actively take steps to prevent prizefights from occurring. There were, then, three competing concerns that animated the early law on prizefighting: preventing injury to the participants; preventing the gathering of large crowds that could quickly turn ungovernable; and, as we will see in the cases discussed below, a countervailing desire to preserve the ability of men to engage in martial combat within certain parameters.

A flurry of prizefighting cases were prosecuted in Canada in the early twentieth century, and a number were of sufficient significance to warrant inclusion in the law reports. One matter that vexed the early court decisions was the true nature of a prizefight. Because the name seemingly requires the availability of a "prize" for fighting, was it necessary, despite the plain wording of the definition contained in the Criminal Code, for there to be a "prize" for a crime to have been committed? The marriage of fighting and commerce was evidently of special concern. The language of the original Criminal Code provisions was somewhat confusing for judges because it first appeared to provide that a prizefight did not require a prize (i.e., the transfer of money or property) in order to be illegal; a different section, however, provided that where the court was satisfied that the fight did not involve a prize but was merely "the result of a quarrel or dispute between the principals," then there was no prizefight per se, and the fight that had occurred could be punished with the lesser penalty of a fine up to $50. In short, a fight for money was to be treated much more seriously than a mere fight arising from a dispute.

Courts were also troubled by whether there was a distinction between a lawful "boxing exhibition" and an unlawful "prizefight."

Perhaps most important, how were courts supposed to navigate the fine line between discouraging "brutal" prizefights and encouraging "good, honest, manly sport"? While everyone agreed that there were situations where the consent of the parties to the blows that they may receive during the course of the prizefight would be insufficient to prevent those blows from being characterized as assaults, they also wanted to ensure that the broad wording of the Criminal Code did not result in overreaching. It was in drawing these fine lines that Canadian courts of the early twentieth century engaged themselves.

In the Quebec case of *Steele v Maber*,[25] the defendant's lawyer was faced with what can charitably be called "hard facts":

> the evidence shews … that the alleged prize fight was advertised as a "Grand Athletic Exhibition between 'Shadow' Maber, champion of Canada, and an unknown;" that the contest would be under the "Marquis of Queensbury rules" for points, for a sum of $200; … it was held in a public hall … on a roped-in platform, that the principals were attired solely in trunks … the proceedings were conducted by a referee; that they were provided with a time keeper and seconds armed with towels and provided with chairs …

Henry Page, the promoter of the fight, had had his own troubles in arranging for the contest to take place. The mayor of Farnham had originally agreed to allow the contest to take place in his town (and received ten complimentary tickets for his troubles), but the mayor was subsequently overruled by the town council; Page blustered his way past the mayor and the secretary-treasurer, implying darkly that Farnham was in danger of sullying its reputation as a "sporting" town. The council reconsidered and relented, allowing the fight to take place. Maber ended up knocking out his opponent in the third round (following a second-round knockdown that left William Henessey, the "unknown" referred to in the playbill, "moaning and twisting as if in great pain" for a seven-count). Confronted with all this, "Shadow" Maber's lawyer put up a brave defence: what occurred on March 20, 1901, was not a prizefight but "an exhibition of scientific boxing," and regardless, the whole thing was a "pure farce and sham" (i.e., the combatants were just play-fighting, and no one was actually injured). Magistrate Mulvena, reviewing the language of what was then Section 92 of the Criminal Code (and what is now Section 83[2]), noted that it seemed fairly straightforward what a "prizefight" was: an encounter or fight with fists or hands between two persons who have met for that purpose by previous arrangement made by or for them. No prior court decisions had modified that language, nor did the debates that took place in Parliament when the law was being discussed offer any indication that anything other than the plain meaning of the language was intended. This looked to all the world — what with the roped-in ring, the timekeeper, the knocking down — like the sort of activity that was intended to be prohibited. Most important, whether or not the boxing itself and the attendant injuries were real or faked, the court decision reflects the deeper concerns at play in prosecutions for prizefights: as Magistrate Mulvena chided, the promoters and contestants "sought to excite in the spectators all the demoralizing and degrading emotions of a genuine prize fight." And so the result: three months in jail at hard labour for "Shadow" Maber, along with various fines for the promoters.

Perhaps uncomfortable with the notion of trying to police the emotions felt by citizens, some judges were considerably less enthusiastic about prosecuting prizefights, however. The enjoyably named case of *The King v Wildfong and Lang*[26] offers such an example of the judiciary having at heart much loftier concerns than the mere question of whether or not the law had been broken. In 1911, the Hamilton Bowling and Athletic Club engaged a number of professional boxers, including the aforementioned Wildfong and Lang, to give a "boxing exhibition" to the "young men of the city" who made up the club's membership. Wildfong versus Lang was scheduled to be the last of four bouts taking place that afternoon, but the chief of police, who was, in the rather unkind phrasing of Judge Snider, "acting on instructions from some person whom he saw fit to obey," announced prior to the fight that he would arrest the men when they appeared to give their "exhibition." When Wildfong and Lang entered the arena, the police duly arrested and charged them. According to the contracts that were entered into evidence, both Wildfong and Lang were to be paid for engaging in the exhibition. There was no "prize" per se (but then one is not required under the wording of the Criminal Code), but they were to receive payment ($125 in the case of Wildfong and a percentage of the gate in the case of Lang) for engaging in ten rounds of boxing. There were to be no points recorded nor a decision rendered, "no prize or reward of any kind to be contested for, nothing to be gained by the winner." Nevertheless, a police magistrate had determined that the wording of the Criminal Code was sufficiently broad to capture what Wildfong and Lang had been about to engage in, and so convicted them. The two appealed their conviction to Judge Snider who, sympathetic to the "not unreasonable" desire of the members of the athletic club that they should be allowed to see "an exhibition of superior skill in boxing," began to parse the wording of the Criminal Code.

Was, queried Judge Snider, a "boxing exhibition" a "prizefight"? Even the deputy chief of police had been forced to admit that, in the course of his "witnessing in different parts of the world genuine 'prize fights,'" there was a distinction between a boxing exhibition and a prize-fight — the latter involves "blows," while the former is "simply scientific boxing." The matter seemed to turn on whether an "exhibition" was truly a "fight." Judge Snider had occasion to look at older cases that had considered the matter, and noted that there was authority for the proposition that "a mere exhibition of skill in sparring is not illegal," but that if the parties intend to "fight till one gives in from exhaustion or injury," then an illegal prizefight has occurred, whether or not gloves were used.[27] Bumping up against issues that would concern courts in later decades (and that will be discussed below), Snider noted that "boxing is, of course, rough sport, but so is hockey, lacrosse and football." The critical element of a "fight" is that there is an intention to injure the other party to the point that he can no longer continue the encounter. And it is that *intention to injure* that renders a fight illegal. While in a game of football a player may be knocked unconscious or suffer a broken arm or leg, that would be not be the *intention* of the player causing such an injury. And if such an injury *were* the result of intentional conduct, then an illegal assault would have been committed and could be charged as a crime.

But the definition of "prizefight" is not limited to "fights" — it covers an "*encounter* or a fight with fists or hands." Is an "encounter" different from a "fight"? No, decided Judge Snider; the two were simply synonyms. Otherwise, "every time one young man telephones another and arranges with him to meet at their gymnasium after office hours and box for a quarter of an hour or so before dinner, both would be guilty of 'prize fighting' and, but for the forbearance of the police, both would have to spend somewhere between three and twelve months in gaol." Surely, said Snider, this could not have been the intention of Parliament. Referencing the *Encyclopedia of Law of England*,[28] Snider noted that boxing or sparring, "if it is an honest and friendly contest with gloves, fairly conducted according to the Queensberry [sic] rules or other like regulations, seems to be perfectly legal" and is not a "prize-fight." Similar to the result in a New Brunswick case,[29] then, Snider drew a distinction between a sporting or exhibition match conducted according to preordained rules and intended to display or hone sparring skills and a fight entered into with the intention of battering the other participant to the point of exhaustion or injury; since Wildfong and Lang were to be engaged in the former and not the latter, the convictions were overturned.

Judge Snider offered his final thoughts, an excellent encapsulation, in perhaps antiquated language, of the conflicting concerns that inform much of the subsequent debate on the nature of consensual violence:

> I wish to make it clear that I am as much opposed to prize fighting and brutality and intentional injury in boxing, football, hockey or lacrosse, as any person can be. At the same time I feel confident that it will be a long time before Parliament will think it wise to so hedge in young men and boys by legislation that all sports that are rough and strenuous or even dangerous must be given up. Virility in young men would soon be lessened and self-reliant manliness be a thing of the past.

We can see in the *Wildfong and Lang* decision an illustration of the dialogue that takes place between courts and legislators: the legislature passes a law that is necessarily cast in broad strokes (or else our statutes, already voluminous enough to weigh down reinforced shelves, would be even longer by orders of magnitude), and the courts are required to tease out a fair and just application of the wording. As Judge Snider noted, surely Parliament didn't intend to criminalize a friendly athletic sparring match between two friends, but on the face of the language, that would be the result. And so the conversation begins, not just between the courts and the legislators, but among the police and Crown prosecutors, as well, with each party listening to what the other has to say, resulting in the fashioning of "the law." In the wake of a decision like *Wildfong and Lang*, then, the police were apt to apply a lighter touch in arresting people for purported violations of the prize-fighting prohibition. But the real world is not always as clinical as dry legal distinctions would imply, with boxing "exhibitions" on the one side and "prizefights" on the other. Attempting to abide by the distinctions described in *Wildfong and Lang* could also lead to questionable decisions that undermine the intention of the law. The *Fitzgerald* case[30] offers an example of the conversation continuing apace but perhaps going a bit off the rails.

The National Sporting Association, a club that operated under a charter granted by the federal government, held a series of sparring contests in January 17, 1912. The police were on hand to keep watch over the proceedings and did not interfere until a bout that took place between Flynn and Williams. Similar to the situation in *Wildfong and Lang*, all of the contestants were paid fixed sums of money to participate, and the bouts were scheduled to occur for a fixed number of rounds. Based on the evidence before the court, no "knockouts" were intended to happen in these demonstrations of skill, but at least one accidental knockout occurred. Once Flynn and Williams took to the ring, however, the nature of the proceedings changed: this was a "furious," "very rough" fight, entirely unscientific, with the two fighting "like bull-dogs from beginning to end." The police charged Fitzgerald with promoting a prizefight; Fitzgerald was convicted and appealed. On appeal, the court applied the *Wildfong and Lang* approach, deciding that, though the fight could even be characterized as "brutal," the better approach was to not criminalize this conduct for fear of discouraging "good, honest, manly sport." Although "unscientific and rough exhibitions should not be permitted by the management of any sporting club," Fitzgerald should not be sanctioned, and the conviction was overturned. The judge approvingly quoted Judge Snider's concerns about suppressing virility in young men and lessening self-reliant manliness.

There thus arose a fine conundrum: following *Fitzgerald*, it was the *intended* character of the encounter that was determinative. Even if the combat became a brutal fight, so long as what was intended to have occurred was an exhibition of boxing skills (with due deference to the apparent societal need to develop robust young men), no prizefight had occurred. But what about a situation where a death had occurred in the ring? Faced with the preceding case law and also with a case where the defendant had killed his opponent, giving rise to a charge of manslaughter, the most authoritative words on the matter came from a charge to the jury delivered by Chief Justice Harvey in the 1913 Supreme Court of Alberta manslaughter case of *R v Pelkey*.[31] Judge Harvey did his best to describe the state of the law as it existed before him. A boxing match would not be considered a prizefight "when it is carried on as an exemplification of what has been called the 'manly art of self-defence'" — but, he cautioned, such a boxing match *might* be a prizefight if it "were typical of what might be designated as the brutal science of attack." Somewhere, then, between the "art of self-defence" and the "science of attack," lay the dividing line between legal and illegal (one could cynically note that both the attack and the defence would need to be present in order for either to occur).

Again, intention was deemed to be the key: if the participants met intending to fight until exhaustion or debilitating injury, then the fight was illegal. Advertisements in the case at hand described the bout as being between Luther McCarty, the "World's Heavyweight Champion," and Arthur Pelkey of Calgary, and was scheduled for ten rounds. Refereeing the bout was one Mr. Smith who, the court noted, "has been trying for 25 years to find out the difference between a prize fight and boxing match" — surely a desire with which we can sympathize by this point. In any event, three thousand people showed up to witness Mr. Pelkey triumph over his opponent and thereby earn the title of World's Heavyweight Champion — unfortunately, though, during the course of the bout Mr. McCarty was injured to the point that he died. On the charge for manslaughter, the jury concluded that an illegal prizefight had not taken place, and the defendant was let free.

In reporting the *Pelkey* case, the editors of the *Canadian Criminal Cases* law reports attempted to annotate the case with a clarifying explanation of the then-existing law but were no more successful than had been Judge Harvey. In light of the confusion reigning among judges and police officers (and, apparently, referees) and the evident hunger among the public to be able to witness prearranged boxing matches, the Criminal Code was eventually amended to incorporate the current language, which allows boxing contests to be held under the supervisory authority of an athletic board or commission established by a provisional legislature. Thus, boxing is now regulated by a web of supervisory bodies, including the Canadian Amateur Boxing Association, Boxing Ontario, and the Athletics Commissioner of Ontario.

The rash of prosecutions from the early decades of the past century fell away not because there were no more prizefights but because the "danger" had been regulated, which is very different from saying that it had been eradicated. The acknowledged danger to the combatants had been ameliorated by the requirement for medical supervision. As for the "many obvious grounds" of mischief to which the earlier English judge referred, those too seem to have been addressed — or at least the authorities became comfortable with them, perhaps as a result of the ability to obtain tax revenue from the proceedings. With the provision of a regulated outlet to enable fight fans to participate in and watch their preferred sport, along with the safety mechanisms of trained referees and medical attendants, reported prizefighting cases lay dormant for over eighty years after 1916. Then along came Thai kickboxing.

Throughout the 1990s, fans of martial arts were exposed to a series of new fighting styles, including kickboxing and "mixed martial arts" (MMA) on pay-per-view television. Unlike traditional "Queensbury" boxing, Thai kickboxing participants were entitled to use kicks and elbows to any part of the body; MMA contests pitted fighters of varying sizes and skill sets against one another, wrestlers against kickboxers, street fighters against jiu-jitsu masters, and a dizzying array of other combinations, all with the intent of showcasing bloodier, more exciting forms of combat than what was increasingly being viewed as the somewhat staid contests between professional boxers (the occasional ear-gnawing incident à la Mike Tyson notwithstanding).

As is to be expected when a market demand is identified, Canadian promoters began to stage MMA bouts and tournaments. In 1998, the Martial Arts Fighting Academy in Mississauga, Ontario, hosted a Thai kickboxing event entitled "Fall Brawl." With approximately two hundred spectators having paid up to $12 each to attend, no medical staff or equipment apparent at the premises, and no licence or authorization to hold the event, the owners of the academy were charged and convicted of promoting an illegal prizefight.[32] A reporter present at the Fall Brawl (who was not charged with committing an offence under Section 83, though *prima facie* his mere presence was a crime under Section 83[1][c]) testified that headgear was not worn by all of the fighters, and kicks to the groin were a common occurrence. The judge trying the case echoed the concerns first mentioned by his predecessors a century and more ago about the fighters themselves and the crowd watching them: "the fight ... was inherently dangerous, and aside from concerns of public order concomitant with any large gathering of people, had insufficient safeguards to prevent serious bodily harm, incapacitation or possibly death of any of the combatants." Times have, of course, changed — whereas "Shadow" Maber received three months' hard labour for being involved in a prizefight, when the promoters of the Fall Brawl were convicted, they received conditional discharges, were ordered to each make a charitable contribution of $100, and their company was ordered to pay a fine of $1,200.

From "Sports" of Violence to Violence in Sports

Darryl Wolski was a hockey fan who noticed that on-ice fights often seemed to generate the loudest and most enthusiastic response at sports bars. Being ambitious and entrepreneurial, Wolski was interested in giving other fans what they seemed to want: unadulterated hockey fights without all the distraction of skating, scoring, or penalties. Thus was born the Battle of the Hockey Enforcers,[33] a tournament where hockey tough guys would clash to determine the last man standing; spectators could attend in person or purchase the show over pay-per-view television. Somewhat similar to the travails faced by Henry Page a century earlier, Wolski encountered a number of difficulties. His original plan to hold the event in Winnipeg was routed after police made it clear to the owners of the Winnipeg Arena that they would seek to bring charges under Section 83 (the prizefight prohibition) if the event went ahead.[34] After a few more false starts in other cities, Wolski was finally able to find a willing host in the city of Prince George, British Columbia, where the Prince George Athletic Commission and the municipal government were willing to let the tournament go forward (though only after initially turning down Wolski's request). On August 27, 2005, approximately two thousand attendees watched as Dean Mayrand battled his way through sixteen participants to a $62,000 first prize finish. Wolski has plans to mount further tournaments.

Embedded in the concept of a prizefight is the notion that the combatants are confronting each other for the express purpose of *fight-*

ing — there isn't much more to a boxing or Muay Thai match than hitting your opponent, whatever lustre may be added by references to the "sweet science." But, as alluded to in the *Jobidon* decision, itself an echo of Judge Snider's much earlier reference to "rough sports," and as any Canadian can tell you, there are some sports where fighting is, though not the dominant element, at least a significant component. Darryl Wolski was perhaps just a bit more honest when it comes to hockey than the rest of us. In determining whether a crime has been committed in the course of a "rough sport," attention must be turned to the issue of the consent of the players.

As a general rule, an act that is otherwise illegal cannot suddenly be made legal just because it occurs within the rules of a sport or during the course of a game.[35] We have seen over recent years a number of vicious assaults taking place during hockey games that have resulted in criminal convictions — as with Boston Bruin Marty McSorley striking Vancouver Canuck Donald Brashear in the head with a stick (McSorley was found guilty of assault with a weapon and received an eighteen-month conditional discharge).[36] There is a significant component of the sports-watching audience that argues that sports figures who engage in questionable conduct on the field of play should be held to account in the courts, regardless of arguments that players have "consented" to a particular level of violence. As early as 1878, manslaughter charges were brought against a soccer player who collided with another player, causing his death.[37] In the 1960s and 1970s, courts began to hold that actions during play could result not only in civil liability[38] but in criminal liability, as well: while all players accept a certain level of hazard, "no athlete should be presumed to accept malicious, unprovoked or overly violent attack."[39] The standard "gloves off" bout of pugilism between enforcers occurring in the course of a hockey game doesn't appear to have resulted in criminal charges being laid. It is when fights arise after play has ended or been halted[40] or off the ice surface (such as in an arena parking lot[41] or dressing room) that the courts have become involved.

The courts have tended to take the view that where an assault occurs during the course of play, it requires either serious injury[42] or unprovoked attacks (whether or not resulting in serious injury[43]) to ground convictions. To participate in a sporting event is not "to enter a forum to which the criminal law does not extend,"[44] but the determination of whether a crime has occurred is a contextual analysis, looking at the amount of force used, the extent of injury incurred, the intention of the accused, whether the game is professional or merely recreational, the age of the participants, and incidents of provocation and retaliation.[45] Severe penalties, however, are rare, except in cases causing death: Minnesota North Star Dino Ciccarelli served only one day in jail for striking an opposing hockey player three times on the head with his stick;[46] Marty McSorley, despite causing Donald Brashear to suffer a severe concussion, received no jail time at all; when Vancouver Canuck Todd Bertuzzi hit the Colorado Avalanche's Steve Moore from behind, breaking three of Moore's vertebrae and giving him a concussion, Bertuzzi pled guilty to assault and received a sentence of one year's probation together with eighty hours of community service. Though the courts pay lip service to the importance of deterring violence, the sentences for high-profile incidents of hockey violence are strikingly lenient, reflecting perhaps the uneasy coexistence of our nominal prohibitions on violence and the public's evident desire to see it.[47]

Despite criticism from many quarters, including professional hockey players, professors, and editorial boards, there is evidently an appetite for the continuation of the hockey brawl and even the unadorned spectacle of violence that Wolski was promoting. Which raises the question: should it be a crime to engage in consensual fights between adults? There does, after all, seem to be a slightly hypocritical air to the current framework. Prizefights are banned, except to the extent that they are sanctioned after having been cleared for health and safety concerns by a provincial licensing board. If we are opposed to violence, why are we willing to sanction it but only up to the point where an arbitrarily determined level of "acceptable" injury and permanent damage is done to the participants? In fact, why is the government involved at all? If consenting adults elect to beat each other bloody, whether for amusement, spectacle, or prize money, of what concern is it to the legislature? There is presumably a governmental interest in ensuring that citizens remain healthy and are not continually being reduced to bloody pulps. There also appears to be some sort of demonstrative effect that arises from displays of violence — the early English decisions referred to above allude to the disruptive mood that comes over crowds gathered to watch fights.

As with other crimes and other times, technology sometimes brings into sharp relief the concerns that drive the varied prohibitions on fighting. In 2006, police in the United States sounded the alarm about the disturbing rise in the number of "fight clubs" (borrowing the title of Chuck Palahniuk's 1996 novel and the subsequent 1999 movie starring Brad Pitt): fighting rings where members engage in bloody hand-to-hand combat, notifying friends and peers by means of cellphones, text messages, and Internet chat relays, and sometimes filming their exploits for dissemination on the Internet or on DVD.[48] In what is perhaps a perversion of what Judge Snider had benignly described in *Wildfong and Lang* as the end-of-day exercise routine of virile young men, these bouts are often bare-knuckle beatings, sometimes devolving into violent assaults on innocent victims who did not agree to participate. Immersed in a world where on-demand savagery is available for download, saturated with violent imagery from boxing matches, bench-clearing brawls on television, movies, mixed martial arts tournaments, and the exploits of their peers, perhaps the lifting of the cap on consensual violence has led to its normalization as part of the social fabric. The assessment of whether that is good or ill, and the inevitable legal response to the problem, is likely to resemble the legal history we have already seen.

Animal Fights

For all the fulminating on the issue of consensual fights, and lest we leave this chapter on too grim a note, our laws also make it very clear that a certain "breed" of non-consensual fights is strictly forbidden, at least in part on the theory that the participants cannot consent: fights between animals. Encouraging, aiding, or assisting the fighting or baiting of animals or birds is prohibited by Section 446(1)(*d*) of the Criminal Code, a subset of the broader provisions relating to the prevention of cruelty to animals. We take this sort of thing seriously. Simply being present at the fighting or baiting of animals is, in the absence of evidence to the contrary, proof that you encouraged, aided, or assisted (Section 446[4]). Somewhat curiously, even more detail is accorded to shooting birds:

> **446.** (1) Every one commits an offence who
> (*f*) promotes, arranges, conducts, assists in, receives money for or

takes part in any meeting, competition, exhibition, pastime, practice, display or event at or in the course of which captive birds are liberated by hand, trap, contrivance or any other means for the purpose of being shot when they are liberated; or

(g) being the owner, occupier or person in charge of any premises, permits the premises or any part thereof to be used for a purpose mentioned in paragraph (f).

As if to prove that we *really* mean it when it comes to birds, a separate section is devoted to the crime of keeping a cockpit. Section 447(1) stipulates that anyone who "builds, makes, maintains or keeps a cockpit on premises that he owners or occupies, or allows a cockpit to be built, made, maintained or kept on such premises is guilty of an offence." In a provision that is almost guaranteed to result in courthouse hilarity, Section 447(2) *requires* a police officer who finds cocks in a cockpit (or on premises where a cockpit is located) to "seize them and take them before a justice who shall order them to be destroyed." In other words, pity the poor police officer who, stumbling across an underground cockfighting operation, in addition to arresting everyone in sight as permitted under Section 446(1)(d) and 446(4), must also chase and capture the birds, then haul them down to the courthouse and present them to a judge or justice of the peace. Actually, after a long day of trying to wrap his or her head around the prohibitions on duels, prizefights, hockey fights, and cockfights, dropping off in court a cage of squawking, feather-shedding, angry fighting chickens might be just the thing to bring a smile to the face of a frazzled peace officer.

3

Saying Bad Things About
People in Power –
Crimes Against the State

On June 6, 2006, a particularly shocking allegation was splashed across newspaper headlines in Canada. Days after seventeen men and boys were arrested in Toronto and alleged to have been conspiring to wage terrorist attacks (including storming Parliament and detonating bombs on Bay Street), the lawyer of one of the accused read in court the allegations that his client had an even more gruesome plan in mind: he was going to behead Prime Minister Stephen Harper.[1]

Oddly, had the plot been successfully carried out, murdering the prime minister would not be considered "treason."

Who dares call it treason? Better, *what* do they dare call treason? Treason is the most well known of the various crimes that are grouped under the heading "crimes against the state" — within the category's name itself is the element that lends these crimes their unique character: they define the contours of what the government has determined are impermissible actions against the government *itself.* The "who" and the "what" of the crime are interrelated to an extent that has historically invited what we now view as abuses of power. The dialectic of the government legislating what you can do to it and then changing and applying that legislation as it sees fit recurs through Canadian history, in accordance with the concerns of the time: rebellions and threats to the person of the monarch in the nineteenth century, commitments to king and country during the First World War, labour strife between the world wars, communist infiltration during the Cold War, separatism, and post-9/11 jihadist threats. Thus, few sections of the Criminal Code offer as clear a glimpse of our past as do the provisions relating to treason, sedition, and other crimes against the state. These sections allow us to use a different lens in examining the law: the law as a mechanism for dealing with dissent and threats to the security of the country.

Section 46(1), which describes the crime of high treason (as distinct from run-of-the-mill treason, handled in subsection [2], discussed below), contains language substantially similar in form to English laws from the fourteenth century:

> **46.**   (1)   Every one commits high treason who
>   (*a*) kills or attempts to kill Her Majesty, or does her any bodily harm tending to death or destruction, maims or wounds her, or imprisons or restrains her;
>   (*b*) levies war against Canada or does any act preparatory thereto; or
>   (*c*) assists an enemy at war with Canada, or any armed forces against whom Canadian Forces are engaged in hostilities, whether or not a state of war exists between Canada and the country whose forces they are.

To reflect the severity of the crime of high treason, it is punishable by an automatic sentence of life imprisonment — the only other crime in the Criminal Code deemed to warrant a similar sentence is murder. There are two distinct aspects of high treason: the first is the protection of the person of the sovereign (i.e., currently Her Majesty Queen Elizabeth II); the second is the levying of war against Canada or assisting an enemy during a state of war or hostilities. The notion of protecting the body of the sovereign is at least as ancient as the Roman law of treason,[2] a derivation of the notion that the monarch was an actual embodiment of the rights of the state. The concepts contained in Section 46(1) are derived from the first anti-treason statute in the English legal tradition, the Statute of Treasons, enacted by Edward III in 1351. That early piece of legislation was somewhat limited in scope in some regards and was supplemented over the ensuing centuries by further legislation that elaborated the scope of what constituted crimes against the state. By 1879, there were so many statutes and cases addressing treason that the English Law Commissioners proposed consolidating them into a single, more easily comprehensible, and accessible form. Canada had passed its own laws addressing treason in 1868 and 1886. These acts, the Treason-Felony Statute and the Treason Act, respectively, incorporated elements of the existing English laws and also sought to address problems particular to a small, sometimes besieged colony, neighbour to a much larger republic to the south whose intentions were sometimes inscrutable, and whose memory of military conflict with indigenous rebels and overseas powers (such as French and English battles) was relatively fresh.[3] So, for example, the Canadian Treason Act made it a crime for a member of the army to correspond with any rebel or enemy of the Queen, to participate in an invasion led by a foreigner, and to conspire to intimidate a provincial legislature.

Because the story of our treason law reaches so far back into history, it can be helpful to sketch the manner in which English law formed part of the law of Canada, or how Canada "received" English law. Each of what would become the Canadian provinces (excluding for purposes of this general discussion the province of Quebec, which is governed by a Civil Code system of laws) inherited English common law (i.e., law as it was created and described in the decisions of English courts) and was subject to English laws passed by the English Parliament in Westminster. The statutory laws applied until what is referred to as the "reception date" (which is different for each province). After the reception date, English statutes did not apply in a colonial province (which henceforth would legislate its own laws), unless the English law in question was expressly stated to apply to the entire British Empire, or it specifically mentioned the relevant colony, or the provincial legislature expressly adopted the statute and made it applicable in the colony.[4] Even after the reception date, English common law decisions continued to be cited as authority — and are to this day, though in a markedly reduced and rapidly declining fashion. The history of Canadian and English law, at least from the Canadian perspective, is a story of an intertwined legal tradition, and it was not until well into the twentieth century, certainly in terms of the crimes against the state, that Canadian law began to mature into its own distinct body of authority.

Canada's first comprehensive Criminal Code, enacted in 1892, incorporated elements of the 1351 Statute of Treasons, the 1886 Treason Act, and even the proposals of the English Law Commissioners. Despite the 1892 reworking of the law, and even a series of subsequent amendments and additions to the concept of crimes against the state, it wasn't until 1953 that some of the most archaic provisions of high treason were done away with. Prior to that date it was still high treason to violate (i.e., rape) the monarch's "companion," or the eldest unmarried daughter of the monarch, or the wife of the heir to the throne. While those remnants of an earlier age have been abolished, the anomalous situation remains that while it would be high treason to imprison or kill the unelected monarch (who is our head of state), imprisoning or killing the prime minister, any member of cabinet, or any other elected official would only be punishable under the otherwise applicable sections of the Criminal Code (such as assault, kidnapping, or murder). One other Criminal Code provision addresses protecting the sovereign: Section 49 prohibits any act intended or likely to cause bodily harm to Her Majesty. But the section also contains one of the remaining Criminal Code provisions most likely to raise an eyebrow: it is illegal to commit an act with an intent to "alarm Her Majesty." The current wording of Section 49 is a much-edited version of the original language that described the crime of alarming the monarch. Our first Criminal Code elaborated on the nature of the offence (and also prescribed a punishment of "seven years' imprisonment, and to be whipped once, twice or thrice as the court directs"), describing it as "producing or having" any weapon or "destructive or dangerous thing" near the Queen, or pointing a firearm (loaded or not) at the Queen. Also encompassed was discharging any weapon or explosive, striking the Queen, or throwing anything at the Queen. All of these details have been stripped away over the ensuing years, leaving a much broader concept of "alarming" Her Majesty. It remains the case that no similar prohibition extends to protect the persons of any of the prime minister, the provincial premiers, or any other elected individual. Apparently, our democratic representatives are made of sterner stuff and can be unduly alarmed or surprised as we see fit.

The concept of high treason also encompasses two distinct concepts of "war" against the state. The first is the notion of "levying war" against Canada, which covers an insurrection or rebellion by Canadians against their government.[5] (Volumes have been written contrasting this approach with that enshrined in the American

Declaration of Independence, which provides that "whenever any Form of Government becomes destructive of [the rights of Life, Liberty and the Pursuit of Happiness], it is the Right of the People to alter or abolish it.") The second form of war-related high treason involves assisting an enemy at war with Canada, or any armed forces "against whom Canadian forces are engaged in hostilities whether or not a state of war exists between Canada and the country whose forces they are." The latter portion of the offence was added in 1951[6] in response to the new nature of armed conflict in the wake of the Second World War.[7] A year earlier Canadian forces became engaged in combat in Korea under the auspices of a United Nations "police action" — no state of war had been declared, but Canadian forces were certainly in harm's way,[8] and endangering them was logically deemed to be an instance of high treason, regardless of the technicalities of the armed conflict.

In moving from "high treason" to "treason," the law becomes somewhat more muddled. When the death penalty was still in effect in Canada, there was a clear distinction between the two forms of treason: high treason automatically got you hanged, whereas death was just one sentencing option for regular treason. With the abolishment of the death penalty in 1975, the primary distinction between high and low treason is a transition from crimes that are punished by automatic life imprisonment to crimes that may or may not be punished by life imprisonment.[9] Section 46(2) describes "treason" as "[using] force or violence for the purpose of overthrowing" the federal or provincial government and communicating military or scientific information to an agent of a state other than Canada that "may be used by that state for a purpose prejudicial to the safety or defence of Canada." Also included in the ambit of treason is entering into a conspiracy to commit high treason or to use force to overthrow a government, or "form[ing] an intention to do anything that is high treason or [using violence to overthrow the government] and manifest[ing] that intention by an overt act."

Again, historical circumstances presaged the modification of the crime of treason. It wasn't until 1953, in the wake of the defection of Igor Gouzenko from the Soviet embassy and his revelation that communist spy rings were operating in Canada, that the crime of espionage (i.e., passing sensitive information to a foreign government) was added to the definition of treason.[10] The most recent comprehensive review of the state of our laws on crimes against the state, conducted by the Law Reform Commission of Canada in the 1980s, recommended a radical overhaul to simplify the provisions. The commission noted that there was considerable overlap and confusion embedded in the provisions. To take an easy example, while they are obviously different concepts, it is unclear why there should be any difference in the punishment for "levying war" against Canada under the "high treason" branch and "using force to overthrow" the Canadian government under the "regular" treason branch — in both cases, someone is trying to dislodge or attack the duly constituted authority of our nation, yet the former gets you an automatic life sentence while the sentence for the latter is entirely in the discretion of the judge and could range from a suspended sentence to life in prison.

The language of the treason provisions is intentionally broad: you do not need to be a Canadian citizen to commit treason, and if you are a Canadian citizen or "a person who owes allegiance to Her Majesty," any treasonable acts are prosecutable whether they were committed in Canada or outside of the country.[11] In other words, within Canadian borders, anyone can be charged with treason if they commit the requisite acts, and a Canadian cannot escape the law's long arm simply by plotting outside of the country. The criminal law regime also imposes procedural particularities that impose limitations on the ability of the government to bring a charge of treason. It takes more than the evidence of one witness to enable a conviction for treason, unless the government possesses actual evidence of the treasonous activity (such as written documents or physical evidence).[12] And where someone is accused of using force or violence to overthrow the government, the proceedings must be commenced within three years of the alleged events.[13] An even tighter timeline faces prosecutors who are confronting an accused who has evidenced his or her treasonous intent by "open and considered speech" (where, for example, someone gets up on a soapbox and tries to rally others in an effort to overthrow the government): police must commence proceedings within six days of the words being spoken.[14]

We can count our blessings as Canadians that the treason sections of the Criminal Code have rarely been invoked. For all their Möbius strip complexity, however, some may regard it as truly mind-bending to learn of when the treason provisions have *not* been called upon. The most recent and perhaps most infamous nominally treasonous episode in modern Canadian history occurred in the 1970s and did not result in a single charge being brought under the treason provisions: the terrorist activities of le Front de Libération du Québec (FLQ). Despite a wave of bomb attacks, a manifesto calling for the violent overthrow of the Quebec government, the kidnapping of a British trade commissioner (James Cross), and the kidnapping and murder of a Quebec cabinet minister (Pierre Laporte), no charges of treason were ever laid. Instead, charges of kidnapping, murder, sedition, and other lesser crimes were laid. The longest term served by an FLQ member was eleven years. As historian and novelist Will Ferguson notes, by 1982 everyone involved in the kidnappings and murders was free from prison; various FLQ members, including some of those directly involved in the murder, were university professors and small business owners and even judges and provincial government chiefs of staff.[15]

Though the connection doesn't appear to have been examined, it is possible that the reluctance to use the treason provisions in the case of the FLQ reflected a familiarity on the part of politicians and prosecutors with the results of the most famous treason case in Canadian history: the hanging of Louis Riel. Treason is at its core a political crime, and the quicksilver shifts of political judgments and allegiances mean that prosecutions of political crimes can result in highly unpredictable consequences. Riel's leadership of the Red River Resistance in 1869–70, which manifested the unhappiness of the Métis, aboriginal, and settler residents of what is now Manitoba over the transfer of their land from the Hudson's Bay Company to the British government and then on to the government of Canada, resulted in the accession of Manitoba to Confederation along with federal guarantees that land would be set aside for the exclusive use of the Métis. Riel had declared a provisional government (i.e., rejecting the authority of the Canadian government) in 1869. In the course of a series of attacks and counterattacks by forces loyal to the provisional government and those in favour of federal Canadian expansion, Riel's forces captured an Irish-Ontarian expansionist named Thomas Scott and, after a farcical "trial," executed him by firing squad. What previously had been a resistance to federal expansion on the margins of the country became a national scandal dividing the country on ethnic and linguistic lines. In broad strokes, Protestant English Ontario sided with the federal government, while Catholic French Quebec sympathized with the French-speaking Métis and their comrades-in-arms. In trying to effect a compromise, Prime Minister John A. Macdonald passed the Manitoba Act, making Manitoba a province, thereby satisfying Quebec, and sent an armed force into the new territory to establish order and, in a nod to his Ontario voters, capture Riel.

Riel evaded capture, however, eventually even being elected to the federal Parliament, despite the legislature's refusal to allow him to take his seat. In 1875, the government offered Riel a pardon if he would go into exile. In the meantime, Riel's success in obtaining land grants for the Métis had proved illusory, as Manitoba was flooded with migrants from other provinces in Canada and the government neglected to observe its earlier covenant. The Métis moved farther west into what would one day become Saskatchewan. By 1884, discontent was again broiling on the Prairies, as the residents of the Northwest Territories suffered through bad harvests, broken government promises, and changes in policy (such as shifting the location of the Canadian Pacific Railway tracks). Following stints in mental asylums and in exile in the United States, Riel was brought back to Canada by the entreaties of Gabriel Dumont to lead the Métis and other Northwest Territories residents in the hopes of re-creating his successes, such as they were, of fifteen years earlier. While Riel began with petitions in late 1884, by the spring of 1885 a full military rebellion against the federal government was underway, prompting a response that included three thousand soldiers and nearly two thousand members of the North-West Mounted Police. On May 15, 1885, in the face of superior manpower, firepower, and a determined and savvy campaign led by General Frederick Middleton, Riel surrendered.

Charged with six counts of high treason for levying war against the Queen contrary to the 1351 English Statute of Treasons, Riel was tried in Regina that summer, convicted and, on November 16, 1885, hanged. The language of each charge against Riel contained wording that Riel was "moved and seduced by the instigation of the devil as a false traitor."[16] There is some debate as to whether Riel was properly charged. George R.D. Goulet, in his book *The Trial of Louis Riel: Justice and Mercy Denied*, argues that Riel was improperly charged under the 1351 English Statute of Treasons,[17] while others charged and tried at the same time as Riel, for treasonous activities arising from the same set of circumstances, were charged under the 1868 Canadian Treason-Felony Statute. Political considerations were likely the primary motivation: the English treason statute provided for a penalty of death for high treason; the Canadian statute, on the other hand, provided for a maximum sentence of life imprisonment. The prime minister was anxious to send multiple messages: to Riel, a long-standing personal enemy; to Ontarians, that the murder of Thomas Scott would not go unpunished; and to those in the West, that resorting to violence to remedy grievances would be dealt with as harshly as the law allowed.[18]

The trial itself, much like the earlier Red River Resistance, fractured the country on linguistic and religious lines. In the face of pleadings from Québécois and foreign politicians to commute Riel's death sentence, Macdonald felt obliged to uphold the jury verdict at least in part to placate his Ontario electoral base. "Riel must swing," goes one of the more colourful sayings attributed to Macdonald, "though every dog in Quebec bark in his favour." Riel's hanging prompted burnings of the prime minister's effigy in the streets of Montreal, and the considered judgment of some historians is that Riel was transformed into a political martyr by Macdonald's refusal to commute the death sentence. Some go so far as to say that Macdonald's refusal was a significant component in the collapse of the federal Conservative Party in Quebec in the 1890s (and the concomitant rise of the Liberal Party to power). Certainly, Quebec politicians weren't afraid to trade on the emotional resonance of Riel's tale: Wilfrid Laurier, one day to be Liberal prime minister of the country, publicly declared in Montreal that, presented with the opportunity, he, too, would have shouldered a musket alongside Riel.

By 1969, the year that Prime Minister Pierre Trudeau personally unveiled a statue dedicated to Riel, a remarkable political turnaround had occurred: a man who not only had raised arms against the government but had been tried and convicted of treason, the gravest offence under our criminal justice tradition, in a duly constituted court of law, was hailed as a Father of Confederation and, at worst, a sort of anti-hero embodiment of frontier scrappiness. In 2002, when the Canadian Broadcasting Corporation (CBC) broadcast a mock retrial of Riel, an overwhelming majority of viewers who watched and voted indicated that they would have rendered a verdict of not guilty. In the CBC's November 2004 "Greatest Canadian" contest, Riel placed eleventh. When crime, justice, and politics intersect to the extent that the crimes against the state provisions mandate, it can be difficult to discern where the demands of one end and the imperatives of the other govern.[19]

If one were to erect a taxonomy of the crimes against the state, treason would at least be regarded as the respectable elder sibling. For the most part, treason at least requires you to *do something* in order to be convicted of a crime. It is the unloved stepchild called "sedition" that brings the entire category of crimes against the state into disrepute. A study of sedition reveals that criminal law is often twisted to serve political ends: it once provided a most useful tool for governments intent on curbing opposition. Much as is the case with "treason," "sedition" is shorthand that refers not to a single crime but to a set of closely related offences: speaking seditious words, publishing a seditious libel, or being party to a seditious conspiracy.[20] The term for the basic technical offence, *seditious libel*, betrays its roots: it once consisted of saying bad things about those in power.[21]

One of the earliest sources of the law of sedition is the evocatively named case *De Libellis Famosis* from 1606, which held that the writing of a poem that defamed the deceased archbishop of Canterbury was a criminal act.[22] By 1704, the courts had determined that defaming the government was a crime, and by the end of that century the first bill was passed in England that codified the matter.[23] When Canada adopted its Criminal Code in 1892, the sedition laws were inherited along with the laws on treason. As they are currently worded, the seditious offences hinge on the concept of *seditious intention*, which is defined in an expansive manner: Section 60 stipulates that "without limiting the generality of the meaning of the expression," a seditious intention is one that advocates "the use, without the authority of law, of force as a means of accomplishing a governmental change within Canada."

When a word or phrase is defined in statute, the drafters of the legislation have a number of different ways of handling the definition. They can define it in a specific manner (e.g., "vehicle *means* …") or in an inclusive manner (e.g., "vehicle *includes* …"). The former device is appropriate if the legislation is intended to have a specific scope (e.g., "vehicle *means* a two-wheeled combustion-engine device for transporting one or two riders" could suffice for a law meant to address motorcycles), while the latter device is used when the legislation is meant to have broad application and be capable of adapting to new situations (e.g., "vehicle *includes* an automobile, a motorcycle and a nautical vessel" would be helpful for a law that is intended to prohibit the use of "vehicles" on footpaths in city parks — it allows courts to adapt the scope of the law to encompass new forms of transportation, such as motorized scooters, as and when they pose a problem). Sedition is one of those crimes that Parliament has historically elected to draft in as broad a fashion as possible — the partial definition that currently exists was not added until 1936. The inclusive nature of the definition is meant to capture not just the possibilities that occurred to the legislators at the time of drafting but the accumulated variations on the concept present in the cases on the topic previously decided, as well as such variations as might be devised in cases to be decided in the future. Hidden within the phrase "without limiting the generality" in Section 60 of the Criminal Code is the Canadian history of sedition. It is not always a proud one. As some have noted, Canada prosecuted more sedition cases than all the other member countries of the British Empire and Commonwealth combined (excluding India, a country that went through an insurrectionist movement of its own, culminating in its 1947 independence). Indeed, in a two-year period during the First World War, Alberta alone witnessed more sedition prosecutions than England had seen in a century.[24]

Even before sedition was set out in the Criminal Code — before there even *was* a criminal code — the early colonial governments of what would soon be Canadian provinces were vigilant in their defence of ... well, themselves. The sedition offences historically had as their concern the protection of the tranquility of the state.[25] A classic English judgment on the matter described sedition as "a crime against society, nearly allied to that of treason ... it embraces all of those practices ... which are calculated to disturb the tranquility of the state, and lead ignorant persons to endeavour to subvert the Government and the laws of the empire."[26] Where treason requires positive action against the state, such as taking up arms or assaulting the monarch, sedition was originally more akin to a thought crime: you did not need to actualize your discontent in any manner other than simply giving voice to it. The phrase "seditious libel" frames the concern: saying bad things about those in power could so agitate other people that they might see fit to act on your criticisms and overthrow the government. Much better, it was thought, to stamp out any such potential trouble at the outset than to address the concerns themselves. A standard definition of seditious intention described it as the intention

> to bring into hatred or contempt, or to excite disaffection against the person of Her Majesty ... or the Government and Constitution ... or either House of Parliament, or the administration of justice ... or to raise discontent or disaffection among Her Majesty's subjects, or to promote feelings of ill-will and hostility between different classes of Her Majesty's subjects.[27]

In a manner that we consider shocking today, seditious libel involved the criminalization of speech or writing that "creat[ed] ill-will, discontent, disaffection, hatred or contempt towards the established institutions of the country."[28]

In Nova Scotia in the first half of the 1800s, there were reform movements and efforts at securing responsible government. Two men, William Wilkie and Joseph Howe, faced criminal prosecution for expressing their criticisms of the governments and the local power brokers whom they opposed. The charges were brought under the English common law and legislation that were both the governing law in Nova Scotia prior to Canadian Confederation. William Wilkie was convicted and sentenced in 1820 to two years' hard labour.[29] While Howe was luckier in that he was acquitted, his story illustrates how the law could be used by those in power to suppress political dissent.[30] Howe was the editor of the *Novascotian*, a prominent fount of criticism and a rallying voice for opposition to a Halifax government described as "corrupt, inefficient and unreformed."[31] In November 1834 and January 1835, in the culmination of a campaign of criticism and exposure, Howe's paper published anonymous letters (signed "The People") that criticized the local magistrates, levelling charges, without naming any individual, of corruption, embezzlement, and incompetence (e.g., "during the lapse of the last 30 years, the Magistracy and Police have, by one stratagem or other, taken from the pockets of the people ... a sum that would exceed in the gross amount £30,000"). After the publication of the second letter, a group of magistrates laid a complaint with the lieutenant-governor and attorney general, seeking a charge of seditious libel against Howe. By March, a grand jury had approved the indictment (based on testimony by the Crown's sole witness: the editor of a rival newspaper sympathetic to the interests of the government) and a trial was commenced.

Members of the Halifax bar were reluctant to defend Howe against the charges. Though they demurred that the case was too similar to the Wilkie case from fifteen years earlier (which Wilkie lost) and therefore Howe stood a poor chance of escaping conviction, observers concluded that they were "intimidated by the degree of government interest in, and sponsorship of, the prosecution."[32] An individual's reputation and financial prospects in such a small community, especially one where a corrupt government stage-managed so many aspects, were likely to be negatively affected by acting in a cause so unpopular with those who were wielding power. Howe, whose formal education consisted largely of having been apprenticed to a printer, was left to defend himself.

The alleged seditious libel was read in court, and Howe began to present his argument to the jury — all six and one-quarter hours of it. His strategy was twofold: remind the jury of the corruption of the magistrates in an effort to distract them, and attempt to convince them of the value of a free press in holding the government to account. The truth of the statements contained in "The People's" letters was largely irrelevant: unlike a regular defamation trial, truth was not a defence to a charge of sedition. The only defence that Howe could avail himself of was that his *intention* had not been seditious — nominally a difficult shield to raise, since presumably the entire point of publishing criticisms of governing officials was to effect a change in the political system or at the very least the identity of those occupying positions of power. Nonetheless, Howe was able to sway those sitting in judgment of him. Despite the fact that the judge presiding over the case informed the jury that his opinion was that "The People's" letters were libellous, the jury returned a verdict of not guilty.[33] Howe's victory was touted (not least by Howe himself) as establishing a commitment to freedom of the press in Nova Scotia, evidencing again the odd element of the dynamic that animates so much of the story of "crimes against the state." Efforts to enforce sedition laws often result in precisely the opposite effect that the authorities intend — a strengthening of resolve and an increase in support for the accused enemies of the state. But behind any salutary effect of Howe's victory lay a darker truth (one upon which the unlucky William Wilkie, while serving his hard labour sentence, had occasion to reflect): the administration of criminal justice was twisted in the Howe case in an attempt to effect a political end — the silencing of criticism. Unlike Wilkie, Howe had been successful in countering the charges, but the mere fact that the prosecution took place at all served an "educational" purpose: if you wanted to publicly criticize the government, you faced the possibility of having to stand in court and defend your words. The government could hope to gain from the intimidating effect of a looming, even if losing, prosecution.

Until fetters were placed on the seditious offences in the middle of the twentieth century, they were sometimes put to ends that are frankly astonishing to current eyes. Particularly at times when political or historical circumstances could be perceived as threatening to the established order, the hoary crime was hauled out and put to its ill-tempered work. Consider the story of Oscar Felton. In late August 1915, during what would come to be known as the First World War, Oscar was sitting in a bar in Okotoks, Alberta. The bartender and other patrons listened as Oscar held forth on his thoughts on the clash in Europe; as one judge hearing the appeal of Felton's conviction noted, Felton "made some very insulting references to Englishmen in language some of which is quite unfit for repetition." Going on, Felton averred that he would not be upset to see Germany cross the English Channel and wipe England off the map. Felton was promptly arrested, charged, and convicted of speaking seditious words.[34] Far from regarding the charged emotions surrounding the war effort as a factor that may have resulted in an overzealous arrest and prosecution, the court determined that the "state of nervous tension and excitement, and intense feeling against the enemy" among Felton's audience meant that "words which, in ordinary times, would have no outward effect in creating disorder, cannot be used now without much greater danger." Having offended those around him, Felton would have been unlikely to use them, the court concluded, unless he had "some intent to stir up trouble." In short, sedition was confirmed: the rantings of an old man in a bar in a small town in Alberta could not go unpunished.

As with the downfall of Oscar Felton, it is the prosaic nature of some of the sedition cases that is almost wrenching. In 1916, George Cohen, a dealer in second-hand furniture who lived in a suburb of Calgary, was reading a newspaper while waiting for a clerk to come back to the tobacco stand where Cohen wanted to purchase some tobacco.[35] Cohen, formerly an officer in the German army, laughed upon reading an account of Canadian soldiers being defeated in battle. Challenged by Wiggins, a neighbouring grocer who was also waiting for the tobacco clerk to return, Cohen told Wiggins it was good news that the Canadians were being beaten, that Canadians were "slaves" forced to follow the orders of King George and Lord Kitchener, then the cabinet minister overseeing the war effort. Horrified at what he was hearing, Wiggins continued to argue with Cohen, who went on to condone the use of poison gas by the Germans and remarked that the bodies of dead Canadians would make good fertilizer on the battlefields of Europe. While Cohen's views and words were undoubtedly odious, we are left to ponder whether it was necessary to devote police and court resources to prosecuting a man for voicing such unpalatable views. In a discomfiting illustration of a court not seeing the forest for the trees, the court hearing Cohen's appeal characterized the case as "upon the extreme limit of the law" of sedition and noted that it was "inclined to wonder why the authorities saw fit to put the country to the expense of a criminal trial" — after all, the decision continued, it was "possible to intern the accused as an enemy alien for the duration of the war." Why, so the reasoning apparently went, bother prosecuting him for sedition, when you could simply imprison him for being German?

In any event, the court dismissed Cohen's appeal, echoing the *Felton* decision by citing "the circumstances not only of the particular occasion [i.e., buying tobacco] but also of the times," and noting that Cohen's language could have stirred up "feelings of ill-will against His

Majesty's peaceable subjects of German origin and have a tendency to create dissension and even riots in such times as these." No evidence was entered that Wiggins, described as "extremely loyal" (i.e., to the King), was prompted to riot by Cohen's noxious musings. Perhaps most damning, in the court's view, was that Cohen felt comfortable sharing his thoughts with a near-stranger: "this was not a case of a quiet conversation between close and intimate personal friends but an open declaration of opinion to a person, only an acquaintance, casually met in a public place." There were rather strict limits, in other words, to the right to declare your opinion in a public place, even if only in a normal conversational tone to one other person.

In the case of Albert Manshrick,[36] it was two separate incidents that resulted in his conviction for uttering seditious words. On two separate occasions, canvassers seeking donations for the Patriotic Fund approached Manshrick. One commented to Albert in July 1916 that the German army was apt to conquer Canada, and Albert responded "let them come, it would be all right." A few weeks later, a different canvasser commented to Albert that some of the Canadian soldiers being sent off to war "will never come back," and Albert responded that he "hope[d] to God none of them comes back." The fact that Manshrick had declined to give money to the Patriotic Fund was not, the judge cautioned, to be used in determining his guilt or innocence. In giving his instructions to the jury, the judge told them that the essence of the crime of uttering words with a seditious intention was whether "the language was calculated, or was it not, to promote public disorder." The jury concluded Manshrick did so intend and duly convicted him. A third indictment, that Manshrick had praised the German sinking of the civilian cruise liner *Lusitania* in 1915, did not result in a conviction — certainly the judge, in instructing the jury on the point, was shocked into disbelief that the accused could utter such "wicked expression of such a horrible thought," and evidently the jury concurred.

It wasn't until a couple of years later that an appellate court in a different case finally conceded the distinction between voicing "disloyal and unpatriotic" thoughts (which though distasteful whether or not expressed in a time of war nevertheless shouldn't result in a criminal record) and actually trying to convince people to overthrow the government by means of violent revolution:[37] Arthur Trainor, living in Strathmore, Alberta, upon hearing of the sinking of the *Lusitania*, had laughed. A colleague confronted him over this reaction, remonstrating that "you surely can't advocate the killing of innocent women, children and non-combatants." Trainor responded that he could indeed, "under the circumstances," chiding his interlocutor, "do not be a hypocrite; you know very well the British are killing women and children by trying to starve them." When Trainor appealed his conviction, Justice Stuart noted that "I cannot understand how a declaration of an opinion in an argument in a country store ... detestable though the opinion is in the hearts of all of us, can be said to have been calculated or expressive of an intention to stir up discontent or disaffection among His Majesty's subjects." Seeking to halt the drift of the earlier cases into punishing mere offensive expression, Stuart lucidly quashed the conviction, noting, "I do not think we should merely say: 'This fellow is evidently a German sympathizer so we will clap him in jail.' ... What I fear in this case is that the accused is being punished for his mere opinions and feelings and not for anything which is covered by the criminal law."

The cases discussed above show a young country in times of political development and war trying to come to grips with a commitment to the unfettered use of language. But the commitment to robust democratic debate and an accommodation of varying political projects often must contend with matters of more import than verbal exchanges or written declarations of contrarian opinion. Sometimes manifesting political action pushes societies and their pledges to free expression, democracy, and the rule of law to the breaking point. The popular imagination has miscast government concern about the threat of communist insurrection as a phenomenon of the 1950s. However, the historical fact remains that it was a generation earlier, in the wake of the Russian Revolution of 1917, that Canadian authorities confronted what they saw as widespread Bolshevik agitation and sought to quell it. The Winnipeg General Strike of 1919 witnessed one of the most widespread and concerted uses in Canadian history of the sedition offences in an effort to suppress political dissent — to this day, the strike and the propriety of the government reaction remain controversial topics. The *Felton* court's reference to the accused not speaking in "ordinary times" can be a licence for the exercise of political power, an attempt to justify a troubling overreach by reference to "exceptional circumstances." The danger is the temptation to consider all circumstances as extraordinary, requiring overbroad enforcement of laws, always with the caveat that circumstances not just beyond our control but out of control are forcing us to do something that we would otherwise abhor. It is with that in mind and by genuinely grappling with the question of whether the government was facing a radical rebellion (or had good reason to think it was) that the events surrounding the Winnipeg General Strike should be interpreted.

Unlike the cases already discussed in this chapter, many of the prosecutions surrounding the Winnipeg General Strike relied on the offence of "seditious conspiracy," a crime that requires an agreement between two or more persons to carry out a seditious intention. In 1919, the government and the media saw conspiracies everywhere. In the United States, an attempted general strike in Seattle in 1918 had been broken, and radical socialist and anarchist political dissidents were engaged in a variety of actions, including the sending of letter bombs to government officials and business leaders. (One such bomb destroyed the front of the U.S. attorney general's house.) As a result of the end of the war, massive demobilization, increasing agitation for recognition and protection of workers' rights, and the evident success of the communist revolution in the Soviet Union, many in business, government, and the media were concerned that similar political violence could take place in Canada.[38] Winnipeg, especially, was on edge: the gateway to the Canadian West was a prosperous, bustling city dependent on thousands of labourers who were beginning to heed the exhortations of union leaders to organize, stand up, and demand their fair share. In addition, the city had a large immigrant community, prompting a certain level of xenophobic unease among more established elements. The Royal North-West Mounted Police and the media were on the watch: "an end to censorship, the overthrow of capitalism, amicable relations with Russia or even a dictatorship of the Canadian proletariat were given top billing by both the police and the journalists. ... [But] while a few radicals suggested that blood might have to flow, none of them advocated the initiation of revolution by force."[39]

On May 15, 1919, a general strike began in Winnipeg.[40] Workers in the metal and building trades had been on strike since April, and the Winnipeg Trades and Labour Council voted to join them in solidarity. Labour leaders had encouraged non-unionized workers to join in the protest, as well, and were successful beyond all expectation. Somewhere between 24,000 and 35,000 individuals (in a city of approximately

200,000) walked out of their jobs, effecting a nearly total stoppage of work: "There was no telephone, telegraph, bread or milk delivery, no mail, garbage, streetcar, taxi, express or freight service, and no regular fire prevention. There was also fear that the city police might soon join the strike."[41] The municipal government refused to negotiate and fired its employees who had left their jobs, as did the post office. Organizing committees (which sometimes feuded with one another) were quickly set up by the unions and strikers to try to manage the chaotic situation. The government was anxious that returning soldiers, who might be able to provide the technical and leadership know-how for an actual attempt to overthrow the government, would sympathize with the strikers and convert that sympathy into action.[42] The strikers attempted to shut down the Winnipeg newspapers in light of their history of anti-union sentiment — a chilling echo of Soviet efforts to muzzle free speech. Anti-strike elements organized into a "citizens' committee" to counter the "strike committee" and began publishing a newspaper that described the strike as obviously revolutionary, whose intention was to usurp the existing civil order and replace it with a Soviet-style workers' dictatorship. The police union expressed its support of the strikers' goals but acceded to the request of the strike committee that its members remain on duty. Throughout all of this, it should be stressed, the official policy of the strike committee was a commitment to non-violence and efforts to avoid mass confrontations that could quickly spiral out of control.

Media reaction across the continent was fierce (some describe it as "hysterical").[43] Winnipeg was described as the opening salvo in a communist-led revolution. Minor labour actions began taking place in other Canadian cities as an expression of solidarity with those in Winnipeg. On May 31, a large parade of pro-strike war veterans flooded the Manitoba legislature and confronted the premier before doing the same to the mayor at city hall — neither confrontation, raucous as they were, resulted in either significant violence or a settlement of grievances. General Ketchen, the officer in command of the military district in which Winnipeg was situated, viewed the city police as collaborators with the strike committee and put in place an initiative to recruit a special force whose members' loyalty would not be questionable. By June 5, two thousand special police were hired, dwarfing the regular police corps of around two hundred officers. On June 10, the first reported violence (mild though it apparently was) occurred when a crowd gathered to listen to a speaker was cleared by mounted officers. As the one-month anniversary of the strike declaration passed, the authorities pledged to take decisive action. In the very early hours of June 17, six of the leaders of the Winnipeg General Strike were arrested from their beds at gun-point, together with four illegal immigrants who were unrelated to the leadership of the strike. During the preceding weeks, General Ketchen had steadily reinforced the Royal North-West Mounted Police, includ-ing militia groups armed with trucks and machine guns.

Finally, on Saturday, June 21, the entire endeavour climaxed in a forceful showdown. A massive "silent parade" was held by pro-strike veterans' groups, in violation of a mayoral ban on parades. Over the course of the afternoon, police reinforcements flooded into the city. Meanwhile, a portion of the crowd, having failed in its efforts to tip a streetcar off the tracks, set the vehicle on fire. Mounted police mar-shalled to keep an eye on the illegal parade ran three charges through the crowd, having been met with a hail of stones and other projectiles. At 2:35 p.m., the mayor read the Riot Act from the steps of City Hall, giving the crowd thirty minutes to disperse. Moments after the mayor finished his proclamation, however, the officer in command of the Royal North-West Mounted Police ordered his officers to fire into the crowd; one man was shot and killed instantly, while a second died later of his wounds. At this point the crowd rampaged, only to be met by hundreds of the special auxiliary police forces, armed with clubs, and the aforementioned militia units, armed with heavy weaponry. The strike was effectively broken, the city essentially under armed occupa-tion and, in the days following, workers began to return to their jobs.

Any number of interpretations have been placed on the events in Winnipeg, with some viewing it as another set-piece battle in the war between capital and labour. Regardless of the rhetorical spin put on the events, the government of the day was facing a challenge to its duly con-stituted authority, and it responded. As the strike dragged on, the federal government of Prime Minister Robert Borden at first pledged a policy of non-interference, but then, in response to the growing media firestorm and resultant concerns expressed by voters and business leaders across the country, began to act. The government's response was multi-faceted but involved two primary elements: a forceful military/police response that effectively re-established government authority on the ground and, as perhaps was to be expected, an enhancement and escalated use of the sedition offences. After the strike had continued for more than twenty days, on June 6, 1919, a bill was introduced in the federal House of Commons that provided for the deportation of anyone convicted of a seditious offence. All three readings of the bill were accomplished in less than twenty minutes, and it was passed and received royal assent on the same day.[44] It was under this change to the Immigration Act that the June 17 arrests of the strike leaders were effected. Within days following the end of the Winnipeg General Strike, an amendment to the Criminal Code was passed: the maximum punishment for seditious libel was increased from two years to twenty years in prison.[45] Although the increased punishment hadn't been passed during the life of the strike, news of its drafting and impending enactment had been circulated in Winnipeg. As if to perfectly encapsulate the effect that heightened social tensions can wreak on the face of the law, eleven years after the end of the strike, with passions having cooled and the memory of the strike having become muted, the maximum punishment was reduced back to its original length.

Although seven of the eight strike leaders arrested and charged were foreign-born, and thus liable to deportation under the new powers contained in the Immigration Act, it was ultimately decided not to deport them but to try them for seditious conspiracy; seven were ultimately convicted.[46] The trial of the first strike leader, R.B. Russell, saw hundreds of political pamphlets (including the *Communist Manifesto*) and labour newspapers introduced as evidence of the conspiracy. Of course, the words used in some of these publications were something less than benign: "when the workers take control ... they will form a Dictatorship which will give the same order to the owners of the world that Lenin gave to the capitalists of Russia: Obey or starve."[47] But the tenor of the times seemed to force radical leaps of logic in the courts. Simply having the documents in one's possession was deemed sufficient to admit them into evidence as showing participation in a seditious conspiracy; as one judge stated during the course of one of the appeals from the convictions, "it will be inferred that he knows their contents *and has acted upon them*" [emphasis added].[48] Russell was convicted and sentenced to two years in prison, the maximum punishment on the books at the time the crime was committed. The remaining six convictions resulted in one sentence of six months and five sentences of one year. One strike leader, A.A. Heaps, was able to win an acquittal.

As a result of their reporting on the riotous events of June 21 in labour publications, a further two individuals, one being J.S. Woodsworth, later to become a Member of Parliament and leader of the left-wing Co-operative Commonwealth Federation (which evolved into the New Democratic Party in 1961), were charged with seditious libel. Fred Dixon, defending himself, was able to secure an acquittal based on his arguments referencing freedom of the press. The charges against Woodsworth followed a more circuitous route: embarrassment resulted when it was revealed that the indictment against Woodsworth included two rather odd examples of his allegedly seditious libel — quotations Woodsworth had included in his writings taken from the Book of Isaiah in the Old Testament.[49] In light of this, and the acquittal of Dixon, the charges against Woodsworth were dropped and he didn't face trial.

The highly charged atmosphere that surrounded the events in Winnipeg, though it dissipated after June 21, 1919, has continued on long after through the academic literature probing the matter. This is likely because of our inability to precisely assess the matter. As noted at the beginning of this chapter, there is an element of unease when we talk about the government, which retained a firm hold on all the levers of power, beginning to punish those who would seek to dislodge the established order; discerning the dividing line between abuse of power and justifiable punishment of genuine threats to our constitutional and legal order can be difficult, whether in the heat of the moment or with the benefit of hindsight. As one chronicler of the strike has stated, "The point here is that the atmosphere of the period was highly prejudicial to, firstly, the decision of whether or not to prosecute and, secondly, the trial of the issue."[50] This is not to say that the concerns about an imminent Bolshevik revolution on the Prairies were insincere: authorities were genuinely concerned that what they were witnessing was the dislocation of constitutional authority. At one point, the lieutenant-governor of British Columbia asked Prime Minister Robert Borden to request the dispatch of a British cruiser to the waters off Vancouver to deal with protesting workers.[51] There was a palpable "Red Scare" and perhaps rightly so: we should take the leaders of the socialist movement at their word that they intended to overthrow the capitalist system and its government; basic respect for their expression of their political ideals demands no less.

In any event, the government reacted wilfully. As mentioned above, in the immediate wake of Winnipeg, the maximum penalty for sedition was increased tenfold, and a "saving clause" was deleted: the language of the sedition offence had previously included a provision that had provided that no person would be deemed to have a seditious intention by reason only that he intends, in good faith, to point out errors or defects in the activities of the Queen or of the government or in the constitution or in the administration of justice — no longer would this "safe harbour" be available for those charged with a sedition offence. At the same time, the Criminal Code was amended to include a new Section 98, which broadened the sedition offences to include belonging to any organization "whose professed purpose ... is to bring about any governmental, industrial or economic change within Canada by use of force, violence or physical injury to person or property, or by threats of such injury, or which teaches, advocates, advises or defends the use of force, violence, terrorism or physical injury to person or property."[52] In other words, even though the strike had been successfully put down using the laws of the time, in the wake of that success the government nevertheless deemed it necessary to make an already vague offence that was open to abuse even *more* nebulous — the argument being that the government needed more tools to fight perceived threats to order.

During the 1920s and 1930s, sedition trials continued to occur with some regularity, particularly in Quebec against Jehovah's Witnesses (discussed in more detail in Chapter 6). In 1923, J.B. McLachlan, a communist and secretary of United Mine Workers of America District 26 in Nova Scotia, was tried, convicted, and imprisoned for seditious libel.[53] McLachlan had written a letter to union members decrying a violent assault by mounted provincial police trying to break a strike by coal miners; in describing "the most brutal manner" in which the police charge had resulted in the beatings and woundings of an elderly woman and a nine-year-old boy, McLachlan called for a sympathetic wildcat strike by his members. In the early 1930s, as the Great Depression ground down the populace, another round of anti-communist activities occupied government attention. In 1931, in a curious echo of the number of charges laid twelve years earlier in Winnipeg, eight leaders of the Communist Party of Canada, including Tim Buck, its general secretary, were arrested in Ontario and charged with violating Section 98 (i.e., belonging to an "unlawful association") and with participating in a seditious conspiracy;

once again, as in Winnipeg, seven were convicted. The conspiracy charges were quashed on appeal, but the other convictions were upheld.[54] Buck was sentenced to five years in prison — by the time of his release from Kingston Penitentiary in 1934, a reported crowd of seven thousand jubilant supporters met him at Union Station in Toronto, cheering and singing as he was "carried in triumph through the streets."[55] The rehabilitation that the legacy of Louis Riel would experience had witnessed its own minor precursor with Buck.

The political tempests that resulted in the widened ambit of the sedition offences and saw their enforcement through the 1920s and 1930s blew strongly but not for long. By 1936, it was conceded that the post-Winnipeg laws were excessive; the maximum penalty for sedition had already been reduced back to two years from twenty, the "saving clause" was reinstated (it is now found in Section 60 of the Criminal Code), and Section 98 was repealed. In addition, the partial definition now contained in Section 59(4) was introduced, giving at least a modicum of guidance as to what constitutes a seditious intention (i.e., advocating the use of force as a means of accomplishing governmental change). Of course, winds blow every which way on occasion: in 1951, as the Cold War settled in, the maximum sentence for committing a seditious offence was raised to seven years, and four years later it was increased to the current maximum of fourteen years.[56]

The story of sedition and crimes against the state in Canada doesn't end there. Two more episodes of interest occurred after the Second World War. Perhaps the most important development in the modern Canadian law of sedition arose from the curious case of Aimé Boucher, a farmer in Quebec who also happened to be an ardent member of the Jehovah's Witnesses.[57] As discussed in Chapter 6, the government of Quebec was engaged in a protracted war of attrition with the Witnesses, and Boucher was the latest to attract criminal charges.[58] (Also discussed in that chapter is the story of the various charges, including seditious offences, which were brought against the Doukhobor sect in British Columbia.) Boucher published and distributed a pamphlet entitled "Quebec's Burning Hate for God, Christ and Freedom Is the Shame of All Canada." With strident and colourful language, Boucher railed against Catholic priests, the invidious efforts of the government in prosecuting his co-religionists, and the complicity of the judiciary in imposing heavy fines and requiring stiff bail postings. He urged people to protest the government's "mob rule and Gestapo tactics" — by praying. Charges of seditious libel followed, and Boucher's determined efforts to appeal his convictions presented the Supreme Court of Canada with such an opportunity to consider important issues that they heard the case and rendered a decision not just once, but twice.[59]

In a progressive and modern judgment that still warrants reading, Justice Rand, having reviewed the existing law and history of seditious libel, rendered a ringing endorsement of the principles of free expression: "Freedom in thought and speech and disagreement in ideas and beliefs, on every conceivable subject, are of the essence of our life. The clash of critical discussion on political, social and religious subjects has too deeply become the stuff of daily experience to suggest that mere ill-will as a product of controversy can strike down the latter with illegality." Merely criticizing the government, even seeking to cause people to hate the government and reject its authority, in other words, is no longer sufficient to warrant a conviction for seditious libel. What is required then is that the publication be intended to result and *capable* of resulting, or *actually result*, in a disturbance of or resistance to the lawfully constituted government (or that the publication would inevitably have resulted in such disturbance or resistance) — a significantly higher threshold than that used to convict Oscar Felton or Albert Manshrick. Following *Boucher*, freedom of expression, even robust, disturbing, and provocative expression, is privileged over allowing the government easy access to the potent weapon of the sedition offences. The ambit of sedition has been greatly curtailed, and it shows: since *Boucher*, there has been only one major set of sedition charges — against five members of the FLQ.

Although on November 4, 1970, the Quebec justice minister had announced the possibility that a number of the FLQ members who had been arrested might be charged with treason and sedition,[60] only five were actually charged with seditious conspiracy. Their defence lawyers were successful in obtaining a motion to quash the charges, though the same charges were laid again against three of the five defendants. Two of the three were acquitted of seditious conspiracy, while the third, Pierre Vallières, skipped town before his hearing could take place. After being in hiding for close to a year, Vallières re-emerged and renounced his support for the FLQ; the prosecution elected not to try him on the seditious conspiracy charge, instead allowing him to stand trial on a charge of uttering seditious words (i.e., advocating the use of force to effect a change in government), for which he received a suspended sentence.

While the seditious offences and treason have largely faded into the historical tapestry, the crimes remain part of the Criminal Code, as do some of the ancillary crimes against the state. They remain a curious amalgam of the mortally serious and the curiously mundane — from waging war against Canada to "alarming" Her Majesty. As a result of their continued presence, not all parts of the story occurred decades ago. In 1996, charges of "intimidating the legislature" (contrary to Section 51 of the Criminal Code) were laid against four students who participated in a protest/riot at Queen's Park in Toronto wherein they broke through police lines on their way towards damaging and occupying the building's lobby. The decision to lay such charges prompted an avalanche of criticism querying whether the government of the day had pressured prosecutors to exhume an obscure charge with the aim of squelching future protests; the charges were subsequently dropped.[61]

As the public has become less tolerant of such manipulations and the speed with which they are exposed and criticized has multiplied with increased media coverage, the Criminal Code provisions have been sparingly used, and the criminal justice approach has been modified in reaction to new developments. Those arrested in connection with the alleged plots referred to at the beginning of this chapter were charged under anti-terrorism provisions of the Criminal Code introduced in the wake of the September 11, 2001, attacks on the United States; half a century ago it is likely they would have been prosecuted under the sedition offences. As has been learned through decades of protest and prosecutions, allowing the government to decide what constitutes a crime against it can result in what in a different context would be called "mission creep": when issues of expression and political action collide with entrenched interests, it is far better that we err in favour of a stalwart commitment to the open and liberal democratic process, and rely on narrowly drafted discrete crimes, rather than open-ended "crimes against the state" with all of the historical weft and warping they entail.

4

Keep Your Pants On

iven just how varied and variable the sexual experience is — it can be transcendent, casual, a matter of commerce, loving, religious, and so much more, ad infinitum — it should come as no surprise that where the law and sex connect, grave confusion and hilarity can often ensue. The common law is an incredible attempt to combine predictability and flux, but it does best with matters that are formulaic and follow a template. Because our cultural relationship with sex is so mutable, and our views regarding what is and is not acceptable are capable of such rapid change, we can be assured that the laws on sex are imperfect and will necessarily give rise to some stories worth recounting.

Perhaps nothing better illustrates our fractious approach to sexual activity than the laws relating to prostitution. It remains the case that prostitution (engaging in sexual activities in exchange for money or property) is not a crime in Canada. Instead, we have tried to make everything *around* prostitution illegal: pimping (technically referred to as "procuring" a person to have sexual intercourse with another person) and all the various activities appurtenant thereto (including living off the avails of a prostitute); keeping or living in a "common bawdy-house" (i.e., in the historical argot, a "whorehouse"); and communicating in public for the purpose of engaging in prostitution (which includes stopping or impeding motor vehicle or pedestrian traffic).[1] As a result of the gaps between those provisions, a lively trade has sprung up in full-colour advertisements in the back pages of weekly alternative newspapers in most cities across the country. Prostitutes are perfectly within their rights to advertise their services through print or on the Internet (because the communications are not taking place in public), engage in private negotiations with interested clients, and then provide sexual services in exchange for money in the privacy of either the homes of their customers, their own homes, or in premises rented from third parties (though the latter two may run afoul of the prohibitions on keeping or being found in a common bawdy-house).

The finely drawn lines of these legal fictions, when everyone knows what we're *actually* trying to deal with, results in the occasional moment of mirth. The artful phrase "common bawdy-house" has been the subject of numerous court decisions, few more satisfying than the 1982 case of *R v Pierce and Golloher*.[2] Mesdames Pierce and Golloher were prostitutes who had been observed to "frequent the area of Queen Street West and Manning Avenue" in Toronto; prospective clients would drive around and either be flagged down by one of the ladies in question or would stop for a chat. After introductions had been made, the customers would be instructed to drive to the parking lot behind 800 Richmond Street West, which had a number of parking stalls, both open-air and some that were covered (because they were cut into the first storey of the building). During the course of the police investigation, Pierce and Golloher had been observed to use a variety of spaces in which to park with their clients — really, whichever ones were not already occupied by parked cars at the relevant time. The investigation included police officers witnessing Pierce and Golloher engaging in various sex acts in the cars, as well as receiving money from the men with whom they had parked. Presumably out of an abundance of caution in gathering evidence, according to the appeals court decision, the police also "seized 23 samples of Kleenex tissues" that had been disposed of by the women on exiting the cars. The tissues were sent to the Centre for Forensic Sciences and, as could be guessed, were found to contain semen. There was, in short, little question as to what was occurring behind 800 Richmond Street West. But, in a rather novel application of the law, prosecutors charged Pierce and Golloher with "keeping a common bawdy-house." Evidently bemused by the notion that a parking lot could be construed as a "bawdy-house," since it lacked the presumably requisite "house"-ness, the trial judge acquitted the women. Undaunted, the Crown appealed to the Ontario Court of Appeal, and the unanimous three-judge panel took the issue very seriously indeed: the written decision of the court includes a table

charting the frequency of use of various parking stalls by the prostitutes over a one-month period.

The Criminal Code defines a "common bawdy-house" as "a place that is (a) kept or occupied, or (b) resorted to by one or more persons, for the purpose of prostitution or the practice of acts of indecency"; the term *place* is defined to include "any place, whether or not (a) it is covered or enclosed, (b) it is used permanently or temporarily, or (c) any person has an exclusive right of use with respect to it." Based on such an expansive definition, the Court of Appeal held that the parking lot could indeed be a "common bawdy-house" — because "any defined space is capable of being a common bawdy-house," provided that there is "localization" of acts of prostitution within the delineated boundaries.

Unfortunately for the prosecution, however, that victory was as far as they were going to get. The crime with which Pierce and Golloher were charged was "*keeping* a common bawdy-house." The court duly turned its attention to the concept of "keeping" and who, precisely, could be found to have "kept" the previously unassuming parking lot behind 800 Richmond Street West. The court determined that whatever Pierce and Golloher had done, they were not keepers of the parking lot/bawdy-house: they "had no right or interest in the parking lot as owners, tenants or licensees," nor was there any evidence that the accused "had any 'say' in what parking spaces would be used or in allocating the spaces" (since they basically just used whichever ones were available to them). While the judges conceded that a trespasser could be a keeper (using as an example the situation where an accused "makes use of an abandoned house or barn for the purposes of prostitution"), this was not one of those cases; as the judges asked rhetorically, "if a prostitute resorts regularly to a farmer's field or to a back alley with her customers, which area can be defined, is she then to be guilty of keeping a common bawdy-house?" The court, presumably sensing that it had left the prosecution on the horns of a dilemma whereby an open outdoor space could be deemed a bawdy-house but it was virtually impossible to convict someone of the crime of "keeping" it since such a space was inherently not capable of control, helpfully suggested that the Crown might have been more successful had Pierce and Golloher been charged with being "inmates" of a common bawdy-house, contrary to what is now Section 210(2)(a). And with that, the language was torqued about as far as it could go and the decision came to an end: the parking lot was a "bawdy-house," and the women were "inmates" thereof. Since Pierce and Golloher hadn't been charged with that offence, however, their acquittal was upheld. We are left to wonder whether the greater crime was what the ladies were doing with their clients or what the judges did to the English language.

Regardless of the low (and even criminal) esteem in which prostitution is held, however, that's not to say the government isn't happy to take its share of the proceeds. In 1964, the Exchequer Court of Canada heard the *Eldridge* case, which pitted the minister of national revenue against the literal Madam Eldridge, who had of late been operating a call-girl operation in Vancouver.[3] The madam and her nine employees had been carrying on business since 1953. It was 1957 before she filed her first tax return in respect of the enterprise, but after listening to her tax advisers and some gentle persuasion from officers of the Department of National Revenue's Taxation Division, she duly prepared returns for the three preceding years and continued to file net worth statements up through 1960. As 1960 drew to a close, the morality squad of the Vancouver Police Department got involved, and in November, Eldridge and her employees were arrested and charged with conspiring to live off the avails of prostitution. They pleaded guilty and were imprisoned for varying terms. Eldridge was still, however, prepared to battle through the courts on the matter of her allowable business deductions for the years 1959 and 1960 — the government, somewhat tellingly, was also willing to fight to the finish.

Gross business income of $77,661.50 and $80,749.00 for the years were held by the revenue authorities to have resulted in an assessment of taxable income of $24,646.75 and $21,703.77. Eldridge complained that a number of critical business expenses hadn't been allowed. In addition to allowable expenses such as payments to the girls for their share of gross revenues (being 50 percent), taxi fares, room rentals, dispatcher wages, and refreshments, Eldridge wanted to be able to claim items of somewhat more indelicate nature. Justice Cattanach went through the items with a bloodless efficiency that should warm the hearts of chartered accountants, libertarians, and entrepreneurs everywhere. Prompted by a remark made by Eldridge to the effect that she thought it "incongruous" that the government was seeking to keep more of her gross revenues and thereby itself hypocritically "live on the avails of prostitution," the court made it very clear that "earnings from illegal operations or illicit businesses are subject to tax" — though not forfeiture (it required an entire series of amendments to the Criminal Code in subsequent decades to render the "proceeds of crime" themselves subject to seizure by the authorities).

The court considered the expenses listed below (the court's decision as to whether each claimed expense was deductible is found on page 205; readers should feel free to make their own guesses as to the court's findings before checking the answers):

- payments made to a telephone company employee in exchange for conducting inspections of Eldridge's telephone lines to determine if the police had tapped her phones;[4]
- "protection" fees payable to law-enforcement officers in exchange for being advised when to avoid certain hotels that were under police surveillance;[5]
- money paid to "men possessed of physical strength and some guile" in exchange for extracting the call girls from "difficult" situations;[6]
- legal fees paid to lawyers defending the girls against charges;[7] and
- payment of $500 to purchase the entire print run of an edition of *Flash* newspaper, which specialized in the publication of

"scandalous stories" and had printed a story describing Eldridge as a "Czarina" of the prostitution trade and claiming that she had been kidnapped and "subjected to loathsome indignities" by her competitors.[8]

The taxation rules surrounding the avails of prostitution strive for even-handedness between the businesspersons whether they conduct licit or illicit activities. Sometimes our laws surrounding sexual activities still fall well short of the goal of equal treatment, however. Canadians of a certain age will recall it was in 1969 that the Liberal government of Pierre Elliott Trudeau decriminalized consensual anal intercourse between adults (at the time defined as someone over twenty-one years of age). Nonetheless, the default position under Canadian criminal law remains that anal intercourse is illegal subject to certain exceptions, and Section 159 of the Criminal Code continues to criminalize anal sex in a variety of situations. The section begins as follows: "159(1) Every person who engages in an act of anal intercourse is guilty of an indictable offence and liable to imprisonment for a term not exceeding ten years or is guilty of an offence punishable on summary conviction."

Up to ten years in jail for anal sex! Regardless of what one thinks about the sexual practices of one's neighbours, presumably everyone can agree that a jail term seems a mite harsh for some orificial adventurousness. The broad sweep of Section 159(1) is circumscribed by the following provisions:

159. (2) Subsection (1) does not apply to any act engaged in, in private, between
(*a*) husband and wife, or
(*b*) any two persons, each of whom is eighteen years of age or more, both of whom consent to the act.

(3) For the purposes of subsection (2),
(*a*) an act shall be deemed not to have been engaged in private if it is engaged in a public place or if more than two persons take part or are present.

Though at first glance subsections (2) and (3) may seem to expand the ambit of permissible anal sex to encompass most conceivable situations, all of the provisions of Section 159 have the effect of criminalizing the following: group sex involving three or more persons that also involves anal activities, and anal sex between persons under eighteen years of age. So two seventeen-year-old male homosexuals who have sex face possible criminal charges, while a heterosexual couple of seventeen-year-olds who engage in sexual intercourse face no similar potential punishment (unless they engage also in anal sex). Since, at the time of this writing, the age of consent for engaging in sexual activity in Canada is fourteen, it remains unclear why anal sex is circumscribed for the additional four-year period. As well, it seems unnecessary to partially legislate with respect to the activities of consenting adults who elect to copulate in groupings of three or more: it is not group sex that is rendered illegal, but only group sex that involves anal intercourse.

The treatment of anal sex (previously known as "buggery" or "sodomy") has a long history in English and Canadian law, and the current provisions are the last vestiges of a crime that once merited death.[9] By the time of the 1969 reforms, which while decriminalizing anal sex between consenting adults also retained the distinction between anal and vaginal sex with someone between the ages of fourteen and twenty-one, it was argued that the distinction was necessary in order to demonstrate the "immoral nature" of homosexual sex and to prevent someone under eighteen from "learning" homosexual behaviour. In 1988, when further reforms of the Criminal Code were undertaken and the age threshold for legal anal sex was lowered from twenty-one to eighteen, the age distinction was nevertheless maintained. (There were some arguments made while the amending bill was in committee that the reason for retaining the age distinction was to aid in preventing transmission of the AIDS virus, but this was such a transparent *ex post facto* non-justification that more than one court has dismissed it out of hand.)[10] The courts that have rejected the constitutionality of Section 159 have noted the hypocrisy in trying to protect those between fourteen and eighteen from anal sex but not from oral or vaginal sex. As the Ontario Court of Appeal chided, even if protecting those in their late teens from anal sex was a compelling governmental interest, throwing people in jail for it may not be the most efficient or effective manner of doing so. Canadian legal history does not contain a high-profile homosexual sex case like Oscar

Wilde's prosecution in England for engaging in sodomy in 1895 (Wilde was sentenced to two years' hard labour), but one need not be famous in order to suffer under an unjust law.

To compound inequity with confusion, the applicability of Section 159 varies across the country. While the Canadian federation enjoys a single Criminal Code (unlike our American neighbours, where each state legislates its own criminal law), each of the Canadian provinces is a sovereign jurisdiction, operating much like ten separate channels all leading to the Supreme Court of Canada. Decisions of an appeal court in one province are binding on lower courts within that province, but are not binding on lower courts (or appellate courts) in other provinces — though appellate decisions often wield strongly persuasive authority. The only court that has jurisdiction to compel a legal conclusion in all ten provinces and three territories is the Supreme Court of Canada — and the Supreme Court has yet to rule on Section 159. Instead, a patchwork of decisions exists: the Courts of Appeal of Ontario and Quebec have concluded that Section 159 violates the Charter of Rights and Freedoms because it discriminates on the basis of sexual orientation, age, and marital status and is therefore unconstitutional, as has a lower court decision in Alberta.[11] Despite these court rulings, the federal government hasn't seen fit to repeal Section 159. As a result, while it is entirely permissible to engage in anal sex in Ontario, Quebec, and most likely Alberta, it remains possible to be convicted under Section 159 in all other provinces and territories.[12] The danger inherent in an unconstitutional law remaining on the books is eloquently pointed out by Donald G. Caswell: because legal knowledge is an imperfect thing, a number of people have been convicted of violating the section even in provinces where the law has been declared unconstitutional. In one case in Ontario, which took place *four years* after the Ontario Court of Appeal decision that deemed Section 159 contrary to the Charter, an accused was convicted by a jury of committing a crime under Section 159, a verdict that was finally overturned on appeal.[13]

A simple true story should suffice to illustrate why leaving an outdated (and unconstitutional) law such as Section 159 on the books is a potential danger: the case of *Lucas v Toronto Police Services Board*.[14] To appreciate the case requires knowing that Section 212(1)(i) of the Criminal Code prohibits giving someone a drug or "intoxicating liquor" for the purpose of "stupefy[ing] or overpower[ing]" that person in order to enable someone to engage in "illicit sex." The provision is meant to be applicable to situations where someone slips a drug into the drink of another person, thereby rendering that person incapable of protesting against an unwanted sexual advance. It appears to be the case that Lucas, a homosexual who was over eighteen years of age, met a fellow homosexual who was under eighteen years of age, and the two had sex while both were drinking. Lucas was arrested and charged with engaging in anal intercourse with a person under the age of eighteen pursuant to Section 159, and also with administering a drug or intoxicating liquor for the purposes of engaging in illicit sex pursuant to Section 212. The sexual encounter hadn't been non-consensual, however — the "illicit" sex that was being used to rely on Section 212 was the act of anal intercourse with a man under eighteen years of age, which is nominally a crime regardless of whether the person under eighteen years consents.

When it was brought to the attention of the Crown prosecutors that Section 159 had been deemed unconstitutional in Ontario, the entire case collapsed: the Section 159 charge was dropped, as was the Section 212 charge, since there was no longer any "illicit" sex that had occurred. Not even a sexual assault charge could be laid since there was no evidence that there had been a lack of consent. In other words, Lucas had been arrested, spent a night in jail, and been put through the expense and hassle of finding a defence lawyer and sitting through multiple court appearances, all for doing something that, had he done the *exact same thing* with a female of the same age (assuming he engaged in vaginal intercourse with her), would not have been a crime, and there would have been nothing he could have been charged with. At the time of this writing, Lucas's lawsuit against the police and Ontario's attorney general appears to be unsettled and untried before the courts.

Notwithstanding any confusion or debate surrounding the issue of anal intercourse, the next crime listed in the Criminal Code is generally regarded as uncontroversial (or at least the fact that it is a crime is uncontroversial):

> **160.** (1) Every person who commits bestiality is guilty of an indictable offence and liable to imprisonment for a term not exceeding ten years or is guilty of an

offence punishable on summary conviction.

(2)   Every person who compels another to commit bestiality is guilty of an indictable offence and liable to imprisonment for a term not exceeding ten years or is guilty of an offence punishable on summary conviction.

(3)   Notwithstanding subsection (1), every person who, in the presence of a person under the age of fourteen years, commits bestiality or who incites a person under the age of fourteen years to commit bestiality is guilty of an indictable offence and liable to imprisonment for a term not exceeding ten years or is guilty of an offence punishable on summary conviction.

The prohibition on bestiality has been part of our criminal law for centuries,[15] and, despite the seriousness with which we should always treat criminal activities, bestiality seems to lend itself to situations that cause the law, profound as it may be, to set itself up for mockery. One of the more recent ruminations on bestiality occurred in British Columbia in 1980.[16] The accused, Triller, was found at one o'clock in the morning "in a position with a golden Labrador dog." Unhappily for the witnesses to the crime, Triller's encounter occurred under a streetlight outside their home. Despite the best efforts of the RCMP Crime Detection Laboratory in Vancouver (which found dog hairs on Triller's pants) and a veterinarian called in to examine the dog, it wasn't clear that Triller had actually managed to engage in intercourse with the dog, though not for lack of trying: he was so intoxicated that the manager of the bar in which he was drinking had cut him off and driven him home. The manager dropped Triller off in his home neighbourhood, leaving Triller to stumble into his amorous conquests. Despite the possible lack of consummation in the relationship, Triller was charged with attempted bestiality, given that his activities "went beyond mere preparation"; but for his own possible inability to perform and/or the undoubtedly strenuous efforts of the dog to avoid the engagement, Triller would have committed the crime and was therefore criminally responsible for the attempt.

Triller's defence lawyer valiantly attempted a number of alternative defences: first, that Triller was too drunk to form the intent necessary to commit a crime. The court rejected this on the basis that the crime is one of a category referred to as "general intent" offences, and no specific intent to commit the crime is required for a conviction. Undaunted, Triller's lawyer tried another tack: "bestiality" requires, so the argument went, not merely sex with an animal, but sex with an animal *of the opposite gender* (the lucky Labrador in question here was male). Confronted with the fact that the Criminal Code doesn't contain a definition of the term *bestiality*, the judge turned to dictionaries (the *Shorter Oxford* defines the term as having an "unnatural connection with a beast"), legal texts (*Wharton's Law Lexicon* defines the crime as "the crime of men with beast"), and earlier cases from jurisdictions as widespread as England, Indiana, and Arizona (one English bestiality case was concerned with whether a duck was an animal — the court concluded it was, and convicted accordingly[17]). The court eventually decided that there was no justification for the view that the crime required an animal of the opposite gender in order to be committed — Triller was guilty as charged.

Subsection (2) of the bestiality provision stipulates that *compelling* someone to engage in bestiality is also a crime — an understandable position. An odd wrinkle in the bestiality provision is subsection (3), which reiterates that bestiality is *still* a crime if you commit it in the presence of a person under the age of fourteen. This is entirely superfluous, of course, and not least because the broader crime subsumes the more particular one: because our sentencing regime invariably provides for sentences for multiple convictions to be served concurrently, even if an accused were convicted of both bestiality and bestiality in front of a thirteen-year-old, he or she wouldn't serve any additional time. Quite what the harm was that was being addressed (was there a spate of people having sex with animals in front of children?) is lost to history. Subsection 160(3) also makes it a crime to "incite" a person under the age of fourteen to commit bestiality. We are left to query why it would be okay to incite a fifteen-year-old to do so.

In addition to laws that address the various permutations in which sex can be had, a somewhat more basic matter is also addressed by the Criminal Code: nudity.

> **174.** (1)   Every one who, without lawful excuse,
>
> > (*a*) is nude in a public place, or
> > (*b*) is nude and exposed to public view while on private property, whether or not the property is his own
>
> > is guilty of an offence punishable on summary conviction.
>
> (2)   For the purposes of this section, a person is nude who is so clad as to offend public decency or order.
>
> (3)   No proceeding shall be commenced under this section without the consent of the Attorney General.

The laws surrounding nudity are surprisingly nuanced. Until 1931, public nudity wasn't a distinct crime in Canada, and any instances of public nudity were generally punished under laws prohibiting acts of public indecency. As described in Chapter 6, the forerunner of the current language was passed into law in 1931 in response to the government's crackdowns on radical Doukhobors who were engaging in mass resistance through public displays of nudity; a new section, 205A, was added that made it a crime to be found in a public place with the intent to "parade" while nude.[18] Whereas a conviction for public indecency carried a maximum sentence of six months' imprisonment, Section 205A provided for a penalty of three years in prison.

The origin of the current nudity provisions (i.e., arising from a highly political government campaign against a rebellious religious sect) means that our current Section 174 retains a relatively unusual provision that results in one of the more interesting twists in the laws regarding nudity: subsection (3) stipulates that in order for any prosecution for public nudity to proceed, the consent of the attorney general of the province in which the alleged offence occurred is required. This was put in place to ensure that the much stiffer penalty of the "nudity" provisions would only be applied in an attempt to squelch the mass resistance of the Doukhobors, and not, unless the relevant attorney general saw fit, to your average person inadvertently out for an afternoon stroll in the buff. As described in the *Niman* case, this requirement both reflects the political origin of the crime and imparts a political element to any prosecutions of it:

> By vesting in the attorney general of each province the discretion of deciding whether or not to prosecute cases of public nudity, Parliament must be taken to be of the view that not all instances of nudity in public require the sanction of criminal law in order to preserve peace and order in our society. Furthermore … [this provides] a safeguard against prosecutions prompted by over-sensitive complainants whose standards of decency and moral conduct significantly exceed the norms of the community in which the complaint arises.[19]

Because the provincial attorneys general often have rather full schedules replete with more important things to worry about than people walking down the street naked, prosecutions for public nudity under Section 174 are relatively rare — without the express prior consent of the attorney general, the charges won't be permitted to stand.[20] The Criminal Code was substantially revised in 1954, and the nudity provisions were simplified to their current incarnation. On the face of it, Section 174 is an example of a tightly drafted law: it prohibits nudity in "a public place," but just in case people get clever and decide to flaunt their wares while standing in their own living rooms (with the drapes open), Parliament thought ahead to address just such inventiveness by including subsection 1(*b*). (In a case that made it all the way to the Supreme Court of Canada, a man who had been observed by his neighbours masturbating near the uncovered window of his illuminated living room across contiguous backyards, but who had no intention of being seen by anyone, was acquitted of charges brought under the closely related Section 173, which prohibits the performance of "an indecent act" in a public place.[21])

Subsection (2) is likewise an attempt to forestall the determined nudist: being partially clothed (for example, wearing a hat or shoes) is meant to be insufficient to avoid a conviction if you're otherwise naked. You would think, then, that Section 174 would be sufficient to criminalize just about any instance of public nudity: if you're completely naked, without the barest stitch of clothing, you're violating subsection (1)(*a*); if you're "partially" clothed with an eye towards evading the "completely naked" requirement of subsection (1)(*a*), well, then you're violating subsection (2). However, when it comes to the law, and especially the law and sex, things are rarely so simple.

It is the additional language in subsection (2) that contains the seeds of its undoing: "a person is nude who is *so clad as to offend public decency or order*." The emphasized language imports a contextual requirement into prosecutions for "partial" public nudity. It is the circumstances in which the nudity occurs that is determinative. Hence, a stripper being naked (except for heels, usually) in a strip club is generally not considered to be a violation of Section 174, because the audience's sense of propriety won't have been offended (quite the contrary, presumably). Strip clubs can also potentially rely on having a "lawful excuse" for public nudity on the basis that the dancing is a form of legitimate entertainment, though again this is a matter for the judge to determine in the context of the situation.[22]

For some residents of Canada's largest city, the issue of public nudity is a perennial recurrence: Toronto's annual Pride celebration, held each June, attracts hundreds of thousands of attendees and parade watchers. Virtually every year, some participants in the parade are "attired" (or not) in a manner that inevitably results in the days following the spectacle to be witness to their own parade of outraged letters to the editor and offended callers to radio shows. How, the question usually goes, can some of the Pride floats feature entirely naked individuals and it isn't against the law? Setting aside the question of whether it *should* be a crime to be naked in a public parade, chalk the lack of charges up to the intricacies of Sections 173 and 174 of the Criminal Code. There are a number of hurdles that would need to be cleared before a conviction could be secured under the public nudity provisions: first, the attorney general would have to agree to the charge being laid; second, if the person had any piece of clothing on whatsoever (even a pair of socks), a court hearing the case would need to be satisfied that "public decency or order" had been offended — a frankly difficult case to make when the nudity has occurred in the midst of hundreds of scantily clad parade participants (often including the mayor and chief of police) being cheered on by thousands of happy audience members.

In 2002, seven men who were part of the TNT!MEN (Totally Naked Toronto Men Enjoying Nudity) contingent in the Pride parade were arrested for "public nudity." Charges appear not to have been laid, and a subsequent letter from the Ontario Crown Attorney's Office confirmed that none would be forthcoming. A press release from the group cheerfully notes the Crown's conclusion that the appearance of the seven, "clad only in footwear and sunscreen," didn't give rise to a "reasonable prospect of conviction."[23] As the TNT!MEN website notes, if you have an ardent desire to be totally naked in front of thousands of well-wishers, do it in Toronto during the Pride celebrations — and wear shoes.

Section 174 isn't necessarily the final word on public nudity, however. The offended parade watcher who was particularly enterprising might try to rely on a closely related provision of the Criminal Code, Section 173, which makes it a crime to commit "an indecent act in a public place." Is public nudity, then, an "indecent act"? The Ontario Court of Appeal had the opportunity to consider the question in a case involving Gwen Jacob, her breasts, and a hot summer day in Guelph, Ontario.[24] Before we get to Ms. Jacob, though, a moment should be spared for the *Niman* case to shed some light on how the legal treatment of nudity has long been treated in a contextual fashion.[25] Judge Swabey wasn't pleased to have Mr. Niman in his court. On March 29, 1974, a police officer had observed Niman running along a street in downtown Ottawa. In and of itself, perhaps this wasn't so unusual as to attract the attention of the officer. Mr. Niman, however, was "clad only with a red scarf around his neck." When confronted by the officer, Niman attempted to plead extenuating circumstances: he was on his way to the beer store to buy a case. Not good enough. Niman was arrested and charged with public indecency. Confronted with these facts, the court was moved to ruminate rather eloquently on the matter before it:

> The facts of this case, when considered without explanation, might lead one to conclude that the mind of the accused was disturbed. Both climate and custom dictate the wearing of clothing in our society.... It is only when one is advised of the accused's explanation

for his nudity that thoughts of unsound mind or sexual abnormality disappear.

For as long as one can remember, springtime in our society has usually been accompanied by a variety of highjinx on the part of students of universities and high schools. Any rationale for such activities must be left to the social scientists to explain but one conclusion that can be drawn from the nature of these activities is that they are, by design, ludicrous and by impulse conceived.... While we have become accustomed to this annual ritual of acting out on the part of young people, the means by which these young people choose to act out never seems to fail to shock the rest of the community. At different points in recent times these activities have included the swallowing of goldfish, the raiding of co-ed dormitories in search for female undergarments, the occupation of telephone booths with record numbers of human beings, the rolling of beds on wheels over record numbers of miles of our highways, and the captivation of the attention of unsuspecting persons through the sudden baring of the posterior accompanied by an expression not unlike the final declaration in a chess match.

As the winter snow began to melt this spring the imaginations of the students turned away from their studies and once again the phenomena of scholarly highjinx erupted on campuses and school grounds. This year's expression of nonsense has taken the form of dashing over pre-arranged routes in the nude.

Niman had accepted a dare that he *streak* (to use the term favoured by the court) to the beer store. As Judge Swabey noted, while the activities would clearly have fallen within the scope of the public nudity provisions, it was unlikely that the attorney general would look kindly on being bothered with this incident and so Niman wasn't charged under those provisions but rather under the procedurally less taxing public indecency provisions. The judge's somewhat grandfatherly and touching meditation on youthful shenanigans was reflected in the outcome of the case:

although Niman was guilty of the offence, he was granted an absolute discharge, leaving him with no punishment and no criminal record.

Nearly twenty years later, a hot, humid day in the summer of 1991 prompted Gwen Jacob to walk "along several Guelph streets with uncovered breasts." She attracted the usual sort of attention, including some from the police — one officer stopped Jacob and asked her to cover her breasts. When she refused, the officer elected not to charge her unless a complaint was lodged with the police. Eventually, there were two complainants, one of whom thought it was inappropriate for her young children (who had been playing in their front yard) to see Ms. Jacob "in her state of undress," and one of whom had been called out of her house by her husband who informed her that a woman was walking the streets without a top. When the first police officer stopped her, Jacob protested that it was entirely unfair that a man was permitted to walk topless in an effort to achieve comfort on a hot day, while a woman who did the same thing was subjected to potential (in her case, actual) criminal charges. As she articulated her position, she had a "constitutional right" to walk in public topless. Once the complaints had been received, Jacob was charged with public indecency (and not public nudity, again likely because the consent of the attorney general couldn't have been obtained), convicted at trial, and sentenced to pay a fine of $75. Jacob appealed twice, all the way to the Ontario Court of Appeal.

Three judges heard the case on appeal. In assessing matters of "indecency," the judges explained, the courts were obliged to use a "community standard of tolerance" test. Somewhat confusingly, the test doesn't ask what is acceptable within a particular community but what the Canadian or *national* community would find acceptable, and it is predicated not on what individuals would deem acceptable for *themselves* to be exposed to but on what they would tolerate *others* being exposed to. And that determination of tolerance is itself predicated on a further requirement: harm. The question in situations of indecency, then, is "what the community would tolerate others being exposed to on the basis of the degree of harm that may flow from such exposure."[26] "Harm" itself requires that the activity in question predisposes people to act in an anti-social manner (by assaulting others, for example).

While the judges on the Ontario Court of Appeal were split among themselves as to whether the notion of "indecency" necessarily required a sexual component (in any event, they all agreed that Jacob's actions weren't overtly sexual, since she hadn't touched her breasts in a sexual manner and there was no commercial element of trying to sell products or services on the basis of sexual attractiveness), they all agreed that there was no harm in what Jacob had done. Any purported harm was nothing more than "grossly speculative" — Jacob did nothing degrading or dehumanizing, her activity was limited in extent, and "no one who was offended was required to continue looking at her."

One judge noted that Jacob's sojourn around the streets of Guelph had caused something of a kerfuffle: more than two hundred people witnessed her, and some were offended, while others were not. Vehicular traffic had been slowed, and "a lot of people walked up from both ends of the street to see what the commotion was about." According to one witness, the car in which she was travelling had almost been broadsided by a van, whose driver presumably had been distracted by the "spectacle" of Jacob's bare breasts. The same judge noted that the "psychological comfort" of a number of witnesses had been affected, and that "the right of parents living in the neighbourhood to raise their children according to their moral beliefs was interfered with by [Jacob] thrusting upon the children a contrary influence which they had no opportunity to avoid." Nevertheless, this didn't rise to the level of "harm" as the courts had interpreted it, and thus, for Jacob, no harm meant no foul. All three judges on the Ontario Court of Appeal agreed that Gwen Jacob should be acquitted of the crime of public indecency.

Though the prerogative of Gwen Jacob to be topless on a hot summer day wasn't quite elevated to the hallowed status of "constitutional right," her stroll through Guelph and its legal fallout were for a time political *causes célèbres*. A Kitchener protest called in solidarity with Jacob after her conviction at trial resulted in its own set of criminal charges and acquittals. At the protest a number of participants bared their own breasts, and the judge hearing that case anticipated the Ontario Court of Appeal holding in the Jacob case. Because there had been no harm, there couldn't be a violation of the community standard of tolerance, regardless of the fact that "most women would not engage in this conduct." The community standard of tolerance test, then, mandates allowing activities to occur even if they aren't approved: absent evidence of harm, there is no "indecency."

By 2005, changing sexual mores would collide with the notions of indecency and the "common bawdy-house" to result in a landmark

Supreme Court of Canada decision addressing sex clubs. Jean-Paul Labaye was charged under Section 210(1) of the Criminal Code with the offence of "keeping a common bawdy-house."[27] As mentioned above, the Criminal Code contains a two-pronged definition of a "common bawdy-house": it is a place kept either "for the purpose of prostitution" or for "the practice of acts of indecency." In Labaye's case, his Montreal club L'Orage was certainly not the former: people weren't paid to have sex with clients. Instead, the purpose of the club was to permit people to meet one another to engage in group sex. In order to enter the club, one was required to be a member (becoming a member was itself a process that required interviews). Once in the club, members were allowed access to a first-floor bar, a second-floor salon, and a third-floor "apartment" where the group gropes took place — the apartment was only accessible via a door equipped with a numeric keypad lock. Everything was entirely voluntary among the members, and no one who wasn't a member could witness the group sex activities that took place on the third floor. The question thus arose: did what was happening behind that locked door constitute "acts of indecency"?

The majority of the Supreme Court reiterated, emphasized, and extended the line of judicial reasoning that had been used in the *Jacob* case: in order for something to be indecent, there needed to be a risk of harm that was incompatible with society's proper functioning. The higher the likelihood of harm, the less likely it was that the activity in question would be tolerated by the community. The decision also erected the framework within which "harm" was to be understood. Activities that would result in unacceptable "harm" are those that cause a loss of autonomy and liberty through confrontation (such as bombarding very young children with images of explicit sex) or activities that harm the participating individuals (such as forced prostitution) or activities that predispose others to engage in anti-social acts (such as continual negative stereotyping that leads to assaults on other people). The *degree* of harm required has also been raised. As the court explicitly stipulates, it isn't sufficient for the harm to "detract" from proper societal functioning — it must be *incompatible* with it. This represents a significant retraction of the scope of government interference in relation to sexual matters and indecency. And the final result in Labaye's case reflected this: all the activity was taking place behind closed doors, in a members-only club, among consenting adults. The only possible danger that the court was convinced existed was the risk of catching a sexually transmitted disease. As the majority decision concluded, "consensual conduct behind code-locked doors can hardly be supposed to jeopardize a society as vigorous and tolerant as Canadian society." Labaye's conviction was overturned and an acquittal entered.

The laws on nudity offer a telling encapsulation of our response to nudity and sex. When the Criminal Code was originally enacted in 1892, public nudity was so rare and the social stigma attaching to it so profound that it wasn't even thought necessary to address a separate section of the law to the matter. From the days Parliament had to pay particular attention to a rebellious Christian sect that insisted on being nude in public in the early 1930s, social mores about the matter have changed to the point where both male and female public nudity are, in certain circumstances, with a nod and wink permissible (or not punishable). One may be tempted to say that judicial condoning (or at least a lack of judicial sanctioning) of group sex reflects a degradation in our stance on sexual matters, but even sex for money was a matter so mundane that fifty years ago a court was clinically determining whether a prostitution business could validly deduct money paid to hired goons. Our legal approach to sex is sometimes confounding and humorous because the subject itself often shares those same features — and neither state of affairs is likely to change any time soon.

5

Blasphemous Pirates in Space

I n addition to formal overlap between various sections ("Canadians would be amazed to learn that if someone deliberately bloodies another's nose the offence is theoretically a matter ... involving no less than fifteen broad categories of offences"[1]), one of the recurring criticisms of the Criminal Code is that it is in need of a good housekeeping — not just to eliminate obsolete provisions but also to streamline even the relevant ones. Why, to take a truly random example, is the crime of "disturbing (i.e., interfering with) religious worship" (Section 176) placed in Part V of the Criminal Code, which is entitled "Sexual Offences"? Nevertheless, if and when the government gets around to rationalizing the law, a good deal of its charm will be lost — eccentricity has its own attractions. There is a historiographical element involved in deleting unused or unnecessary provisions. In a sense, reading the Criminal Code and other laws is akin to an archaeological dig — each provision is the legal vestige of the historical incidents that culminated in its enactment. Somebody, somewhere, must have done the "bad thing" that prompted our legal system to respond with a law prohibiting it. With an eye for both eccentricity and history, then, and in the absence of any other unifying theme, this chapter offers a brief tour of some of the more strangely compelling portions of our criminal law.

Looking Back

Before strolling through current Canadian crimes, it is worth reminding ourselves of some of the laws that we have managed to remove from the books over the years. Our first Criminal Code, introduced in 1892 (referred to in this chapter as the "1892 Code"), offers an easy resource for determining what concerned Canadian lawmakers a century and more ago. We learn, for instance, that it was once illegal to "incite Indians to riot." Section 98 of the 1892 Code made a criminal of anyone who "induces, incites or stirs up any three or more Indians ... to make any request or demand [of the government] in a riotous, routous, disorderly or threatening manner." Our current Criminal Code continues to have provisions relating to the crime of piracy (Sections 74 and 75), but it was once a crime to *not* fight pirates who were attempting to board your ship. If you were attacked by a pirate at sea and you failed to "fight and endeavour to defend [yourself] and [your] vessel from being taken by such pirate," Section 130 of the 1892 Code could have resulted in your being imprisoned for up to six months. A string of sections was also addressed to gambling, perhaps the most interesting of which was Section 203, which made it a crime to gamble on "any railway car or steamboat."

A recurring theme in the 1892 Code was the specification of crimes against women. While kidnapping was a crime (Section 264), there were also two separate crimes relating to kidnapping women. Section 281 made it a crime to abduct a woman "with intent to marry or carnally know" her; similarly, Section 282 made it a crime to abduct an "heiress" — male heirs were evidently on their own. "Seduction" was apparently a significant problem in the late nineteenth century: no less than four separate sections are devoted to the matter. Sections 181 through 184 provided for the following crimes: seducing any girl "of previously chaste character" under sixteen years of age; seducing with a promise of marriage any girl "of previously chaste character" under twenty-one years of age; seducing any female ward or employee; and seducing any female passenger "of previously chaste character" on a vessel (whether by promise of marriage, threats, exercise of authority, solicitation, or the making of gifts or presents). At least with respect to the last of those crimes, however, it was a valid defence if there was "a subsequent intermarriage of the seducer and the seduced." Returning to the preoccupation of the

1892 Code's drafters with aboriginals (or "Indians"), while there was no general prohibition on prostitution or pimping, Section 190 of the 1892 Code did make it illegal for an "Indian woman" to be a prostitute or for the "keeper of any house, tent or wigwam" to allow an Indian woman to prostitute herself therein.

Canoeing While Drunk and Other Water Sports

Canadians have long prided themselves on not only the staggering beauty of our natural environment but also our enthusiastic participation in outdoor activities. In looking at current crimes, we begin with a set appropriate to the Canadian milieu. The summer of 2006 saw a minor tizzy of attention paid to what some might think was an otherwise benign act: operating a canoe while under the influence. To the surprise of some, it was discovered that it has been illegal in Canada to paddle a canoe while intoxicated since 1961. Section 253 of the Criminal Code makes it an offence to operate a motor vehicle or vessel while impaired by drugs or alcohol. While a definition of the term *vessel* is provided in Section 214 of the Criminal Code, it is so broadly worded that the concept includes non-motorized floating devices such as canoes, kayaks, and rubber dinghies.

No one seemed to pay much attention to these sections of the Criminal Code until a member of the Ontario legislature, Liberal MPP David Zimmer, managed to get a private member's bill passed that strengthened Ontario's impaired driving laws to close a loophole: Ontario's Highway Traffic Act had previously provided that anyone who was convicted under the Criminal Code of driving a motorized vehicle while impaired would have his or her licence automatically suspended for one year. But the criminal law is broader than that: it makes it an offence to *drive a vehicle* while drunk *and* to operate a vessel while drunk. So Zimmer's bill expanded the wording of the Ontario legislation to apply to boats and vessels, in alignment with the Criminal Code.

An enterprising *Maclean's* reporter caught on to the fact that one result of Zimmer's bill meant that people in Ontario caught drunk in their canoes and convicted would have their driver's licences suspended for one year.[2] Although Zimmer hadn't been aware that this would be one result of his efforts, the police advise that it's no laughing matter.

Staff Sergeant Brad Schlorff, with the Ontario Provincial Police, noted that "across North America, about 35 percent of all boating fatalities occur in non-powered vessels, primarily canoes and kayaks." To date, it doesn't appear that anyone has been convicted of the offence.

Part of the Canadian self-image involves outdoor activities at the lake, so perhaps it should come as no surprise that, in addition to the prohibition on canoeing while drunk, our Criminal Code contains a number of other provisions related to boating. Thus, an entire section (Section 250) is devoted to water sports. Subsection (1) makes it a crime to tow behind your boat any person on water skis, a surfboard, water sled, or other object if there is not also "another responsible person keeping watch on the person being towed" — so no water-skiing unless there are two people in the boat, one to drive and one to keep watch. Subsection 250(2) enshrines in law the rather commonsensical notion that you shouldn't water-ski at night. It is a crime to operate a vessel while towing a person on water skis, a surfboard, water sled, or other object "during the period from one hour after sunset to sunrise." Just as the law operates around the clock, criminal regulation of outdoor activities doesn't end with the turning of the seasons. Section 263 makes it a crime to make an opening in ice (for the purposes of, for example, ice fishing) that is accessible to the public without safeguarding the opening so as to prevent people from falling in.

Witchcraft

Presumably, we can all stand behind the prohibition on defrauding people. But do we really need a prohibition on witchcraft?

> **365.**   Every one who fraudulently
> > (*a*) pretends to exercise or to use any kind of witchcraft, sorcery, enchantment or conjuration,
> > (*b*) undertakes, for a consideration, to tell fortunes, or
> > (*c*) pretends from his skill in or knowledge of an occult or crafty science to discover where or in

what manner anything that is supposed to have been stolen or lost
may be found,

is guilty of an offence punishable on summary
conviction.

At first blush it would appear that we are permitted no witchcraft
or sorcery, no fortune-telling, and no use of a "crafty science" to find
lost objects. But the prohibition isn't quite so broad. Section 365 only
prohibits doing such things *fraudulently* and, in the case of sorcery,
witchcraft, enchantment, or conjuration, *pretending* to do so — if
you're *genuinely* telling fortunes or *actually* a sorcerer, then you might
be okay. The requirement that the activity be "fraudulent" in nature is
a relatively recent development. Prior to 1954, when the language was
amended, simply pretending to practise witchcraft or undertaking to tell
a fortune was sufficient to constitute a crime. Fortune tellers are hardly
relegated to an underground economy, however. A stroll through most
large Canadian cities will reveal at least a few neon signs enticing those
who want some insight into their futures or some help in finding a lost
heirloom; the Yellow Pages also offer a plethora of providers of similar
services. Like some of the other crimes discussed in this book, such as
prizefighting, the prosecution of fortune-telling was once relatively frequent but has declined markedly in recent years. This is a function of
both the gravity with which the offence is treated and certain decisions
that make it more difficult for prosecutors to obtain a conviction.

Legal prohibitions on witchcraft have a long history in Anglo-
Canadian law. In 1541, the first legislation addressing conjuring
and witchcraft was passed in England, and the roots of the current
Canadian law on the matter can be seen therein:

It shall be Felony to practise, or cause to be practised
Conjuration, Witchcraft, Enchantment or Sorcery, to
get Money; or to consume any Person in his Body,
Members or Goods; or to provoke any Person to
unlawful Love; or for the Despight of Christ, or Lucre
of Money, to pull down any Cross; or to declare where
Goods stolen be.[3]

It was a crime in 1541 "to declare where Goods stolen be" by means of sorcery and it remains the case today in Canada. English laws against witchcraft were modified and expanded throughout the sixteenth and seventeenth centuries. By 1735, the English Witchcraft Act had language largely similar to that in our current Criminal Code (excepting the requirement for fraud), and as late as 1890 that act had been held to be in force in Ontario and convictions were obtained pursuant to it.[4] The language was so broad that simply telling a fortune was sufficient to warrant conviction, even if the person whose fortune had been told testified that he hadn't been duped or defrauded. In 1892, when Canada's first Criminal Code was enacted, it contained a prohibition on witchcraft and fortune-telling, using the language of the 1735 Witchcraft Act. The late nineteenth century and early twentieth century in particular saw a number of prosecutions and reported cases in Canada. The Ontario Court of Appeal in 1901 tried to limit the broad sweep of the language by requiring that to be convicted of the crime, the fortune teller had to intend to delude or defraud his or her customers;[5] the intent was to provide an exception for such harmless activities as fortune-telling booths at fairs, as it was presumed that no one took such endeavours seriously enough to warrant criminal prosecution. Those individuals who were more industrious in their fortune-telling enterprises, however, could expect a visit from the police until well into the 1980s.

Various efforts were made by fortune tellers to comply with the language of the law, including having customers sign an acknowledgement that what was being done was "merely an examination of the lines of their hands and giving information in respect thereof in accordance with books on the subject of palmistry" — not so much a "crafty" science, in other words, as an actual science, spelled out in books. Such diversions weren't successful. Helen Stanley of Edmonton was engaged in the business of "palmistry" and had even obtained a licence to carry on her business from the municipal licensing department. When she was charged with fortune-telling in 1952, she tried to hold up her business licence as a defence against conviction. The judge was as unimpressed with that gambit as he was with her evident inability to foretell her own bad luck, and Stanley was convicted.[6]

In 1955, in order to bring the legislation more in line with what various court decisions had indicated, the Criminal Code was amended to require that an accused be acting "fraudulently" in order to be convicted of the crime — no longer would telling fortunes per se be illegal, only doing so with the intent to defraud. The first reported decision under the new language came in 1975, when an Ontario judge dismissed charges against a Mrs. Dazenbrook. While the accused "advertised that she told fortunes and charged for such services," and she "implied that she had the power to tell fortunes, and probably expected her assertions or representations should be believed," it was nevertheless the case that the prosecution hadn't shown that "she told fortunes *with intent to delude or defraud others*."[7] The judge didn't specify what the prosecution could have tendered as evidence to show such an intention, but no further Ontario prosecutions are reported.

In Quebec, however, a handful of other prosecutions are reported, including one case that made it all the way to the Supreme Court of Canada in 1987, though the latter decision showed a remarkable level of credulity for the purported power of those who would predict the future. In 1981, one fortune teller was convicted of the crime after charging $10 to tell fortunes; the court was satisfied that the accused had acted with intent to defraud her customer, and she was accordingly convicted.[8] In the *Labrosse* case three years later, where the accused had been charged for telling fortunes at a cost of $15 per appointment, the trial judge was of the opinion that because there is no possibility that someone can possess the power to predict the future, any fortune-telling was inherently fraudulent, and Labrosse was therefore guilty as charged.[9] Though the Quebec Court of Appeal seemed to agree with this conclusion, the Supreme Court of Canada, while confirming the conviction, opened the door to being proved wrong. "On the facts of this case," held the Supreme Court, it isn't open to the accused to claim that she honestly believed that she had, in her words, "special powers to predict the future." But if someone *did* tender sufficient evidence to satisfy a judge that he or she believed in his or her own ability to practise sorcery or predict the future, then it couldn't be said that they had acted fraudulently. As interesting as a successful defence would be from a legal standpoint, there are surely even more important reasons to eagerly await news of someone who beats the charges on that basis.

Blasphemy

The roots of the crime of "witchcraft" can be found in medieval notions of heresy and blasphemy. And just as sorcery remains a crime, so too does blasphemy:

296. (1)   Everyone who publishes a blasphemous libel is guilty of an indictable offence and liable to imprisonment for a term not exceeding two years.

(2)   It is a question of fact whether or not any matter that is published is a blasphemous libel.

(3)   No person shall be convicted of an offence under this section for expressing in good faith and in decent language, or attempting to establish by argument used in good faith and conveyed in decent language, an opinion upon a religious subject.

Being derived from old English common law and statutes from the sixteenth and seventeenth centuries, the nature of the crime of blasphemy remains firmly Christian in its conception: "It is blasphemy to publish any profane words vilifying or ridiculing God, Jesus Christ, the Old or New Testament, or Christianity in general with intent to insult and shock believers or to pervert or mislead the ignorant or unwary."[10] Early reported English prosecutions for the crime involved situations where virtually any form of questioning Christian doctrine was sufficient to ground a charge of blasphemy. Over time, this staunch approach was relaxed, with English courts seeking to allow for the non-provocative good faith discussions of sincerely held beliefs, even where those beliefs conflicted with religious orthodoxy. This impetus is reflected in subsection (3) of the provision, which allows for nominally blasphemous statements provided they are made using decent language. By 1883 the law had developed to the point where merely denying the truth of the Christian religion wasn't enough to constitute blasphemous libel: what was required was offensive attacks on the religion or its Scriptures, "calculated to outrage the feelings of the general body of the community."[11]

English prosecutions for blasphemy continued throughout the nineteenth and twentieth centuries, including one prosecution as late as 1922.[12] Though the crime of "blasphemous libel" has been present in Canadian law since the first Criminal Code in 1892, it is, thankfully, not one that has ever been prosecuted with real vigour. Which is not to say that it has *never* been prosecuted in Canada. In 1926, Ernest Sterry was convicted of blasphemous libel and sentenced to sixty days in prison for publishing pamphlets that contained among other "scandalous, impious, blasphemous, profane and indecent matters" the following, in describing "the God of the Bible": "This touchy Jehovah, whom the deluded superstitionists claim to be the creator of the whole universe, makes one feel utter contempt for the preachers and unfeigned pity for the mental state of those who can retain a serious countenance as they peruse the stories of His peculiar whims, freaks and fancies and His frenzied megalomaniac boastings." As the court described it, Sterry's writings were such as to be "to the high displeasure of Almighty God, to the great scandal and reproach of the Christian religion, to the evil example of all others in like case offending, and contrary to the Criminal Code."[13] One assumes that the final imprecation was the least of Sterry's worries. Attempts by Quebec authorities to prosecute a member of the Jehovah's Witnesses in Quebec for publishing pamphlets that attacked the Catholic Church and the pope didn't bear fruit — the court found that nothing in the pamphlet attacked God or Christianity per se, and so the elements of the offence weren't present.[14]

The most recent prosecution in Canada for blasphemy appears to have occurred in Quebec in 1935, which tested the scope of the exemption in Section 296(3) and involved an Anglican priest, the Reverend Victor Rahard, who in 1933 pasted a poster attacking the Catholic Church on the side of his church — "in full view of passersby and especially of Roman Catholics and French Canadians who compose at least three-quarters of the population of the City of Montreal."[15] The poster attacked the "papist religion" and the hubris of the "Roman clergy" and

the "Roman Church," which wished to displace "the commandments of God" with "her own commandments," commandments that were "not of God nor of universal morality nor of the conscience. They bind no one and their transgression may be considered as an act of enfranchisement in regard to usurped authority." Relying on Biblical allusions, Rahard described Catholic churches as dens of commerce: "If Christ should return to visit all His churches He could still chase the merchants from the temples by crying 'My house is a house of prayer and you have made it a den of thieves.'"

Was the language used by Rahard an expression of an argument "in good faith and in decent language"? This question could be answered by posing another question: Is the language used intended to insult the feelings and the deepest religious convictions of the great majority of the persons among whom we live? If so, they are not to be tolerated. Answering both questions in the negative, the court found that Rahard had acted in bad faith and he was found guilty of blasphemy. The sentence imposed on the Anglican wasn't reported.

As with some of the other laws described in this book, the blasphemy provisions may prompt nothing more than a shrug of the shoulders — it's been over seventy years since a blasphemy charge was seen in court, so what's the harm? Consider the controversy that raged around the world in the winter of 2005–06. In September 2005, a Danish newspaper, *Jyllands-Posten*, published a set of cartoons that some Muslims considered offensive. By the following February, death threats, bomb threats, riots, and attacks on embassies had spread across the globe. Nearly all Canadian media outlets refused to reprint the cartoons, despite arguments that they would simply be providing context to a news story. In its February 27, 2006, edition the *Western Standard* news magazine decided to publish the cartoons, together with commentaries both in favour and opposed to the decision. The legal recourse against the magazine was limited to a human rights complaint filed in Calgary against the publishers. As frivolous as that complaint might have been, and even in light of the expenditure that the publishers were forced to undertake in order to hire counsel to defend themselves against it, things could have been much more serious: they conceivably could have been charged with blasphemous libel under the Criminal Code.

It remains an open question as to whether the crime of blasphemy could have been relied on in that case. Though the language of Section 296 doesn't mention Christianity, the case law on the section is very clear that it only applies to language and images that attack the Christian faith and its sacred objects. That being said, the nature of the crime has transformed over the centuries by means of judicial decisions, and there is no obvious impediment to a court deciding that the crime extends to statements that would be deemed blasphemous by a faith other than Christianity. The most likely defence against a blasphemous libel charge would be to claim that Section 296 is contrary to the guarantee of freedom of expression found in the Charter of Rights and Freedoms. But as a pluralistic, secular society that purports to cherish our right to free speech, the question remains whether it should even be a possibility that someone be brought into court on charges perhaps better relegated to a more devout past.

Illicit Advertising

Perhaps you've had the decidedly uncomfortable experience of having to explain to a child the meaning of those impossibly upbeat but decidedly vague commercials broadcast on television for such "performance enhancing" pharmaceutical products as Viagra and Levitra. You can try to dodge the questions next time around by pointing out that Section 163(2)(d) of the Criminal Code makes it an offence to advertise "any means, instructions, medicine, drug or article intended or represented as a method for restoring sexual virility." The same section goes on to prohibit advertising for any cures for venereal diseases. Note that it is not a crime to actually *use* a drug that purports to restore sexual virility or cure venereal disease — just to advertise it. A somewhat similar situation exists in Section 163(2)(c), which makes it illegal in Canada to sell or advertise "any means, instructions, medicine, drug or article intended or represented as a method of causing abortion or miscarriage." It has been entirely legal in Canada to actually *have* or *perform* an abortion since 1988, but it remains a criminal act to advertise for it. Subsection 163(3) provides a defence to the charges: no person can be convicted if "the public good was served by the acts that are alleged to constitute the offence."

The entire history of Section 163(2)(c) and (d) (subsections [a] and [b] deal with obscene materials and "disgusting objects or an indecent show," topics about which an entire separate book could be written) is a Canadian relic. Language prohibiting advertising of abortion aids has been present in our laws since the 1892 Code and was an entirely Canadian innovation: the English criminal laws on which the first code was modelled didn't contain a similar prohibition. The original language actually addressed the matter at both ends. It prohibited any advertising for articles that were meant to prevent conception as well as those meant to cause an abortion. Birth control was not, it can be concluded, considered a topic worthy of public discussion.

Although relatively little attention has been paid to the provisions over the decades, a few cases have been reported, primarily dealing with advertisements for contraceptive aids. In 1936, Dorothea Palmer was an employee of the Parents Information Bureau and carried on sales activities in the town of Eastview, Ontario.[16] Part of her duties involved going door to door, introducing herself as nurse and engaging the female of the household in conversation about the "spacing of children" — in other words, the frequency with which the woman wanted to bear children. If the mother expressed an interest, Palmer would demonstrate her organization's product, consisting of "tube, nozzle and jelly." The meeting would be followed up with "a sample box containing a nozzle and tube of contraceptive jelly, an envelope containing 3 condoms … and a pamphlet containing information, instructions and comment upon various methods of contraception," with the expectation that the recipient would pay for the box and future "refills," as it were. Palmer was charged with advertising a contraceptive device.

In a remarkably progressive judgment for the time, the judge acquitted Palmer on the basis that her actions were serving the "public good." The judge reasoned that the populace of Eastview was largely poor or working class, a group that, unlike "the rich and middle class people who can afford to go to a doctor," was unable to easily access birth control. Although the language is perhaps unrefined for current sensibilities, the judge noted that "the poorer classes are generally breeding large families … [t]he mothers are in poor health, pregnant 9 months out of every year. Several witnesses in this case had 9 or 10 children and were aged 30 to 35 years, husband on relief or on small salaries." These women *wanted* information about birth control, reasoned the judge, so what was Palmer's crime in providing it to them?

Nearly twenty-five years later, Keystone Enterprises of Winnipeg, Manitoba, wasn't so lucky, despite its best efforts.[17] Keystone had engaged in a mass-mailing campaign soliciting customers to satisfy their need for "personal hygienic sundries and supplies." All recipients had to do was simply fill in the order form, and Keystone would send "latex prophylactics and the personal hygienic supplies popular to all adult Canadians." To ensure that no one got the wrong idea about what it was selling, Keystone assured readers that "all our rubber goods are sold for the protection of health only," and the advertisement carried the disclaimer that "should this be contrary to your beliefs, kindly accept our apology and disregard this advertisement."

Confronted with this promotion, coupled with the fact that persons signing the order form had to attest that they were twenty-one years of age or older, the magistrate hearing the case agreed with the Crown prosecutor that the articles being advertised were intended to be used as a method of preventing conception. Evidently hoping to defend the pristine honour of his hometown, the judge further noted that he took offence at the notion that the goods were being sold for the "protection of health": "This to me denotes an insult to the respectability of our community and I may say that our city is noted for being one of the cleanest on the continent." Notwithstanding the affront, the court decided to take pity on the accused: though Keystone was held to be guilty as charged, only a $25 fine was levied. As the judge noted, prosecutions under the section are "rarely, if ever, laid." While the prohibition on advertising preventative birth control devices has since been removed from Section 163(2), it remains the case that it is possible to be charged merely for advertising products (for restoring sexual virility or curing venereal disease) that it is otherwise perfectly legal to ingest.

Currency

We take money seriously, and with good reason. It makes the world go round, after all. An entire part of the Criminal Code, Part XII, is devoted to "Offences Relating to Currency." While some of these provisions should come as no surprise to anyone, such as the prohibitions on making or possessing counterfeit money (Sections 449 and 450), other components of the rather comprehensive sections are more obscure. Some of the sections have clear historical origins: since it was once the case that coins actually contained silver and gold, it was necessary to prohibit the "clipping" of coins, i.e., shaving or otherwise diminishing the coin so as to lighten it (thereby diminishing the value of the coin), as remains with us in Section 455. It is also a crime to possess, without lawful excuse, the gold or silver clippings themselves, as well as to possess gold or silver dust (Section 451).

Section 457 makes it functionally illegal to take pictures of paper money — so photographing, photocopying, or printing anything that is "in the likeness of" current Canadian paper bills is a crime. The section does, however, contain language that creates some "safe harbour" exemptions so that not *every* reproduction of paper money is a crime. Some of the exceptions apply to the RCMP and employees of the Bank of Canada, who may be required to reproduce money in the course of their duties (such as anti-counterfeiting law enforcement). Subsection 457(4) creates a general exemption for the printed likeness of paper money, provided that the reproduction is either 75 percent smaller than a real bill or 50 percent larger and where the reproduction is in black and white only; if the reproduction is in colour, that is also acceptable (assuming it is of the required size), so long as it is printed on only one side of the page. Those who feel the need to print up fake money (say, for a charity casino) or to take accurate-sized pictures of money (such as in an advertisement for a bank) can also apply for a licence to do so from the Bank of Canada. The bank's primary concern is that pictures of money not be of such high quality that they could be used by counterfeiters as an aid in their illegal endeavours.

The Bank of Canada has put in place guidelines and policies that provide guidance on how to address the bank's concerns and avoid any problems under the Criminal Code and other laws (the bank also holds copyright in coins and paper money, so reproducing them on film or in a picture is technically also an infringement of copyright).[18] Generally, the bank won't object (and hence doesn't seek to enforce its copyright or have criminal charges laid) where the reproductions are of such a nature that they would be of little use in counterfeiting (i.e., they are photographed on a slant or angle and not flat to the camera, or are marked with the word *specimen* or something similar), and there is nothing in the reproduction that, in the words of the bank, could "tarnish the dignity and importance of currency to Canadians." When the bank refers to the "importance of currency to Canadians," it isn't messing around. Section 456 makes it a crime to "deface a current coin." So don't scratch your quarters.

I Predict a Riot

The expression "reading the riot act" connotes a stern warning or reprimand for misbehaviour. Those who use the phrase may not realize that it is still possible in Canada to *actually* be read the Riot Act, and that it happens on a relatively frequent basis. Sections 63 through 66 of the Criminal Code make it illegal to participate in an "unlawful assembly" (a group of three or more who assemble with a common purpose and conduct themselves in a fashion that causes other people to think they will "disturb the peace tumultuously") or a "riot" (an unlawful assembly that has actually *begun* to "disturb the peace tumultuously"). The precursor to the Riot Act provisions was passed into law in England in 1714. Originally called "An act for preventing tumults and riotous assemblies, and for the more speedy and effectual punishing the rioters,"[19] it remained on the English books until 1973 when it was repealed and its provisions subsumed into other statutes. In Canada the law survives in the Criminal Code. It is from Section 67 that the colloquial expression "reading the riot act" is derived. The section stipulates that a judge, mayor, sheriff, or prison warden (or their respective deputies), upon being informed that "twelve or more persons are unlawfully and riotously assembled," must go to the site of the riot, approach as near as is safe, satisfy themselves that a riot is occurring, and then

> ... command silence and thereupon make or cause to be made in a loud voice a proclamation in the following words or the like effect:

> > Her Majesty the Queen charges and commands all persons being assembled immediately to disperse and peaceably depart to their habitations or to their lawful business on the pain of being guilty of an offence for which, on conviction, they may be sentenced to imprisonment for life. GOD SAVE THE QUEEN.

And yes, the capital letters are in the text of the Criminal Code. Reading the Riot Act (or "proclamation," as it is formally called) is serious business. Participating in a run-of-the-mill riot is punishable by a maximum sentence of two years (Section 65). Once the Riot Act has been read, rioters have thirty minutes to disperse. Failure to disperse within that time is punishable by a maximum term of life in prison (Section 68).

Our Animal Friends

Our criminal law not only regulates relations between humans but also addresses our interactions with the animal kingdom, though in a sometimes odd manner. No one should be surprised that Section 446 prohibits cruelty to animals, but evidently further elaboration is required. Section 445 makes it a crime to kill, poison, or injure an animal, punishable by a maximum of six months' imprisonment. Cows, however, get their own distinct treatment in a few different instances. Section 444 makes it a crime to kill, poison, or injure cattle, and increases the penalty to a maximum of five years; similarly, while theft is governed by Section 322, Section 338 makes it a separate crime to steal a cow (or to alter a brand or mark on a cow). The inventiveness of defence lawyers should never be underestimated. In the *Allen* case, where the accused had killed a farm animal, the defence argued that what Allen had killed was a "heifer" and not "cattle" within the meaning of the Criminal Code.[20] The court of appeal noted that a heifer was simply a young cow that hasn't borne a calf, and so the conviction was upheld. Those opposed to species-ist treatment of fauna should also keep in mind that it remains an entirely separate crime, punishable under Section 323, to steal oysters.

Quis Custodiet Ipsos Custodes?

Variously translated as "Who will guard the guardians?" or "Who will watch the watchers themselves?", the Latin query in the above subheading is attributed to the Roman poet Juvenal and has been the subject of endless political theory debates for more than two thousand years. How does a state handle those who are necessary for the preservation of the state itself? What special laws, if any, are required to deal with the military and police forces, those whose function it is to enforce the laws themselves and ensure the continued existence of a free political entity? It is a fundamental power of the Canadian Parliament that it can enact laws to ensure "the Peace, Order, and good Government of Canada" — a power that expressly includes governance over military and criminal law matters.[21] In erecting a framework of laws that govern the country, Parliament has also been required to implement laws that address the particular position of those whose job it is to enforce and protect the laws themselves — the guardians or watchers whose task is to ensure that there is peace and order, such that the rest of us have an opportunity to ensure that there is good government.

"Military justice" is a euphemism indicating a particularly harsh brand of punitive corrections. Whether or not that is an apt description of the sentences handed down by military courts, Canada has an entirely separate justice system that applies to members of the Canadian Forces. The National Defence Act[22] erects the organization of the Department of National Defence and the Canadian Forces. Within the National Defence Act exists the Code of Service Discipline, which creates the Canadian military justice system,[23] a system of "Judge Advocates General" (JAGs), or military lawyers, which may be familiar to viewers of various prime-time television dramas or Tom Cruise movies. The Criminal Code and the military justice system intersect in Section 5 of the Criminal Code, which provides that "nothing in this Act affects any law relating to the government of the Canadian Forces," which is intended to make it clear that the Criminal Code doesn't displace the military justice system.

The Criminal Code and the military justice system aren't mutually exclusive spheres. A member of the Canadian Forces can be charged with a crime and tried by civilian courts, and a civilian can, in certain circumstances, be tried by military courts (military courts have jurisdiction, for example, over persons who accompany an active service unit of the Canadian Forces, such as reporters).[24] An accused cannot be tried twice, however. A member of the Canadian Forces couldn't be acquitted by a civilian court, for example, and then retried by a military tribunal for the same offence.[25] The Code of Service Discipline sets out the crimes over which Canadian military courts have jurisdiction — offences that are military in nature, such as mutiny, disobedience of a lawful command, or desertion. On the other hand, certain very serious crimes that are committed by a member of the Canadian Forces in Canada, such as murder and child abduction, cannot be tried in military courts and are reserved solely to the civilian criminal courts.[26] If, however, a member of the Canadian Forces were to commit one of those serious crimes *outside* Canada, he or she would be subject to punishment in the military court system.[27]

The military justice system is not the end of the line even for someone convicted by a military court. As noted by more than one academic, "just as war is too important to be left to the generals, so military justice is too vital to be entrusted to judge advocates [i.e., military lawyers]."[28] Military court decisions can thus be appealed to the Canadian Court Martial Appeal Court, which is staffed by civilian judges.

Because members of the Canadian Forces are charged with a special duty, they can be charged (criminally) with failing to adhere to a much higher standard of behaviour than the rest of us. Military commanders (i.e., those in charge of a vessel, aircraft, fort, or unit) are required to exercise their "utmost exertion" in engaging the enemy, must "fight courageously," and must assist allies to "the utmost of [their] power." Failure to do so is a crime punishable on a sliding scale: an automatic sentence of life imprisonment if the officer acted traitorously, up to life in prison if the officer acted out of cowardice, and dismissal with disgrace or other punishment in all other cases.[29] There are also other crimes that anyone who is subject to the National Defence Act can commit: failing to use "utmost exertion" to carry out an order of war, discouraging action against an enemy, abandoning a defence post, assisting the enemy, abandoning war *matériel* in the presence of the enemy, cowardice, and leaving a post or being asleep or drunk while at a post.[30] It is a military offence to be captured and made a prisoner of war through "want of due precaution," disobedience, or neglect of duty. Once captured, any member of the Canadian Forces is under a duty not to aid the enemy and is also required to attempt to escape and rejoin his or her comrades-in-arms.[31]

As the foregoing helps to illustrate, the Code of Service Conduct creates a comprehensive code that covers virtually any discreditable conduct in which a member of the armed forces can engage, from plundering homes or bodies during war operations, engaging in mutiny, or spying for the enemy, to using "traitorous or disloyal words regarding Her Majesty" and engaging in "insubordinate behaviour" (which is defined as using threatening or insulting language to, or behaving with contempt towards, a superior officer). The Code of Service Conduct also devotes a separate section to the offence of "drunkenness," which is punishable by up to two years' imprisonment. The military probably having some experience with those who are unwilling to follow orders, a fair bit of thought has been devoted to efforts to avoid the carrying out of duty. Not only are "malingering" and feigning a disease or infirmity prohibited (and punishable by a term of up to life imprisonment when in active service), but so are aggravating or delaying the cure of a disease or infirmity. To deal with the most dedicated of dodgers, it is also prohibited to wilfully injure yourself or another person, or to allow another person to injure you, if the intention is to render you or the other person unfit for service.

Just as our system of laws make special provision for persons *in* the military, it also has specific laws that address how those of us on the *outside* can interact with members of the Canadian Forces. A series of sections in the Criminal Code makes a crime of matters such as inciting mutiny among members of the Canadian Forces or, for a traitorous or mutinous purpose, "seduc[ing] a member of the Canadian Forces from his duty and allegiance to Her Majesty" (Section 53). Once a member of the Canadian Forces has deserted his or her post, it is illegal to knowingly "aid, assist, harbour or conceal" the deserter (Section 54). Because the Royal Canadian Mounted Police has for long stretches of Canadian history functioned as a quasi-military force, it is also a crime to "persuade or counsel" a member of the RCMP to desert or go AWOL (absent without leave) or to aid or harbour an RCMP deserter.

Maintaining discipline among members of the armed forces isn't restricted to just the Canadian military, however. Section 62 of the Criminal Code makes it a crime to interfere with the loyalty or discipline of a "member of a force," and also to publish or say anything that advocates "insubordination, disloyalty, mutiny or refusal of duty." A "member of a force" means not just members of the Canadian Forces, but the naval, army, or air forces of *any* country who are lawfully present in Canada. It is thus a crime to publish a tract calling for American or British soldiers to disobey orders if those soldiers are lawfully present in Canada (as they sometimes were during both world wars). It is also a crime to wear a military uniform (or one that is confusingly similar) or any medal, ribbon, or other decoration (or any imitation of the foregoing) unless you are lawfully entitled to do so (i.e., you are a member of the applicable armed forces or were the actual recipient of the award in question). This prohibition extends also to the uniforms and medals of the armed forces of foreign countries.

Lost in Space

This chapter began with a backward glance at some historical laws. To end we turn to face the future. It was alluded to early in this chapter that all laws are reactive — a *response* to behaviour and activities that our elected representatives have decided are deleterious to our continued well-being. No one sat down and dreamed up all the possible crimes that *could* be committed and then created laws to prevent them. The laws were implemented because the activities were occurring and we decided to punish them. However, since every generalization is inevitably subject to some sort of caveat, it should come as no surprise that one has arisen for this, as well. Not every element of our criminal law was enacted in response to a particular incident — sometimes our legislators are proactive, even, you might say, visionary.

To appreciate the scope of their foresight, it must first be acknowledged that it has historically been a principle of criminal law that it only applies to acts committed within the territory of the state — you can't be charged in Canada for a theft that was committed in, for example, France (though there may be extradition treaties that permit the police to detain you and transport you to that other country if the authorities in that other country request it).[32] However, Parliament can pass a specific law that extends Canadian criminal jurisdiction beyond the borders of the country, thereby empowering the Canadian law-enforcement apparatus to arrest, try, and punish for crimes committed elsewhere. Parliament has done so for a number of the most serious of crimes: matters such as hijackings, torture, war crimes, and crimes against humanity. Canada, in other words, won't allow itself to be a safe haven for those who have done these things elsewhere.

Sometimes, though, we need to cast our eyes on vistas even farther removed and let our imaginations run wild to deal with the sort of crimes that previously would only have been in the domain of science fiction writers. Hence Sections 7(2.3) through 7(2.34) of the Criminal Code, enacted in 1999. Those sections make it very clear that anything that is a crime if performed here in Canada could also land you in jail if committed in a somewhat more exotic location, specifically an international space station. Thus far, there have (perhaps disappointingly) been no reports of any need to file charges in reliance on these sections.

6

Race, Religion, and the Law

In a time when matters of race and religion occupy such a significant portion of our public discourse, coupled with the generally ahistorical approach the mass media brings to such matters, it can be tempting to think our preoccupation with such concerns is a new phenomenon. Surely, goes this line of thinking, in previous decades when the country was somewhat more homogenous in its makeup, race and religion weren't as prevalent a matter of debate and anxiety. Such a conclusion would be incorrect. Because, as we have seen, the law is simply another vector along which societal issues are addressed, our history is replete with legislation and cases that uncover a perpetual cultural and governmental concern with race and religion.

As was the case with some of the sedition cases discussed in Chapter 3, it is useful to occasionally remind ourselves of where we have gone wrong in the past in order to ensure that we don't make the same mistakes in the future. The past few decades have seen an increasing public awareness of racist aspects of Canadian history. By the summer of 2006, for example, the federal government took steps to formally apologize for and offer monetary investments in anti-racism and cultural reconciliation programs in response to protests over the "head tax" that Chinese immigrants were forced to pay during the late nineteenth century and early twentieth century. This chapter won't recount the more notorious episodes, such as the interning of Canadians of Italian, Japanese, and other descent during the world wars, but instead will focus on a handful of nearly forgotten (at least to the general public) strands of our legal history, which are no less interesting (and sometimes shameful) for their lack of prominence.

It was once a crime in Canada to participate in certain kinds of dancing — a story that springs from the confluence of race and spirituality. In 1884, the federal Indian Act was amended to prohibit the "Potlatch" and "Tamanawas" celebrations and dances that took place among certain West Coast aboriginal nations.[1] Any person, whether aboriginal (*Indian* was the term generally used at the time) or not, was prohibited from engaging in, assisting in, encouraging, or celebrating these aboriginal customs, which were a mix of cultural expression and spiritual/religious affirmation. A minimum sentence of two months' imprisonment was set out, with a six-month maximum. By 1895, the prohibition had been extended beyond the two named events to include any "festival, dance or ceremony of which the giving away or paying or giving back of money, goods or articles of any sort forms a part."[2] The latter aspect of the ceremonies, described as an "insane exuberance of generosity" by Liberal Opposition Leader Edward Blake during the debates regarding the 1884 amendments,[3] seemed to particularly offend federal sensibilities. While the aboriginal mindset frowned upon the acquisition of material goods and viewed the giving away of surplus items as an opportunity to develop familial and tribal ties, such treatment of valuable commodities was almost alien to the prevailing European-derived view. A paternalistic concern for preventing the exposure of aboriginals to "debauchery of the worst kind" (in the words of Prime Minister John A. Macdonald, in his arguments advocating for the adoption of the dancing ban) also shot through the debates.

A number of rationales for prohibiting the dances and ceremonies were advanced, though the fundamental impetus appears to have been an attempt to suppress aboriginal culture in order to supplant it. The policy of the Department of Indian Affairs at the time was to encourage cultural assimilation and replace aboriginal language, culture, and religion, whether by means of residential schools, Christian missionaries, or discouraging (and even prohibiting) the use of aboriginal languages for communication.[4] Some of the arguments used by agents of the department to justify the prohibitions were particularly spurious: the dust kicked up by the dances spread diseases; dancing resulted not only in mental and physical deterioration but also in destitution, misery, sickness, and death among young and old alike.[5] Economic concerns were also paramount. It was thought necessary to replace the reluctance to acquire personal property and the desire to give it away with a proclivity for ownership and rational selfishness,[6] and also to avoid activities that would result in the frenzied participants not being as available for work as they might otherwise be.

Thus it was that any purported commitment to freedom of religion was exposed as a lie, a fact that wasn't lost on those charged and convicted of the crime of dancing in contravention of the Indian Act. Convictions and imprisonment were imposed on aboriginals at all levels of their social hierarchy, from lay members to elders to tribal chiefs. Although there is a relative paucity of comprehensive records, some authorities recount that, in one four-year span beginning in 1900, at least fifty arrests and twenty convictions were tendered, and in subsequent decades hundreds of aboriginals were charged and convicted.[7]

The law itself didn't remain undisturbed in the midst of the enhanced enforcement. In 1914 and 1918, the language was amended and expanded to criminalize any "Indian dance" that didn't take place on a reserve (i.e., whether or not it involved the "giving away" of money or property) and also prohibited participation by an aboriginal in any "show, exhibition, performance, stampede or pageant" while the participant was garbed in "aboriginal costume." The nature of the offence was also changed, no longer requiring a criminal trial in court: a justice of the peace or an agent of the Department of Indian Affairs could now handle the entire process, depriving those charged of the traditional protections available to accused in a court appearance. The scope of the crime was widened yet again in 1933 by deleting the words "in aboriginal costume." As Prime Minister Arthur Meighen explained, this was intended to make it more difficult for aboriginals to evade the ban by making minor alterations to their attire.

Throughout the decades of government suppression, tribal customs didn't die out entirely, and aboriginal communities were inventive in their efforts to keep their traditions alive. Aside from performing the dances in private homes and far from the prying eyes of Indian Affairs agents, they would sometimes divide a potlatch ceremony into its constituent parts, performing each component days or even months and many miles apart from the others. One innovative strategy involved blending the ceremonies with government-approved Christian church proceedings.[8]

It wasn't until 1951 that the legislative barriers to celebrations of the ceremonies would be dismantled, as a minor part of an omnibus reform to the Indian Act and the laws relating to the treatment of aboriginals.[9] Despite more than fifty years and thousands of work-hours dedicated to the eradication of aboriginal dances and ceremonies, the available evidence shows that deleting the ban on aboriginal dancing was hardly discussed by Parliament. For all that it had occupied the efforts of bureaucrats and prime ministers, the prohibition lapsed in a surfeit of inattention, a particularly Canadian violation of religious freedom taking leave of this world without the official remonstration properly due it.

The Prairies in the first half of the twentieth century saw a massive influx of immigrants from diverse racial or ethnic backgrounds. Asians and aboriginals, Eastern Europeans and Englishmen, among many others, all found themselves warily circling one another in an attempt to carve out the Canadian future. Just as aboriginals had learned that unfamiliar facets of race and religion could result in legal repression, race alone was sometimes enough to spawn government action. Saskatchewan was home to a law that forbade Chinese immigrants from employing white females, which gave rise to a bold legal challenge by Yee Clun, the owner of a restaurant and rooming house.

During the First World War, Regina had a Chinese population hovering around 100 persons out of a total population of about 35,000, a number that grew to around 250 persons by the time of the Second World War.[10] Nevertheless, the Chinese, and especially the entrepreneurs among them, were the subject of particular attention from both provincial and federal legislatures. Racialized fears of Asian immigration resulted in federal head taxes being imposed on Chinese immigrants, starting at $50 in 1885 and rising to $500 by 1903, on the way to a complete ban on Chinese immigrants imposed in 1923 (and finally lifted after the Second World War). Because Japan was a military ally of the British Empire, a similar head tax on Japanese immigrants wasn't feasible, but agreements between the governments restricted Japanese immigration to 400 persons per year.[11]

Despite their small numbers, the presence of Asian immigrants prompted what now can only be described as bizarre overreaction. A web of federal and provincial laws acted to restrain the activities of Chinese immigrants. They were denied the right to vote and, in British

Columbia, denied the right to work in such disparate endeavours as mining and the public service, while also prevented from obtaining licences to operate laundries, sell liquor, work in construction, practise law or, in a final indignity, receive unemployment relief.[12] Sometimes the prohibitions affecting Chinese immigrants were even more strikingly banal, if no less pernicious in their effect.

In 1912, the government of Saskatchewan enacted An Act to Prevent the Employment of Female Labour in Certain Capacities.[13] Despite its rather arid title, the legislation contained a remarkable prohibition:

> No person shall employ in any capacity any white woman or girl or permit any white woman or girl to reside or lodge in or to work in or, save as a *bona fide* customer in a public apartment thereof only, to frequent any restaurant, laundry or other place of business or amusement owned, kept or managed by any Japanese, Chinaman or other Oriental person.

In short, Asians (whether immigrants or Canadian-born) couldn't hire white women to work in their businesses. The Saskatchewan legislation was enacted in the wake of union petitions demanding such legislation, which was also supported by other small business owners in the province.[14] The provision didn't prevent Asians from operating businesses (as reflected in the language of the law, restaurants, laundries, and rooming houses were the primary activities in which Asian immigrants were engaged), but it did place them at a significant competitive disadvantage. In a society that frowned on interaction with Asians, being able to hire white females as waitresses and clerks could be critical to the survival of a business.[15] There was also a moralizing element to the demands for such a law, since it was believed that Asians in a position to exercise influence over white females would inevitably lure them into a lifestyle of vice and iniquity.

Shortly after the law was enacted in Saskatchewan, vociferous protests from the Japanese government (which included the Japanese consul-general travelling to Regina to speak with the provincial attorney general responsible for drafting the law) were successful in securing an amendment to delete references to "Japanese" and "other Oriental person[s]" — from then on, only Chinese business owners would be prevented from hiring white women. Somewhat more favourable responses came from some of Saskatchewan's sister provinces: Manitoba passed a similar law in 1913, though it was never proclaimed into force and was finally repealed in 1940; Ontario passed a similar law in 1914, but it didn't come into effect until 1920; British Columbia also passed similar legislation in 1919.[16]

The first trials occurred shortly after the enactment in 1912 of the Saskatchewan statute, when two Chinese-Canadian men who owned restaurants and a rooming house in Moose Jaw were charged with employing three white waitresses and chambermaids. The defence strategy focused on the vagueness of the term *Chinaman*. Did it cover only those who were born in China, or also those who were descended from Chinese parents? Would it apply to a naturalized immigrant, or did the accused need to still be a Chinese national? The police magistrate who conducted the trial concluded that, whatever interpretation one wanted to put on the word, the accused Quong Wing and Quong Sing were each indeed a "Chinaman" and had therefore violated the law. The convictions were upheld on appeal all the way through to the Supreme Court of Canada. A different case in Saskatoon that same year witnessed a slightly different spin being attempted by the accused's lawyer. Because the women hired by one Mr. Yoshi were described as "Russian" and "German," the challenge was to determine whether they were properly considered "white women," a matter that wasn't entirely conclusive in the highly charged racialized atmosphere of the time. The magistrate hearing the case adjourned it to consider the question and then answered in the affirmative on his return: Germans and Russians were indeed Caucasian, and so Yoshi was convicted.[17]

By 1919, the Saskatchewan legislature amended the legislation again to delete the reference to "Chinaman," thereby making it a matter of municipal licensing to determine in what circumstances "white women" could be employed in restaurants, laundries, and rooming houses. Because of the continuing prejudice held by some members of the community, the effect on Chinese business owners was largely the same as before the 1919 amendments: they still couldn't hire "white women," only now they had to incur the time and trouble of making an application to the licensing authorities in order to be told so.

Yee Clun owned one of Regina's most popular and acclaimed restaurants, and in 1924, following the implementation of the complete
ban on Chinese immigration in 1923, he made his request for a licence
to hire white females. Clun's application had the support of a number
of his white neighbours, including the city licence inspector, police
officers, and a member of the city council. But Regina City Council as
a whole wasn't enthusiastic about granting the request, voting to give
preliminary approval to the matter, subject to ratification at the next
council meeting. Concerns about encouraging intermarriage among
different racial groups were raised by, among others, the Woman's
Christian Temperance Union, the Regina Local Council of Women,
and the Regina Women's Labour League, and the second city council
meeting to consider the matter was flooded with requests to make
submissions on the matter. The meeting was inconclusive, and so the
matter was held over for nearly two months until the next council
meeting. At that next meeting, the third to be devoted to considering
the matter, Yee Clun's application was denied.

The Chinese community of Regina pooled its resources and
retained a lawyer to appeal the matter. During the court proceedings,
the mayor and other members of the city council who had voted against
Clun's application explained that they were concerned that, because
Clun's business also employed Chinese males, there was a danger that
would be posed to their white female co-employees. Of course, other
restaurants in Regina also employed Chinese males and white females
side by side, and city council hadn't deemed it necessary to restrict such
commingling, but those restaurants were owned by white businessmen.
The judge hearing the appeal, offended by the discriminatory practices
being paraded in front of him and decidedly unpersuaded by the arguments marshalled by the mayor and the councillors who supported
him, ordered the city to issue a licence to Yee Clun.

But the matter didn't end there. By 1926, the Saskatchewan legislature
amended the law once more, expanding the number of businesses that
would require a municipal licence in order to hire white females, and
also, in a bitter swipe at the Yee Clun decision, empowered municipal
councils to revoke any licence that they had already granted and, further,
barred any right of appeal from any such revocation or refusal to grant a
licence. It isn't clear whether Regina City Council revoked Yee Clun's
licence after being given the power to do so, but it did seek to prosecute

him for tax evasion, a conviction that was overturned on appeal. The "white women labour protection laws," although their wording was carefully denuded over time of the overtly racial language, remained on the books for decades following their enactment. Ontario's version was finally repealed in 1947 after years of confusion as to whether it had, in fact, been proclaimed and passionate denunciations from the media and the Chinese embassy. British Columbia didn't repeal its version of the law until 1968, and Saskatchewan's law, the original and inspiration for the others, remained in effect until 1969.[18]

The story of Rosa Parks, a black resident of Montgomery, Alabama, who in 1955 refused to give up her seat on a bus to a white person in accordance with a city bylaw and thereby provided one of the sparks of the American civil rights movement of the 1950s, is well known. Unfortunately much less familiar is the story of Viola Desmond, a Nova Scotia resident who in 1946 was subjected to the racist "colour-bar" policies of New Glasgow's Roseland Theatre and fought back through the courts, and whose example should serve more widely as an inspiration for those who wish to stand up to discriminatory laws and regulations.

Desmond was travelling to Sydney when her car broke down in New Glasgow. In order to pass the time while she waited for her car to be repaired, she decided to watch a movie at the Roseland. The Roseland had two seating areas: a main floor for which tickets were forty cents and a balcony that had tickets at thirty cents. Desmond requested a downstairs ticket, but the cashier gave her a balcony ticket together with her change. Not realizing that she hadn't been given the ticket for which she had asked, Desmond proceeded towards a seat on the main floor. The usher, after checking her ticket, stopped her and explained that she had an "upstairs" ticket and wouldn't be permitted to sit downstairs. Hoping to clear up matters, Desmond went back to the cashier and asked to exchange her balcony ticket for the main-floor ticket she had originally requested.

The response came back: "I'm sorry, but I'm not permitted to sell downstairs tickets to you people."

It is worth recalling the environment in which Viola Desmond found herself confronted with this segregation. She was alone, away from home, and being confronted by strangers, with no one to assist her. Nova Scotia had suffered from a series of racist incidents over the preceding decades, including race-based riots in Truro and New Glasgow. In 1946, there were no human rights codes and no Canadian federal Bill of Rights or Charter of Rights and Freedoms. No civil rights movement of any endurance or discipline was extant from which she could derive inspiration or emotional sustenance. Nonetheless, Viola Desmond promptly walked back inside and took the seat for which she had asked and was willing to pay. The usher asked her to vacate her seat, as did the manager. She refused. Finally, a police officer was called, who promptly physically removed her from the theatre and placed her in jail overnight, where she was made to share a cell with male prisoners. The next day, without being given an opportunity to retain a lawyer, nor having been informed of her right to seek bail or an adjournment in order to prepare her case, she was charged and convicted of violating a provincial statute that governed the licensing of movie theatres and playhouses, and ordered to pay a fine of $20, together with costs of $6 to the theatre manager.

There is a somewhat grim, if revealing, irony in the charge. The relevant act, the Theatres, Cinematographs and Amusements Act, didn't have any language in it that spoke about racial segregation of seating arrangements. It did, however, require ticket buyers to pay an amusement tax. The amount of tax payable was a function of the price of the ticket: on the downstairs ticket of forty cents, three cents tax was included, while on the upstairs ticket of thirty cents, two cents tax was included. Desmond had tendered $1 to pay for her ticket and had been given seventy cents in change, though she had asked for the forty-cent ticket and was willing to pay for it. The discrepancy between the amount she paid and the activity she undertook was what grounded the charge and conviction. Because she had sat downstairs, despite not having been charged the required forty-cent price, she hadn't paid the appropriate amount of tax — Viola Desmond, in other words, was arrested, charged, put in jail, tried, convicted, and fined $26 because she had technically failed to pay *one cent* in taxes.

Viola turned to the Nova Scotia Association for the Advancement of Colored People, founded a year earlier in 1945. As the news of her treatment became public knowledge, editorials denouncing the actions of the Roseland Theatre and the police were written as far away as Toronto. A lawyer was retained to argue Desmond's case, though the legal precedents they were faced with weren't terribly promising. A previous lawsuit against the Roseland by another black woman who had deliberately challenged the theatre's seating policies in 1942 had failed.

A 1911 lawsuit against a Regina restaurant that openly charged black customers double what white customers were charged for the same meal had also been dismissed. Various cases across the country, including at least one that had reached the Supreme Court of Canada, had upheld the right of owners of theatres, restaurants, and bars to set their own rules in conducting their business, including the determination of their own racial preference policies, whether in respect of seating, pricing, or refusal to provide any service whatsoever.[19] A handful of cases, however, had held otherwise: while declining to find that such race-based treatment was a violation of law, they were prepared to accept the argument that a breach of contract had occurred.[20] Confronted with these inauspicious heralds, Desmond's lawyer elected not to challenge the right of the Roseland to bar Desmond from the ground-floor seating. Instead, he sought to quash the conviction on the basis that it had been procedurally unfair and that there was insufficient evidence to support it. Advanced on technical legal grounds, the case fell on them, as well: a four-judge panel dismissed the attempt. To this day, the sense of lost opportunity among some academics and activists is palpable.

Just as race alone was sometimes a sufficient catalyst to involve legal sanction, so too was religion. Two religious sects in Canada, the Doukhobors and Jehovah's Witnesses, have been the target of governmental and legislative action and discrimination. The case of the Doukhobors, and particularly the zealous sub-sect known as the Sons of Freedom, is a story of fanaticism, violent terrorism, and mass reprisal — and, oddly enough, nudity. It is worth contrasting the Doukhobor story, which flared into violence and suffering caused by radical Doukhobor fanatics, with that of the Jehovah's Witnesses, who were decidedly more peaceful and yet faced the more vigorous crackdown and much more broadly aimed efforts at suppression. The Jehovah's Witnesses have been the subject of some of the most concentrated governmental attacks on a particular group of religious adherents in Canadian history, especially in the Province of Quebec. As some commentators have remarked, the story of the Witnesses is one that shows Canada both at its worst and at its best. Although the mistreatment of these Canadians was at times abominable, it is also the case that the very fact of their victimization was a significant catalyst of the efforts that resulted in the passing of the Canadian Bill of Rights and, eventually, the Charter of Rights and Freedoms, groundbreaking legislation and constitutional platforms that enshrined our fundamental rights and freedoms against governmental abuse.

On January 20, 1899, the first of what would eventually number 7,427 Doukhobors arrived in Canada.[21] The religious group (whose name derived from a Russian word meaning "spirit wrestlers") had been granted a migration permit from Tsarist Russia, where the authorities had been more than eager to see the back of them. The group was an ascetic peasant splinter sect from the Russian Orthodox Church, which pledged absolute pacifism, vegetarianism, and abstinence from alcohol; held their property in common; and refused to recognize the authority of either church or state. Because Doukhobor men refused to serve in the Russian military, they had been the subject of multiple episodes of public prosecution, continually being forced to move their communities into ever more remote locations, at least until such time as the Russian government decided to take an interest in their activities again.

The Doukhobor desire for a new home coincided nicely with the Canadian government's hunger for settlers to populate the Canadian prairie. After an unsuccessful attempt to settle in Cyprus, Doukhobor representatives negotiated with the Canadian government, which agreed to give each adult male 160 acres of fertile land — nearly 750,000 acres in what is now Saskatchewan and Manitoba were to be set aside for Doukhobor use. Canada also agreed to exempt the Doukhobors from military service, passing an order-in-council that granted the Doukhobors privileges similar to those held by Quakers and Mennonites, namely an exemption from the Militia Act, which otherwise required adult males to answer calls for conscription in the event of armed conflict.[22] Contained within the agreement reached by the Doukhobors and the Canadian government, however, were requirements that would eventually blossom into a literal conflagration. A registration fee would have to be paid to the government, vital statistics would need to be provided to the government for census purposes, taxes would need to be paid, and each Doukhobor would need to become a Canadian citizen, which required the swearing of an oath of allegiance.

Within the Doukhobor community, while some of the new immigrants began to break away from the communal lifestyle and attempted to establish an existence and lifestyle independent from the increasingly strange dictates of the sect leadership, a group of particularly zealous believers began to interpret communications they received from the Doukhobor leaders (who remained in Russia) as invocations to mass resistance against Canadian authority. Trouble began in 1900 when the Doukhobors refused to record their landholdings in their individual names; they also refused to register births, deaths, and marriages, or to allow their children to attend government-funded schools, all on the basis that the government was a Satanic instrument. One letter denouncing both materialism and materials derived from the earth prompted devout members to hand over all their money to the authorities, refuse to use metal farm implements, and turn loose all of their livestock — many of which were promptly eaten by coyotes, with the remainder being captured by the North-West Mounted Police and auctioned off (the proceeds of the auction were placed in a trust fund for the benefit of the Doukhobors). The Canadian government, and particularly the North-West Mounted Police who frequently encountered the community in their efforts to maintain order in what was then still the Northwest Territories, were increasingly baffled by the actions of the more fervent Doukhobors.

In 1903, some members of the Doukhobor community began efforts to effect a mass migration to a warmer climate, large groups of them marching south or towards government offices in an effort to prompt the government to relocate them. They also began to protest efforts by more mainstream Protestant denominations to proselytize among the Doukhobors, and to protest government efforts to make them comply with the vital statistics and land registration requirements. To make matters even more interesting, many Doukhobors decided to take part in these marches and protests in the nude. The nudity seems to have been derived from multiple justifications: it was an expression of their desire to return to the "simplicity of Adam and Eve" in furtherance of the command to forgo material things;[23] some viewed it as a demonstration of the necessity of living in more comfortable environmental conditions; while others, particularly the more fanatical leaders of the protest currents within the community, recognized that mass displays of public nudity were decidedly unsettling to both their non-Doukhobor neighbours and the authorities who were stymied in their efforts to deal with dozens and hundreds of naked protestors. Exposing themselves was a potent psychological weapon — by provocatively making themselves vulnerable, they magnified the impact of their public displays.

The use of nudity as a means of protest wasn't condoned by all members of the Doukhobor community, and so rifts began to fracture the community between law-abiding and radical elements; the latter began referring to themselves as "Sons of Freedom." In the summer of 1903, when the first instances of mass nude protests occurred, the police tried to determine the most effective way of handling the public nudity. The protests weren't violent; they were just disturbing. In the town of Yorkton, the police rounded up twenty-eight men and seventeen women and children and housed them in an immigration hall. After the protestors refused to obey police orders to dress themselves, police nailed the doors of the hall open and hung bright lamps in the hall to attract mosquitoes. Forced to choose between remaining naked and enduring ravenous clouds of bugs or putting on clothes and avoiding the problem, the group chose modesty. The adult males were charged and convicted of public indecency and sentenced to three months in prison. [24] Although a certain amount of comic relief can be had in recounting some of the Doukhobor stories, it is worth remembering that their activities involved not just the consenting adult members of the sect but children, as well. Many of the police reports and some of the later commentaries particularly stress the suffering of the children, who were not only forced to parade naked but also to observe the stringent dietary requirements of their parents — the group marching to Yorkton subsisted on grass and leaves.

Although mass use of public nudity faded in the wake of the 1903 arrests and convictions, many Doukhobors continued to refuse to register their landholdings in individual names or swear the oath of allegiance required for citizenship, and so the land that had been allocated to the community began to be withdrawn from them and parcelled out to other Canadians who were willing to abide by Canadian laws. Unhappy with the situation confronting them on the Prairies, some Doukhobors, led by their spiritual leader Peter Verigin (the "Lordly"), began moving to British Columbia in 1907 in a continuing effort to avoid government authority and to establish an isolated self-sufficient religious community.

Some of those left in Saskatchewan and Manitoba started to act in increasingly strange fashion. In the fall of 1907, a group of nearly one hundred Doukhobors began marching east, reaching Fort William, Ontario. On New Year's Day, 1908 (which is, you will recall, in the middle of winter, not a particularly pleasant time in Northern Ontario), eighteen of them burned their clothes in public and then started a forty-day hunger strike, which resulted in one death. As the weather got better, more public nudity occurred in Fort William, and nineteen Doukhobors were arrested in April and sentenced to six months in prison. Because no prisons in Ontario would accept the prisoners, the entire group of seventy Doukhobors were sent back to Yorkton, where matters became even more bizarre. The Doukhobors refused to put on clothes and so they were confined to the Yorkton Agricultural Hall, where they made constant efforts to escape. Still unsure how exactly to handle the matter, the Saskatchewan government finally built a fenced compound near Orcadia, Saskatchewan, and the group was moved there — it was, in short, a religious-based detention camp. Hunger strikes, battles with police, committals to insane asylums, and the removal of starving children from their fanatic parents carried on for the balance of the summer.[25]

The new Doukhobor community in British Columbia didn't fare much better; if anything, the story of the sect took an even darker turn, culminating in large-scale imprisonments, arson, and murder. Approximately five thousand Doukhobors had moved to British Columbia, where a thriving community had been created on land purchased by Verigin. Fruit farms, a sawmill, a brick manufacturing plant, and even a jam factory that was to become renowned for its product were established.[26] Nonetheless, the primary contentious issues remained: a continued refusal to register births, marriages, and deaths and a reluctance to send their children to state-run schools. The old schisms between hardline believers and more accommodating Doukhobors also continued to split the community, with the former calling for more radical rejection of societal norms and Canadian laws.

In 1914, in an effort to address the concerns raised by some British Columbia residents, the provincial government passed the Community Regulation Act, which provided that where violations of the laws relating to vital statistics and school attendance were breached, the entire community of Doukhobors could be held criminally responsible, permitting the seizure of property held by any individual Doukhobor in satisfaction of unpaid fines levied on another Doukhobor. An attempt at negotiations between Verigin and the government delayed enforcement of the law for a number of years, but the matter soon flared out of control.

Tensions between the Doukhobors and their neighbours were exacerbated during the First World War and in the years following. The pacifism of the sect and their consequent ability to evade military service was a particular flashpoint, as was the government's general inability or reluctance to enforce tax and other legal obligations on the community. Much of the subsequent trouble revolved around schooling. An accommodation was reached by the provincial government whereby the Doukhobors would be entitled to send their children to schools within their own communities, but the schools were paid for by general government funds — in other words, non-Doukhobor taxpayers were financing the building and running of schools reserved exclusively for Doukhobors. This prompted reactions on both sides of the issue: for the wider community, it was an insistence on enforcing school attendance requirements and anger at the special treatment being accorded to Doukhobors; for radical elements of the Doukhobor community, it was fury that the "taint" of the outside world was being permitted into the schools and a refusal to countenance their children's attendance even at these Doukhobor-run but government-funded facilities. On one side, the government began enforcing in earnest the Community Regulation Act by arresting Doukhobors and testing them for insanity; on the other side, radical Doukhobors started setting fire to the government schools. Eight schools were burned in a one-year period beginning in the spring of 1923.[27]

In 1924, the leader of the Doukhobor community, Peter Verigin, was killed in an explosion on a Canadian Pacific Railway train. Verigin's maid and seven others also died. The cause of the explosion was a bomb planted under Verigin's seat. While some Doukhobors blamed the government for assassinating their leader, other investigations concluded that it was an act of murder carried out by splinter factions within the Doukhobor community who rejected his (however cynical) attempts to conciliate with Canadian authorities. In the wake of the murder, Verigin's son (also named Peter, but referred to as the "Purger") took over leadership of the community, and the radical Sons of Freedom continued to become even more aggressive in their defiance.

By the late 1920s, school burnings were a regular occurrence, causing school attendance by Doukhobor children to plummet (evidently both as an expression of support for the anti-schooling elements in the community and as a precaution intended to keep the children safe).

Also making a comeback were fervent demonstrations of mass public nudity. In August 1929, more than one hundred naked Doukhobors were arrested after a protest in Nelson, British Columbia, charged with public indecency, and sentenced to six months in jail. The provincial government also initiated an effort to remove Doukhobor children from their parents under the auspices of child welfare legislation and place them in government schools. The move to take their children aggravated the relationship between the government and the Doukhobors, prompting the Sons of Freedom to foment even more vituperative rhetoric about government persecution.

The school burnings and the public demonstrations of nudity also spread from British Columbia to the remaining Doukhobor communities in Saskatchewan. Provincial demands for federal action prompted a 1931 amendment to the Criminal Code that created a distinct crime of public nudity and provided for a three-year term of imprisonment (increased from the six-month term that had been the maximum punishment for "public indecency," previously the only crime with which the nude protestors could be punished), and also inserted a requirement that any prosecution under the law first obtain the consent of the provincial attorney general before proceeding. The new tougher law was called upon in short order.

In May 1932, the younger Peter Verigin was convicted of perjury (arising from a civil lawsuit that Verigin had filed against another non-radical Doukhobor) and sentenced to eighteen months in prison. The imprisonment of Verigin prompted what one commentator referred to as the "mobilization of [a] nude army" of Sons of Freedom. By the end of the month, 725 men, women, and children were arrested for participating in nude demonstrations. The numbers were so large that the federal government created a special penal colony to hold the adults on an island off the coast of British Columbia. The arrested children were parcelled out to foster homes and correctional institutions.[28] By the middle of the 1930s, because of a lack of government funds arising from the Depression as well as a public outcry over the fact that more money was being spent on re-educating Doukhobor children than on non-Doukhobors who were suffering from unemployment and economic dislocation, the island prison was dismantled and the Doukhobor children were returned to their communities in British Columbia.

Over the next three decades, until the early 1960s, the Sons of Freedom continued to engage in terrorist activities — burning schools and homes and bombing bridges and electricity lines. The nude protests continued, as did subsequent efforts by the government to neutralize the more radical and destabilizing elements in the Doukhobor community. In 1950, five Doukhobor leaders were convicted of seditious conspiracy and sentenced to two years' imprisonment on the basis that the leaders had signed a document that contained "emphatic exhortation to refuse to register births, deaths and marriages under provincial law." In 1951, the then-current leader of the Sons of Freedom Doukhobors, Michael Verigin (referred to as the "Archangel"), was charged and convicted of seditious conspiracy for encouraging his followers "to disobey, defy and subvert His Majesty's laws" and was sentenced to two years, though he died shortly after sentencing.[29]

The year 1962 saw the last surge of actions against the Sons of Freedom. Although seventy members of the "Fraternal Council" of the Sons of Freedom were acquitted of charges of seditious conspiracy and intimidating the provincial legislature,[30] thirty-six sect members were convicted of attempted arson and conspiracy to commit arson and sentenced to twelve years in prison.[31] Since the early 1960s, there haven't been any major outbreaks of arson, bombing, or nude protests by the Sons of Freedom Doukhobors. The most radical elements of the community appear to have learned that their campaign of arson, hunger strikes, and intimidation of their co-religionists didn't result in their purportedly desired result: originally of wanting to be moved en masse out of the country and finally of having the government exempt them from any obligations under the law.

The Canadian Doukhobor saga remains controversial, with some people viewing the more than fifty years of confrontation as a blot on the Canadian historical record (a view that, in light of such disturbing incidents as the construction of the penal colony on Piers Island and the enforced distribution of Doukhobor children among child welfare agencies, is not without its merits). Others view the matter as a government confronted with a fanatical insurrectionist sect that cynically abused its own children in an attempt to further its ends. Regardless of the position one takes, it is indisputable that terrorist acts of arson and bombing were carried out by radical elements within the Doukhobor community. By the account of Simma Holt, one of the primary chroniclers of the Doukhobor story, more than one thousand separate criminal acts (including more than 250 acts of arson in 1962 alone) cost more than $20 million (in 1964 dollars) in damages and law-enforcement costs.[32] Perhaps because of the diminutive size of the community and its self-imposed outsider status, the Doukhobor story isn't extensively known, nor did it, outside of the extremely narrow realm of nudity law, result in significant legal developments. No such claims, whether regarding the violence of their movement or the legal significance of their treatment, can be made about the Jehovah's Witnesses — a distressing verdict on both counts.

It was only in 1931 that the Christian sect known as Jehovah's Witnesses decided to call themselves by that name. Prior to that, the group was known as "Bible Students" or "Russellites," after the founder of the movement, Charles Taze Russell. Beginning in the 1870s in Pennsylvania, Russell expounded the belief that Jesus Christ would return to this world in 1914 (after 1914, it became a doctrinal belief among Witnesses that Christ did, in fact, return invisibly). The Witnesses are a literate group who promulgate their beliefs in a number of publications, including their official magazine, *The Watchtower*, and are infamous for their method of door-to-door canvassing as a means of spreading their word.

Believing in a literal Kingdom of God and Kingdom of Satan, the Witnesses weren't shy in explaining their belief that the Roman Catholic Church was the tool of the Devil for the deliverance of evil in this world. The worldview of Jehovah's Witnesses isn't as resolutely rejectionist as that of the Doukhobors. Although they won't vote, they do pay taxes. And though they refuse to serve in the armed forces of any nation-state and won't salute any flag or sing national anthems, they otherwise consider themselves subject to civil laws.[33]

Their status as a community apart from the society around them has resulted in singularly energetic efforts on the part of governments around the world to persecute the group — despite this, their numbers have grown from tens of thousand primarily in the United States to millions around the world.[34] The sometimes intense overreaction of governments and the admirably staunch manner in which the sect has fought back through the courts and through political lobbying have meant that cases involving the Witnesses have changed jurisprudence throughout the world, especially in the United States and Canada.

Canadian law and history first intersect in a meaningful way with the Witnesses during the First World War. Because of their pacifist beliefs, and in the face of impending conscription, *The Watchtower* in November 1915 published an excerpt from the Militia Act, which stipulated that "persons who, from the doctrines of their religion, are averse to bearing arms or rendering personal military service" would be exempt from military service if they filed a sworn affidavit setting out the basis on which they were claiming exemption. Shortly thereafter, hundreds of adherents filed their affidavits, prompting a public outcry. One paper even called the Witnesses "a cover for pro-German anti-recruiting propaganda."[35] Although no immediate action was taken against the Witnesses as a group at the time, Russell was prohibited by Canadian border agents from entering the country to address his followers. Later during the war effort, two Witnesses publications were banned by order of the federal cabinet: a book written by Russell's successor entitled *The Finished Mystery*, which railed against the Catholic Church, militarism, and organized armies, and the monthly newsletter of the group. Simply possessing either was punishable by fines up to $5,000 and a maximum jail term of five years. By July 1918, all publications of the Watch Tower Bible and Tract Society (the official printing body of the Witnesses) were banned, and a number of sect members were fined and even imprisoned for owning them.[36]

After conscription was instituted in July 1917 by means of the Military Service Act,[37] the position of the Witnesses became more precarious, and their treatment more humiliating. While the Military Service Act contained conscientious objector exemptions similar to those present in the earlier Militia Act (upon which many Witnesses had relied in filing their exemption affidavits), the new law extended the exemption only to members of an "organized religious denomination existing and well recognized in Canada" on or before July 6, 1917. In the *Cooke* case,[38] a court confirmed the decision of a military tribunal that the International Bible Students Association (then the formal name for the Witnesses) didn't qualify as a sufficiently recognized religious denomination. The Witnesses were therefore liable to be drafted. When they refused to wear uniforms or bear arms, they were court-martialled, imprisoned, and in some cases beaten.[39]

By 1920, the ban on publication and possession of Watch Tower Society publications was lifted. As the country moved through the Great Depression and into the Second World War, however, government persecution of the Jehovah's Witnesses across Canada became even more zealous. Eager to disseminate their creed, the Witnesses were entrepreneurial enough to take advantage of new means of communication: they broadcast radio shows, exhibited movies, and even pressed records containing speeches. In 1928, the federal government revoked the radio broadcast licences of the Witnesses on the basis that the content of their broadcasts was very nearly seditious as they exhorted that "all organized churches are corrupt and in alliance with unrighteous forces, that the entire system of society is wrong and that all governments are to be condemned."[40]

It was in Quebec that the Witnesses found themselves in a virtual war of attrition with the authorities. Quebec society between the wars was fairly described as church-dominated. The Catholic Church controlled most of the hospitals, schools, and civil society organizations such as charities; indeed, seated beside the lieutenant-governor on the floor of the legislature was the cardinal of the province, on a throne.[41] As a result, the near-fanatical antipathy that the Witnesses reserved for the Catholic Church was especially concentrated in Quebec, where it also found its least receptive audience. The Witnesses were often gratuitously offensive in their provocations: the publications of the Witnesses sometimes depicted "the Pope as a whore and priests as fat pigs."[42] These pamphlets prompted at least one charge for "blasphemous libel" (still found in the Criminal Code at Section 296) — the prosecution was unsuccessful, however, because the court found that nothing in the pamphlet attacked God per se.[43]

As the activities of the Witnesses in Quebec increased, a different line of attack was tried: the old warhorse of seditious libel was trotted out. During the 1930s, multiple convictions were obtained on the basis that the Witnesses' publications and activities (which included stopping Catholic parishioners on their way to church to tell them they were being duped by Satan) were, under the then-existing wording of the crime, "disturb[ing] the tranquility of the State, by creating ill-will, discontent, disaffection, hatred or contempt towards ... the established institutions of the country."[44] Governmental suspicion of the group wasn't limited to Quebec. The RCMP kept the Witnesses under surveillance beginning in 1933, and approximately one hundred Witnesses were arrested each year during the decade for their proselytizing.[45]

With the onset of the Second World War, the federal government enacted wartime regulations that declared illegal numerous organizations. At first the ban extended to fascist and communist organizations, but in July 1940, the federal cabinet, at the urging of numerous Members of Parliament both inside and outside Quebec, made the Jehovah's Witnesses an illegal organization, making membership a crime punishable by fines and imprisonment and permitting the government to seize all assets of the group. Nearly thirty Witnesses were charged and convicted in 1940, and $100,000 worth of property was confiscated.[46] Defending the ban, Liberal Prime Minister Mackenzie King read a statement in the House of Commons arguing that "the literature of Jehovah's Witnesses discloses ... that man-made authority or law should not be recognized if it conflicts with [their] interpretation of the Bible ... the general effect of this literature is ... to undermine the ordinary responsibility of citizens, particularly in time of war."[47]

However confrontational their literature was, however, the matter that most differentiated the Witnesses from their neighbours was their refusal to salute the flag or sing the national anthem (both actions were seen by Witnesses as idolatrous). Especially during a time of war, this was viewed as akin to treason. As is often the case with religious sects, it was the children of the Witnesses who bore the brunt of the backlash — it being standard practice to commence each school day with the singing of "God Save the King." (It is interesting to note that, prior to the war, Ontario school regulations actually exempted the children of the Witnesses from having to sing the national anthem — in September 1940, however, school boards in the province were instructed to suspend all children who refused to sing or salute the flag.)[48] Jehovah's Witnesses students across Canada were regularly suspended or expelled from school for their refusal to take part in the morning activities,[49] and in the absence of any other signs of neglect, the expelled or suspended children were taken from their parents and placed in foster homes.[50]

Numerous Opposition politicians in Ottawa, including future prime minister John Diefenbaker, argued strenuously for the lifting of the ban on the Witnesses. The ban was eventually removed in stages: "Jehovah's Witnesses" were deleted from the regulations in October 1943, the "International Bible Students Association of Canada" was removed from the list in June 1944, and the "Watch Tower Society" again became legal in May 1945. As Diefenbaker remarked, over the course of the war there had been nearly "five hundred prosecutions of Jehovah's Witnesses, none of which had to do with subversive activities."[51]

As the war ended, so did the official federal proscription of the Witnesses' organizations. In Quebec, however, prosecutions for sedition continued apace, and many municipalities began relying on bylaws to prohibit the Witnesses from canvassing door to door and distributing literature. One particularly fervent member of the religion, Laurier Saumur, faced more than one hundred charges ranging from sedition to distributing religious literature without a licence.[52] Two Supreme Court cases of particular importance also involved Witnesses: *Boucher* and *Roncarelli*. As described in Chapter 4, *Boucher* was the case that modernized the Canadian law of sedition, with the Supreme Court holding that simply criticizing the government or even bearing an intention to create hostility and ill will between different groups of Canadians wasn't sufficient to ground a conviction for sedition — freedom of expression, even unpopular or offensive expression, was to be privileged over the desire of the government or other state institutions to curtail criticism. It was *Boucher*, together with the case of Frank Roncarelli, that ultimately signalled the death knell of Quebec government persecution of Jehovah's Witnesses.

The premier of Quebec, Maurice Duplessis, a devout Catholic, having regained power after the end of the war, was determined in his efforts to prosecute the Witnesses and oversaw a campaign that resulted in hundreds of arrests, disruptions of the Witnesses' meetings and ceremonies, and general harassment. Frank Roncarelli, a Montreal restaurateur and a member of the Jehovah's Witnesses, posted bail for more than four hundred of his co-religionists who had been arrested.[53] The premier took umbrage at this act of defiance, going so far as to publicly warn Roncarelli against posting bail for any others. When Roncarelli continued to post bail for his fellow Witnesses, Duplessis decided to flex his political muscle: he ordered the chairman of the Quebec Liquor Commission to revoke Roncarelli's licence, thereby putting Roncarelli out of business in December 1946.[54]

This time, the premier took matters one step too far. A sustained public outcry followed this blatant abuse of power, and Roncarelli launched multiple lawsuits against the Liquor Commission and the premier.[55] The case wound its way through the courts for more than a decade, as the premier's legal team attempted various manoeuvres to stymie Roncarelli's victory at trial. It took until 1959 for the Supreme Court of Canada to render its decision in the case and confirm what had been obvious to many for so long: Duplessis had acted capriciously, maliciously, and entirely without justification. As the *Montreal Star* editorialized about the decision, it restrained "the exercise of arbitrary authority and establishes the supremacy of the rule of law in this country."[56] The long tenure of official molestation of the Jehovah's Witnesses was coming to an end.

One of the deficiencies in our legal system that allowed the campaigns of discrimination discussed in this chapter to occur was the absence of an enumerated bill of rights. This is not to say, of course, that the presence of a bill of rights is in itself sufficient to prevent discrimination, but the entrenchment of guaranteed rights and freedoms (to free expression, to religious worship, and from arbitrary arrest, among others) is a critical element. During the course of the twentieth century, mainstream social and political views on the use of the instruments of law and state to the detriment of identifiable groups changed dramatically, often shepherded by the political lobbying of the persecuted groups themselves. The Jehovah's Witnesses were particularly active in agitating for a bill of rights, and did everything they could to call attention to the actions being taken against them across Canada. In 1948, a petition for a bill of rights that specifically named the actions of the Quebec government against the Witnesses secured more than half a million signatures.[57] John Diefenbaker, in his efforts to introduce a federal bill of rights (which eventually bore fruit in 1960), often invoked the mistreatment of the Witnesses for rhetorical effect.

The eventual entrenchment in 1982 of the Charter of Rights and Freedoms in our constitutional order was the culmination of a long process of persecution, activism, and court battles. Determining causation across the sweep of history isn't always exact, but we can say with certainty that it took an assessment of the sometimes appalling treatment of Canadians by our legal system in order to arrive where we are today. Whether the future treatment of Canadians is better is ultimately up to us — and we shouldn't allow it to be said that we didn't learn lessons from our past.

7

It Doesn't Take a Thief — Or, Not All the Interesting Stuff Happens in Criminal Court

For all the arcana unearthed by a jaunt through Canadian criminal law, it remains a fact that many, if not most, lawyers will never open a copy of the Criminal Code during the course of their professional lives. Drafting contracts in an office or arguing a divorce proceeding in court might not be the sort of legal activity that inspires prime-time drama on television, but such mundane pursuits have left gems sprinkled throughout our legal history. The legal profession has long sought to cultivate and display a sense of propriety and dignity — hence such features as the formal robes worn by judges and lawyers appearing before superior courts. But the law being both the product of human endeavour and the forum where ingenuity and artlessness collide, a certain charming gaudiness will inevitably emerge if one looks hard enough. Courts are sometimes where the human condition is cast into sharp relief, and where judges are obliged to attempt, in their own necessarily imperfect way, to snatch justice (or a semblance of it) from the snapping jaws of conflict between plaintiff and defendant. It doesn't always require a crime to have taken place for the law to be a forum for human foibles. Hopefully, none of us will ever be embroiled in the situations like some of those that have resulted in the cases discussed in this chapter, but we shouldn't let that stop us from enjoying them all the same.

The Incredibly Odd Buzzer Case

You can tell you're going to face a bad day in court when the judge describes the situation before him as having "evolved out of a mess, turned into a mess and the end result is a mess." When he goes on to say that "each side likely bears 75 per cent of the blame … (an overlapping of at least 50 per cent)," it's probably time to excuse yourself from the courtroom. But even with those warning flags having gone up, it's unlikely anyone, least of all the parties involved, could have guessed quite how the decision in *Wittlin v Bergman* was going to turn out.[1] The case involved ownership of Coby's Cookies Inc. By 1994, the Wittlin brothers owned 20 percent of the shares in Coby's Cookies, while Bergman and companies allied with Bergman owned the remaining 80 percent of the shares. The relationship between the two camps was the source of the "mess" comment made by Justice Farley. While originally the parties had collaborated as friends and business partners, poisonous animosity now ruled. Each side wanted nothing more than to be rid of the other and each had completely lost all trust in the other's intentions and activities. Bergman had offered to purchase the Wittlins' shares for $209,000 — the Wittlins had scoffed and demanded $527,272 (how such a precise figure was arrived at is not disclosed in the written decisions), a price that Bergman was unwilling to pay.

Situations such as this where there has been a complete breakdown in the relationship are textbook examples that corporate lawyers use to illustrate the need for what is called a "shareholders' agreement" — a contract between shareholders of a corporation that addresses various matters surrounding how the business will be run, including, critically, what dispute resolution mechanism will be relied upon if the relationship between shareholders is irretrievably damaged. Shareholders' agreements often include provisions that allow one party to buy out the other party, sometimes in accordance with a predetermined formula. Unfortunately for the holders of Coby's Cookies shares, no such agreement had ever been entered into. Short of abandoning their investment entirely and leaving the business to their new enemies, their only practical alternative was to bring an application in court. They could try to seek relief under a provision of the Business Corporations Act referred to as the "oppression remedy," which allows shareholders, when they feel that other shareholders have acted in a manner that is "oppressive" or "unfairly prejudicial," to ask a court to grant an order requiring the parties to act in accordance with the court's demands. The language of the section grants the courts extremely wide-ranging abilities to grant such orders as the court sees fit. No one had any idea what the court would see fit to do in this case.

The Wittlin brothers had sought an order forcing Bergman to buy the Wittlins' shares at their requested price. The judge didn't think it appropriate to force Bergman to purchase the shares or to predetermine the price at which the shares should be bought, so he crafted a somewhat more inventive "mechanism" (to use his description) — enter the buzzer. The parties to the lawsuit and their lawyers were to construct a "buzzer which may be operated by one of two buttons." Each side was to hold one button, and they were to arrange themselves in such a fashion that "only the faces … are to be seen by the other," so that there was no way for the other side to determine when the button was going to be pushed. When one button was pushed, the system would be overridden so that the other button couldn't also be pushed. The device was also to be equipped with a stopwatch, which would help determine the share price. The price of the Wittlin shares would start at their desired amount of $527,272, and then drop by $1,000 every six seconds (so, if the button was pushed after one minute, the purchase price would be $517,272).

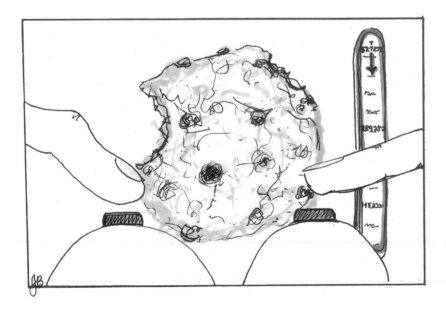

To make things more complicated, once the button was pushed, the party that did *not* push the button would have the option to decide who bought the shares. If Wittlin pushed the button, Bergman would have two options: buy the Wittlin shares at the price determined by the button mechanism, or punt the option back to Wittlin to buy Bergman's shares at the same price per share. If Wittlin was unwilling to buy Bergman's shares after Bergman had punted to Wittlin, Wittlin could force Bergman to buy the Wittlin shares, but at a 20 percent discount to the original price determined by pushing the button. For example, if Wittlin pushed the button at the two-minute mark, the preliminary purchase price would be $507,272 (i.e., $20,000 less than the starting price). At this point, Bergman could either purchase the Wittlin shares for $507,272 (thereby acquiring 100 percent control of the company) or require Wittlin to purchase Bergman's shares (i.e., 80 percent of the Coby's Cookies shares) for a price equal to $2,029,088 (i.e., four times the preliminary purchase price). If Wittlin was unwilling to purchase the Bergman shares, Wittlin could then force Bergman to buy the Wittlin shares for $405,817 (i.e., 20 percent less than the preliminary purchase price).

Besides being somewhat baffling, it was manifest that someone would be prejudiced by the arrangement: it was unfair to Bergman to have to face the risk of being bought out of a business that he had no desire to leave, and the Wittlins faced the prospect of having their purchase price being almost certainly reduced by 20 percent no matter when the button was pushed. They didn't have the funds to buy the Bergman shares, so Bergman could simply game the system by punting the option to purchase to them, after which they would in turn force Bergman to buy their shares at a 20 percent discount. Both parties were unimpressed with the proposed solution and appealed the decision. The Ontario Court of Appeal was similarly nonplussed and overturned it, substituting a much simpler mechanism: the corporation would purchase the Wittlin shares at a price determined by an independent business valuator. Finally, Coby's Cookies could continue on without any potentially debilitating animosity among its shareholders — and without the need for a nerve-wracking episode of duelling thumbs.

The Million-Dollar Comma

Lawyers charge for their services by the hour — not by the word, though it may sometimes seem otherwise to their clients. Clients call asking for documents to formalize what to the clients seem like relatively straight-forward transactions —business partnerships, for example. They are therefore somewhat surprised to see lawyers provide them with thirty-page, single-spaced documents, replete with dozens of articles, subsec-tions, and cross-references, and littered with capitalized terms each accompanied by its own specific definition. This, contends the client, is surely overkill. Pity the lawyer who is obliged to patiently explain to his or her client the necessity of all the wordsmithing, the seemingly excruciating and unnecessary attention to detail — *I'm not doing this work because I'm bored*, thinks the lawyer. *I'm doing it because I have to in order to protect your interests*. In the future, lawyers confronted with intransigent clients who are perplexed at why their counsel is spend-ing hours proofreading their contracts (at a dollar rate per minute that can be truly mind-boggling) should supply them with a copy of the case involving Rogers Communication and Aliant.[2] Rarely has an unpreten-tious comma had such an eye-opening impact.

Aliant owns utility poles throughout the Maritimes, which are quite lucrative pieces of property, at least for companies such as Rogers that require access to them. Rogers entered into a fourteen-page agreement with Aliant, granting Rogers the right to use 91,000 poles for cable lines at an annual rate of $9.60 per pole. When the contract was signed in 2002, Rogers thought it was agreeing to a five-year initial term, due to expire in 2007. But in early 2005, Aliant served notice to Rogers that the contract was being cancelled, effective one year from the date of notice (i.e., the date of termination would occur in early 2006, a year ahead of schedule), and that if Rogers wanted to continue to use the poles, it would need to enter into a new agreement based on current market rates, which had in some cases more than tripled to $28 per pole. Both Rogers and Aliant pointed to the contract, which contained the following clause: "[This agreement] shall continue in force for a period of five years from the date it is made, and thereafter for successive five year terms, unless and until terminated by one year prior notice in writing by either party."

When the folks at Rogers read that sentence, they interpreted it to mean something like "this agreement is in force for five years, until

2007 — after that, it will renew itself for further five-year periods, unless, in the fourth year of any given five-year period, one party notifies the other that it is terminating the contract effective one year after giving notice." On Rogers's understanding of the wording, the contract would be in place until at least 2007 and, in the most generous interpretation, couldn't be cancelled until 2011. Aliant, needless to say, had quite a different take: in their view, the contract had a nominal initial term of five years, but it could be terminated at any time simply by giving one year's written notice — they could have terminated the contract in 2003 had they seen fit to do so. The differing interpretations revolved around the second comma in the portion quoted above — did the language following the comma ("unless and until terminated …") apply to the first five-year term (i.e., from 2002 to 2007) or only to the five-year terms after 2007?

Because the matter involved the communications industry, which is federally regulated, the first resort of the parties was not to the courts to solve their dispute, but to a panel of the Canadian Radio-television and Telecommunications Commission (CRTC). The CRTC, citing "the rules of punctuation," held that Aliant's position was the correct one: the contract could be terminated at any time after it was entered into, simply by the delivery of one year's prior written notice. Total cost to Rogers of the comma in question? Approximately $2.1 million. That's what it cost Rogers to learn this lesson, but we can get it for free: both you and your lawyer should have paid attention during grammar lessons in school.

Liar, Liar, Pants on Fire

Don't break your promises. If you swear you're going to do something, basic morality compels you to do it. It seems a fairly simple edict, and most of us at least pay lip service to it. But since at least the dawn of democracy, citizens have marvelled at the willingness of politicians to break their promises; perhaps even more amazing is the relative impunity with which they do so. There have been times, however, when individual Canadians have had enough of the lies and taken it upon themselves to seek some accountability through the courts for yet one more promise broken by a politician. Fortunately for the politicians, and unfortunately for the rest of us, the courts have tended to side with the oath breakers.

Beginning on one side of the aisle, in 1988 John Ruffolo had had enough. He had watched Brian Mulroney state on television during the 1984 federal election campaign that Mulroney would improve postal service if elected. Furthermore, Ruffolo had received written campaign materials from the Progressive Conservative Party that indicated the party wouldn't implement free trade with the United States. Ruffolo claimed that he had relied on these promises in deciding to cast his vote for the Progressive Conservative candidate in his riding — and four years later, postal service hadn't improved and the federal government was moving forward with free trade. What else to do but sue for breach of contract and negligent misrepresentation?

Ruffolo had tried this once before. He had attempted to sue Mulroney in a court in Kitchener, Ontario, for breaching the promise about improving mail delivery, claiming $90 in damages for "hardship incurred from the breach of this promise." That action had been dismissed, and the court even declined to give any reasons. Undaunted, Ruffolo tried again by launching a lawsuit in Toronto's Small Claims Court against Mulroney and the Progressive Conservative Party, this time addressing both the postal service promise and the free trade promise.[3] Perhaps hoping to put a nail in the coffin of any future actions, Judge Thomson released a comprehensive decision, analyzing the various issues raised by Ruffolo's case, but the result was disarmingly simple: case dismissed.

Ruffolo's lawsuit failed for a number of reasons. First, there could be no contract between a voter and a candidate for political office. At law, to create a contract there must be two elements present: the intention to create a legal relationship between the parties (i.e., an intention to enter into a contract), and what lawyers call "consideration." By "consideration" is meant that there must be something of value exchanged between the parties in order for the contract to exist. If you enter into an agreement with a plumber to repair your leaky faucet, the "consideration" flows two ways: you are agreeing to give the plumber money and the plumber is agreeing to render services. When it comes to an election campaign, said Judge Thomson, neither condition is met. The candidate certainly isn't intending to enter into a contract with an individual voter (especially in a case like this, where Mulroney had never even met Ruffolo), and there is nothing of value that is being exchanged.

The second reason the judge gave for dismissing Ruffolo's lawsuit was that no "negligent misrepresentation" had occurred. Negligent misrepresentation falls under a body of law separate from contracts that is called "torts." The theory of negligent misrepresentation provides that where a person possesses special skill and ability and makes statements that draw upon that skill or ability, the speaker can be liable for damages that result to a person who has relied on the statements of the speaker if the speaker didn't exercise reasonable care in making the statements. In other words, the speaker has what is called a "duty of care" towards listeners whom the speaker knows or ought to know will be relying on the statements of the speaker. If an accountant, for example, prepares financial statements for a company and negligently makes a mistake in those financial statements, the accountant will be liable to an investor in the company who read the financial statements prepared by the accountant and relied on them in deciding to invest in the company (and then lost money because the fiscal health of the company was something less attractive than was portrayed in the financial statements).[4] Ruffolo argued that Mulroney and the Progressive Conservative Party had misrepresented the state of their own minds: they lied, knowing that they had no intention of doing the things they promised to do (or had an intention of doing the very opposite of what they promised).

Even though he ultimately dismissed the case, let it not be said that the judge was under any illusions about the integrity of your average politician or the value of promises made during an election campaign. The negligent misrepresentation claim must also fail, wrote the judge, because the statements of Mulroney and his party were not statements of fact but statements of intention — and a statement of intention couldn't reasonably be relied on in this case. Stating a truth for the ages, Thomson wrote that "it is not reasonable to rely on a statement ... in the context of an election" and that "a statement of intention is often mere puffery in an election campaign. Even the most gullible of voters would be foolish to rely solely on the statement of a candidate without further investigation as to past action and current policies." The statements were essentially just a sales pitch, in other words, and everybody *knows* that politicians are, to put it generously, wont to change their minds, so there's nothing that can be done if they, in fact, decide to do so. There was no contract, Ruffolo couldn't reasonably have relied on Mulroney's promises, and in any event Ruffolo hadn't suffered any damages that could be calculated. Ruffolo's only remedy? To change his vote in the next election.

The other side of the aisle saw a similar situation much more recently. Love him or hate him, most observers would agree that when Mike Harris, Ontario's former premier, said he was going to do something, he did it (but let the record show that there were a large number of people who would have been quite happy if he had neglected to follow through on his promised policies). One Harris promise that was implemented was the Taxpayer Protection Act, 1999,[5] which stipulated that no Ontario government could increase an existing tax or introduce a new tax unless a public referendum was first held that authorized such increase or introduction. Political conservatives rejoiced: the law seemed to handcuff the ability of the government to raise taxes. It is, however, a basic power of the legislature to amend or repeal any law that the legislature has previously passed, simply by passing a new law (the exception is for constitutional laws, such as the Constitution itself and the Charter of Rights and Freedoms, which have built-in amendment mechanisms that often require something more than a simple majority vote in the legislature).[6] If the Harris Conservatives were defeated in a future election, it would always be available to the new government to simply repeal the Taxpayer Protection Act, 1999, and then raise taxes.

By 2003, another provincial election was underway in Ontario. Keen to ensure that taxes weren't going to be raised, the Canadian Taxpayers Federation (CTF), a group that lobbies against government waste and in favour of lower taxes, and also no doubt aware that the *Ruffolo* decision meant that campaign promises don't constitute an enforceable contract, took action that it thought would result in an iron-clad promise on the part of candidates. In the midst of the campaign, on September 11, 2003, the CTF and Liberal Party leader Dalton McGuinty (who looked to be well positioned to replace the Progressive Conservative Party in power) held a joint press conference, during which McGuinty signed a document entitled "Taxpayer Protection Promise." The document consisted of the following language:

> I, Dalton McGuinty, leader of the Liberal Party of Ontario, promise, if my party is elected as the next government, that I will:

Not raise taxes or implement any new taxes without
the explicit consent of Ontario voters; and

Not run deficits.

I promise to abide by the Taxpayer Protection and
Balanced Budget Act.

The document seemed relatively straightforward. It was perhaps a
more formal version of the elder George Bush's election promise from
1988: "Read my lips — no new taxes." But just as Bush had broken his
promise, once in office McGuinty broke his. In connection with the new
government's first budget, delivered in May 2004, a new piece of legislation was passed that created an exception to the Taxpayer Protection
Act, 1999, allowing the government to implement a new "health pre-
mium";[7] once that law became effective, a second law was passed that
actually implemented the new tax.[8] The CTF promptly sued McGuinty
and the government, alleging breach of contract and negligent misrepresentation.

At the end of 2004, the decision of the Ontario Superior Court
of Justice was released, and to the extent that *Ruffolo* did not do so,
CTF v McGuinty appears to put to rest any possibility of ever successfully suing a politician for breaking a campaign promise.[9] The written
pledge that McGuinty had signed was rejected as a contract, since it
"was not a promise made to anyone in particular and was not framed
as an agreement or a contract between two parties." Furthermore, "few
people would consider that all of the promises made and pledges given
[by politicians and their parties] constitute legally-binding agreements
between the candidate and the [electorate]." The court also worried
that if an election promise could be enforceable by voters by a court
action, "our system of government would be rendered dysfunctional ...
this would hinder if not paralyse the parliamentary system" — of course,
perhaps the threat of such lawsuits would be an added incentive for politicians to, you know, *keep their promises*. Regardless, the court accepted
the argument of the government that the principle of "supremacy of
Parliament" meant that election promises do not create legally enforceable rights. As the court stated, "It is a well-settled principle that, when
elected into government, commitments previously made by a Minister

regarding future conduct cannot fetter that Minister's freedom" to act in a manner inconsistent with those prior commitments — in short, by their very nature, governments cannot be held accountable for political promises.

In any event, there was no enforceable contract for much the same reason that Ruffolo was stymied: no consideration had been exchanged. The CTF tried to argue that McGuinty and the Liberals had received favourable publicity from the press conference and pledge signing, but the court dismissed this as insufficient to constitute "consideration." The court also dismissed the negligent misrepresentation argument, largely on the basis that to allow such claims "would raise the spectre of unlimited liability ... [and] would have a chilling effect ... once elected, members would be concerned about the representations they made during their election campaigns and would not consider themselves at liberty to act and vote in the public interest on each bill as it came before the legislature." It thus remains the case that in Canada election promises can't be enforced, even those that have been put in writing and signed in full view of the television cameras. It remains up to Canadian voters to decide whether they will agree with the hands-off approach adopted by the courts.

You Son of a ...

Defamation, subdivided into *libel* (written materials that are injurious to a person's reputation) and *slander* (verbal statements that have the same effect), has long been a complex and constantly evolving area of law. The proliferation of online media and the ease with which someone with a grudge can print up and distribute defamatory accusations means that this is one topic that will remain a rich vein for lawyers and legal commentators to mine.[10] When confronted with a defamation case, one of the fundamental inquiries that a judge must undertake is whether the defendant's statement about the plaintiff was, as a matter of law, defamatory. If someone calls you a "cheap bastard," is that defamatory? Probably not.[11] If he accuses you of stealing money from your employer? Almost certainly yes. There remains, however, a rather large number of expressions whose defamatory nature is somewhat less than clear — at which point the court must canvass prior case law to decide how to treat them.

A fired hotel manager in Edmonton sued his former employer for calling him "stupid," "dumb," and an "idiot" to co-workers, and the language was held to be defamatory.[12] In the late 1970s, a group of guards working at a correctional facility in Edmonton sued the *Edmonton Sun* newspaper, together with a reporter and columnist at the paper. The paper had published articles in reaction to the actions of the guards while interacting with reporters and photographers who had gone to the facility to obtain information about a hostage-taking situation. The guards had asked members of the media who were present not to take pictures and had confronted and detained certain photographers and reporters. The *Sun* articles expressed outrage that this had happened, referring to the guards as "goons" and "bumbling yo-yos." Moreover, the guards "haven't got the brains to be Nazis, the discipline to be jackboots or the mentality to philosophically endorse either of the above." The court concluded that the guards had indeed been defamed and held the paper liable.

Notwithstanding the foregoing cases, Canadian lawsuits have seen some rather colourful language be deemed *not* defamatory. In a case sure to warm the hearts of disgruntled clients everywhere, a Saskatchewan court determined that saying a lawyer "does not know his asshole from a hole in the ground" and that he had obtained his licence from "somewhere in a K-Tel box" was not defamatory — "uncalled for," perhaps, but not defamatory.[13]

One of the more interesting defamation cases to occur in Canada is the 1992 case of *Ralston v Fomich*,[14] which pondered the eternal question: is it defamatory to call someone a "son of a bitch"? What if you call them a "sick son of a bitch"? Ralston and Fomich were municipal aldermen. During the course of a council meeting on a land use matter, Fomich opined that Ralston was a "sick son of a bitch." Though Fomich apologized during the meeting, after its conclusion he reiterated to reporters that "You can quote me that in my personal opinion Ralston is a sick son of a bitch." Ralston sued, prompting a rather lengthy disquisition on the nature of the phrase in question. While Ralston's lawyer initially ventured that "son of a bitch" is actually blasphemous in origin (evidently on the basis that the phrase was derived from medieval references to Jesus), the court rejected this contention. "Son of a bitch," the court concluded, was perhaps impolite, but otherwise "not capable of any defamatory meaning."

Fomich didn't get off the hook, however. To the contrary, in rather resplendent consideration, the judge opined that the phrase is a "translucent vessel waiting to be filled with colour by [its] immediate qualifier.... Thus, one has sympathy for a poor son of a bitch, admiration for a brave son of a bitch, affection for a good old son of a bitch, envy for a rich son of a bitch ..." But Fomich had called Ralston a "sick" son of a bitch. That adjective constituted a line that had been crossed — the court concluded that "sick" impugned Ralston as mentally ill or perverted. Would calling someone a "*sick* son of a bitch" lower the reputation of the plaintiff in the esteem of the general public? Indeed it would, concluded the judge, and thus Fomich was liable for defaming Ralston. We can assume that Fomich rues those four extra letters to this day.

The Good Kind of Swearing

Even those who have never been inside a courtroom are likely familiar with the procedure for the swearing of an oath: you've watched on television or the movie screen as a witness is asked to place his or her right hand on a Bible and promise to tell the truth. The exact wording of the oath varies from courtroom to courtroom, but it is intended to bind the consciences of witnesses by having them affirm before a higher power that they won't lie. In a polyglot society like ours, however, courts have long had to take account of the fact that not everyone is Christian or otherwise willing to swear on a Bible, and for those persons "swearing on a Bible" wouldn't serve to "bind their consciences" in the requisite fashion. Some legislation governing the giving of evidence in court assumes that a person will either be willing to swear on a Bible or is an atheist; the Canada Evidence Act, for example, provides that a witness can either swear an oath *or* make a "solemn affirmation" in the form "I solemnly affirm that the evidence to be given by me shall be the truth, the whole truth and nothing but the truth." Other legislation, such as Ontario's Evidence Act, says that if a witness objects to being sworn by holding a copy of the Old or New Testament, an oath can be administered "in such manner and form and with such ceremonies as he or she declares to be binding."

Allowing for alternative oaths isn't some new innovation ushered in during the past few years pursuant to some sort of obsession with "political correctness" — Canadian courts have long taken note of and tried to accommodate differing belief systems.[15] Providing the alternative of the affirmation to swearing an oath was originally done to accommodate Quakers, who objected to swearing an oath on the basis that doing so implied that the obligation to tell the truth didn't apply at all times. In the *Ah Wooey* case from 1902,[16] the court had to address the need to obtain the oath of a Chinese witness, Chong Fon Fi, who wasn't Christian. The court's interpreters informed the judge that Chong Fon Fi believed in the binding power of oaths, and that in his home Chinese province of Canton, the most grave form of oath was referred to as the "King's Oath" (the court noted that it had a different name "as white people call it": the "chicken oath"). Swearing the oath involved writing the oath (in Chinese) on a piece of paper, which included the following wording: "If I falsely accuse [the prisoner] I shall die on the street, Heaven will punish me, earth will destroy me, I shall forever suffer adversity, and all my offspring be exterminated." As the report of the case relates, the court and jury accompanied the witness outside the courthouse, where the oath-taking ceremony was performed, but only after a chicken had been obtained. The ceremony involved a block of wood, three incense sticks, and a pair of Chinese candles being stuck in the ground and lighted. The witness read aloud the oath, then cut off the head of the chicken, and finally burned the piece of paper on which the oath had been written. The law report notes that an alternative Chinese oath, called (presumably by white people) the "saucer oath," also existed. It involved the witness kneeling and holding a "China saucer," then breaking the saucer after which the court clerk was to read the following: "You shall tell the truth, and the whole truth; the saucer is cracked, and if you do not tell the truth, your soul will be cracked like the saucer."

From the Grave

Wills and trusts, perhaps because they invoke and require contemplation of our own mortality, are not often a topic of conversation. They are also often intensely personal, requiring us to wrestle with complex and emotional matters such as awarding a wayward child a portion of an estate or determining who among surviving relatives should be entrusted with a prized possession. Thus a will that is the subject of prolonged consideration can't help but bear the imprint of the testator, the person who is making the will. Their hopes and fears for their heirs and for the legacy they leave will inevitably colour the terms of the will. And those who are left behind often feel a compulsion to observe the terms of the will, perhaps as a final demonstration of respect for the person who has passed on. Which raises a question: what do you do when the person making the will was prejudiced or racist and the terms of the will are also?

Some testators have been concerned with ensuring that their estates are handled in a fashion that accords with their personal religious and political views as expressed while they were alive. So, for example, Canadian courts have upheld the validity of wills that required a beneficiary to be "of the Lutheran religion" or to "rejoin the Catholic Church and practise the Catholic faith" in order to be entitled to receive property from an estate.[17] The common law has historically sought to preserve the complete freedom of a testator to do with his or her property as he or she saw fit. Capricious or spiteful limits on gifts have long been upheld by courts,[18] on the rationale that the beneficiary of the will has a choice: either abide by the condition on the gift or forgo the gift. No one is forcing such people to do anything, and the courts won't interfere with the freedom of a testator to dispose (or not) of property.

There has also historically been a countervailing principle at common law that property can't be the subject of a complete prohibition on transfer. So, for example, a will can't state that a house is being given to the testator's daughter on the condition that she never sell it — such a condition will be struck as invalid, though the gift itself will still be carried out. That being said, courts have generally upheld *partial* restrictions on transfer and use: a will that allowed a beneficiary use of certain property unless the beneficiary became a member of the Roman Catholic Church was held to be enforceable.[19] Canadian courts have also upheld restrictions on the transfer of land. In 1948, the Ontario Court of Appeal deemed valid a restrictive covenant on the sale of land that provided that the land could never be sold, leased, or occupied by "any person of the Jewish, Hebrew, Semitic, Negro or coloured race or blood."[20] Such restrictions on transfer are now prohibited by provincial human rights legislation and statutes that address the transfer of land, but no similar legislation addresses the validity of wills.

After the introduction of the Charter of Rights and Freedoms in 1982, courts have tended to frown upon conditions in wills that seek to give effect to racial or religious discrimination from the grave. While the Charter only regulates government activities, the Supreme Court of Canada has held that the common law must be interpreted in a manner that is "consistent" with the values expressed in the Charter. So, in 1995, the will of a United Church clergyman in Newfoundland provided that the beneficiary of his estate, his niece's son, must in order to become the heir "remain in one or the other main stream [sic] Christian Churches" — Jehovah's Witnesses and Mormons being specifically excluded. The judge held the condition to be invalid, noting that a provision "which restricts the religious affiliation of any person" is contrary to public policy.[21]

Even trusts that were created long before the Charter came into existence and that are discriminatory have had their terms revised in order to comport with current sensibilities. The Leonard Foundation Trust was established in 1923 with the purpose of providing scholarships to children, but not to those who "are not Christians of the White Race, and who are not of British Nationality or of British Parentage, and all who owe allegiance to any Foreign Government, Prince, Pope or Potentate or who recognize any such authority, temporal or spiritual" — in other words, only white Protestant children of British descent need apply. The document establishing the trust had evoked the necessity of ensuring the vitality of Protestant Christianity and the superiority of the "white race." In 1990, the Ontario Court of Appeal declared the trust invalid, and then reconstituted it as an educational trust without the offensive restrictions.[22] Because the Leonard Foundation Trust was a public trust, it remains an open question as to whether similarly discriminatory language in a private family trust would be invalid, but it can safely be concluded that trends are certainly pointing in that direction. Cases dealing with attempts to bind property by means of discriminatory clauses have occurred with much less frequency in recent decades, hopefully a function of the fact that not only has the expression of such sentiments become less acceptable but the holding of such sentiments has become more rare, as well.

8

Most Foul

The Canadian experience with murder has often been an ambivalent one. Positioned next to the United States, which has the highest murder rate among industrialized countries, Canadians are sometimes lulled into thinking that our comparatively low murder rate (currently running at roughly 650 murders a year, or 2 per 100,000) is therefore similar to that of other countries. Unfortunately that is not the case, as our rates of violent crime and murder are generally at the high end of the scale when compared to Western European countries, Australia, and industrializing nations in South America and Asia.[1] While the absolute number of murders in Canada has often been low relative to our population (in the late nineteenth century, there were only a handful of murder charges and convictions; most years saw at worst a couple of dozen charges, and 1894, for example, recorded only eight convictions[2]), our history has nonetheless resulted in the development of a unique legal framework in which the crime is handled. Readers should be cautioned that, just as murder is among the gravest of crimes, some of the subjects discussed here (including the killing of children) don't make for the most pleasant reading.

To begin, a survey of terms is in order. The Criminal Code defines *homicide* as causing the death of a human being, and divides culpable homicide (i.e., homicide that is blameworthy and punishable by law) into the categories of *murder, manslaughter,* and *infanticide.* To be classified as murder, a homicide must be intentional (i.e., you meant to cause the death, or meant to cause bodily harm that is likely to result in death, or did something unlawful that you know is likely to result in death). Murder is further divided into *first degree* (where the killing is planned and deliberate) and *second degree* (all other murders).[3] Infanticide, on the other hand, is a very specific crime: it is the killing of a newly born child by the mother of that child, when the mother "is not fully recovered from the effects of giving birth to the child and by reason thereof or of the effect of lactation consequent on the birth of the child her mind is then disturbed."[4] All other culpable homicides (i.e., those that are not murder or infanticide) are manslaughter.[5]

Suicidal Tendencies

As with the law relating to assaults (discussed in Chapter 2), a person can't consent to being killed: Section 14 of the Criminal Code stipulates that any purported consent doesn't affect the criminal responsibility of the person who inflicted death on the deceased. So if person A is severely depressed and begs person B to kill A, and B does kill A, B won't be able to raise A's consent as a defence. Despite the fairly clear wording of the Criminal Code on this point, there is evidently another defence that is available in very limited circumstances: the suicide pact. In the *Gagnon* case, decided in 1993, the accused was charged with first-degree murder.[6] The relationship between Gagnon and his girlfriend, Annie, was in dire straits. Annie's twelve-year-old daughter was making their lives miserable because she refused to accept Gagnon's relationship with her mother, despite efforts by Gagnon and Annie to develop some sort of friendship between Gagnon and the girl. Neither Gagnon nor his girlfriend could bear the thought of being without the other, so they agreed to commit suicide together. The method by which they would carry out this pact was unusual: both were to be lying in bed, Annie on top of Gagnon, and Gagnon would hold a large-calibre pistol behind her back and fire it, with the intention that the bullet would pass through Annie's body (thereby killing her) and into Gagnon's body (thereby killing him). Gagnon and Annie had prepared letters explaining their decision, and evidently in order to avoid having Annie's children walk in on their dead bodies, had called the police moments before Gagnon pulled the trigger. But when Gagnon fired the gun, while he killed Annie and seriously wounded himself, Gagnon wasn't killed. While Gagnon conceded that he couldn't rely on Section 14 as a defence, he argued that there was a common law defence that provided that the existence of the "suicide pact" was sufficient to clear him of any wrongdoing.

Both the trial court and the Quebec Court of Appeal agreed with Gagnon and acquitted him of the crime of murder. A suicide pact, the court concluded, is a valid defence to a charge of murder where the deceased and the accused were in a common mental state whereby they had irrevocably intended to commit suicide together by the same act, and where the risk of death was equal for both parties. In other words, the accused couldn't rely on this defence where the pact involved the accused killing the other parties to the pact and only subsequently killing himself. There had to be a single act that caused multiple deaths; for example, if A and B entered into a suicide pact whereby they would route the exhaust from the tailpipe of a car into the car itself where they would be sitting (thereby inducing carbon monoxide poisoning), A couldn't be charged with murder because A had turned on the ignition and started the car. The court's reasoning was premised on the notion that Gagnon's intention hadn't been to kill Annie but to commit suicide; Annie's death was a concurrent result.

This line of argument requires the court to examine another murder-related aspect of the Criminal Code: the laws surrounding suicide. While "committing suicide" isn't a crime (for the obvious reason that in the case of a successful suicide there would be no one left to charge with the crime), the Criminal Code originally included a provision that made "attempted suicide" a crime, punishable by up to two years' imprisonment. The crime of attempted suicide was repealed in 1972, but its sister provision remains: Section 241 makes it a crime to counsel a person to commit suicide or to aid or abet a person in committing suicide. As the Court of Appeal in *Gagnon* held, Gagnon *could* have been charged (and likely convicted) under Section 241 because he aided and abetted Annie in committing suicide, but the prosecution had elected instead to charge Gagnon with first-degree murder, and his genuine participation in the suicide pact precluded his guilt of that crime.

The Mind Alone

Section 228 of the Criminal Code provides one of the more intriguing defences to a charge of culpable homicide:

> **228.** No person commits culpable homicide where he causes the death of a human being
> (*a*) by any influence on the mind alone, or
> (*b*) by any disorder or disease resulting from influence on the mind alone,
> but this section does not apply where a person causes the death of a child or sick person by wilfully frightening him.

It is not, therefore, a crime to scare people to death (by, say, prowling in their bushes) — unless the person in question is a child or is ill. The language raises the question of why it *would* be okay to scare a healthy adult to death, but there has been little treatment of the section in reported cases, even though it has been present in the Criminal Code from its earliest version. The provision is also a uniquely Canadian one: there is no similar antecedent provision in English criminal law. Prior to enactment of the 1892 Criminal Code, there were diverging decisions on whether frightening someone to death was culpable homicide. Some cases held that causing the death of another by exciting the emotions through language or actions, whether the resulting emotion was fear, anger, or grief, was neither murder nor manslaughter.[7] In other instances, such as the 1878 *Dugal* case, scaring someone to death was sufficient to result in a manslaughter conviction.[8] The accused, Dugal, had been fighting with his brother when the boys' father tried to interfere. The accused, holding a kitchen knife, had advanced threateningly towards the father, whereupon other witnesses to the fight had stepped in to prevent Dugal from attacking him. The father was led from the room in a state of "great agitation and weakness" — and twenty minutes later he died (in the medical parlance of the time, he had died from a "syncope," an event or condition akin to a heart attack).

In an attempt to clarify the somewhat confusing precedents, Parliament decided to enact the predecessor to the current Section

228. The cases that have been reported since that time illustrate that the plain meaning of the provision makes for some disturbing judicial decisions. The first reported case to result in an acquittal under the provision occurred in Winnipeg in 1913 when the accused, Howard, jostled with another man while attempting to disembark from a street car with his wife and children.[9] Howard was frustrated that other passengers were blocking the exit of his family, and he exchanged words with the man, calling him a "chump." From there, matters escalated to the point that Howard punched the other man in the face. No further punches were traded, and Howard got off and continued on his way. Witnesses testified that the man was smiling after his encounter with Howard, and that they didn't think he had suffered any lasting damage. Unfortunately, not long after Howard left, the other man lost consciousness and died; Howard was tracked down and charged with killing the deceased.

Expert medical testimony concluded that Howard's punch was *not* the cause of death; rather, the feelings of "anger or excitement" that were felt by the deceased during his confrontation with Howard had caused him to suffer a fatal brain aneurysm. The doctors testified that the autopsy revealed that the deceased suffered from a condition that caused the flow of blood through his veins to be accelerated to the point where his arteries were weakened. The increased stress from the tangle with Howard was the proximate cause of death, and one doctor opined that even if no punch had been landed, the deceased would have died "from the excitement," as it were. The magistrate dismissed the charges in reliance on what is now Section 228: the death had been caused by an "influence on the mind," namely the anger or excitement felt by the deceased, and not by any action on the part of the accused. The decision was also greatly influenced by what the magistrate described as "an incident which raises human nature in one's view." The son of the deceased had spoken with Howard before trial, indicating that he didn't hold Howard responsible for the death of his father and bore him no ill will, demonstrating that the son was "possessed of the same kindly disposition and character that his father had."

Unfortunately, the remaining cases that deal with Section 228 offer no similar uplifting tales. Perhaps the most disturbing application of the "influence on the mind alone" defence occurred in Alberta in 1981 when an accused with the last name Powder, together with a friend, broke into the home of a seventy-year-old man. When confronted by the home-owner, the three engaged in a scuffle, with the result that the elderly man died. In the words of the court of appeal, he died from "stress and fright." On appeal the accused was ordered acquitted of manslaughter (he was still found guilty of break-and-enter).[10] Other attempts to rely on Section 228 have been less successful. In a modern re-enactment of the *Dugal* case, a judge in Ontario directed an acquittal in a case where the accused had struck his mother in the face, prompting the deceased to attempt to stop the assault — the accused pushed the deceased, who suffered a fatal heart attack.[11] The trial judge concluded that the death was a result of "stress" arising from an emotional situation and not a result of the push. The judge also concluded that the deceased, though he had suffered a recent heart attack, wasn't sufficiently ill to fall within the exception provided for children and the sick. The court of appeal disagreed, remanding the case for a new trial.

In one of the most recent cases seeking to rely on the defence offered by Section 228, the police found a dead woman in a hotel room, having essentially drunk herself to death. Over the course of twelve hours, she had consumed approximately thirty ounces of hard liquor, giving her a blood alcohol level of .91. (By way of comparison, the legal limit for impaired driving is .08.)[12] It was discovered that the accused and the deceased had occupied the hotel room during the night of October 11, 1987, and the early morning of the next day. It turned out that this wasn't the first time the accused had found himself in such compromising circumstances: over the previous decade, six female aboriginals had been found dead in hotel rooms from overconsumption of alcohol, while police had intervened in the hotel room drinking binges of four others. In each of the ten prior cases, the accused had been the only other person present during the drinking sprees.

By the time of the last four cases, police had decided to stake out the hotel rooms where the accused and the women were holed up. On one occasion, an officer testified, they heard the following uttered by the accused: "Have a drink, down the hatch baby, 20 bucks if you drink it right down; see if you're a real woman; finish that drink, finish that drink, down the hatch hurry, right down; you need another drink, I'll give you 50 bucks if you can take it...." What the police had on their hands, in other words, was a killer with an inventive modus operandi. He convinced his victims to drink themselves to death. The accused

raised Section 228 as a defence: all that he had done was *encourage* the women to drink — an "influence on the mind" if you will, and not any physical act that resulted in their deaths. Thankfully, both the trial judge and the court of appeal disagreed and found the accused guilty of manslaughter arising from criminal negligence — the accused, after all, had purchased and supplied all of the alcohol being consumed.

A Year and a Day

One of the salient characteristics about Canadian criminal law is that there is no limitation period for serious crimes. Most jurisdictions around the world put in place what are referred to as "statutes of limitation" for both civil and criminal law, which restrict the ability of plaintiffs or prosecutors to begin court proceedings after a certain period of time has elapsed. The goal is to encourage the commencement of actions while evidence and memories are still fresh, and to give people comfort that they aren't being threatened by a lawsuit stemming from a long-forgotten incident that happened thirty years ago. In Ontario, for instance, the general limitation period on a breach of contract claim is two years. If you purchase a car and the seller violates the terms of the contract, you can't wait six years and then sue — you have to do it within two years of finding out about the breach.[13] Even some minor criminal offences (referred to as those punishable on "summary conviction") are subject to a limitations period: a prosecution can't be commenced more than six months after the activities that constituted the crime occurred, unless the accused otherwise agrees.[14] Major crimes, however, such as assault, theft, and armed robbery, aren't subject to any limitations period. If you beat someone up, you can be arrested and charged for it whether the police catch up with you a week or forty years later. This is a reflection of the seriousness with which significant violations of the criminal law are treated: you shouldn't be able to avoid punishment just because you've been skilled at evading detection or capture.[15] That being said, until very recently there was one major crime that *did* have a limitations period: killing another person.

Until 1999, Section 227 of the Criminal Code read as follows:

> **227.**   No person commits culpable homicide or the offence of causing the death of a person by criminal negligence ... unless the death occurs within one year and one day from the time of the occurrence of the last event by means of which the person caused or contributed to the cause of death.

It was the case for most of Canadian history that to be charged with homicide, your victim needed to die within one year and one day of your doing whatever it is you did to kill him or her. If you attacked someone and beat him into a coma, and he died four years later without waking from that coma, you couldn't be charged with homicide for his death (though you could certainly be charged with aggravated assault). To make the law even more affecting, if your victim had died one year and *two* days after you assaulted him, you were still off the hook. The "one year and one day" rule was derived from medieval English common law and had been incorporated into the first Canadian Criminal Code. The origins of the common law rule are thought to have been largely practical: in a time of rudimentary medical knowledge, proving causation (i.e., that the actions of the accused were the proximate cause of the death of the victim) was haphazard at best. The arbitrary limit of one year and one day was thus offered as a common law defence to a charge of homicide.

England abolished the year and a day defence in 1996, and Canada followed suit in 1999.[16] As the Canadian House of Commons committee considering the repeal heard, the arbitrary nature of the rule and the fact that it contradicted our lack of limitations periods on all other serious crimes compelled its abolition. Two other developments also militated in favour of removing the availability of the defence: advances in medical technology meant that victims could survive in a debilitated state for longer periods of time before succumbing to their injuries, and more threateningly, it was now possible to cause death by means of deliberate infection with a long-term fatal agent such as the HIV/AIDS virus. In order to avoid the prospect of not being able to successfully prosecute a killer in light of those developments, Section 227 was repealed. For those foreign jurisdictions that haven't repealed the availability of the year and a day rule, murderers are still getting away with, well, murder. As recently as 2003, a defendant in Wisconsin walked free when the victim of his assault died after spending two years in a coma.[17]

The Smallest Victims

The Criminal Code devotes numerous sections to matters revolving around murder and infants, particularly the smallest of all infants, namely those who have literally just been born. As noted above, "homicide" is the killing of a "human being." What constitutes a "human being" for these purposes is partly addressed by Section 223 of the Criminal Code, which provides that a "child has become a human being ... when it has completely proceeded, in a living state, from the body of its mother." Being "in a living state" doesn't require that the infant has breathed or that it has an independent circulation — merely that it isn't deceased when it emerges fully from its mother's womb. It is as a result of the wording of this section that abortion providers aren't charged with homicide (as noted above, performing abortions has been entirely legal in Canada since 1988) — if aborted in the womb, the fetus isn't a "human being" within the meaning of the homicide provisions of the Criminal Code.

Section 223(2) stipulates that "a person commits homicide when he causes injury to a child before or during its birth as a result of which the child dies after becoming a human being." This subsection has been applied to cases where an obviously pregnant woman has been attacked and the fetus she was carrying died shortly after birth as a result of injuries inflicted on the mother — the accused in such cases could be convicted of manslaughter for the death of the infant.[18] It is important to note, however, that the section requires the baby to have been born alive in order for the attacker to be guilty. If the child dies in the womb, there isn't a "human being" for purposes of the Criminal Code that has died.

As described at the beginning of this chapter, infanticide is a crime restricted to very specific circumstances involving the mother of an infant. Section 233 provides that where a mother "is not fully recovered from the effects of giving birth" to a child and as a result her mind is "disturbed" and she by a "wilful act or omission" causes the death of the "newly-born child," then she is punishable by up to five years in prison.[19] A somewhat convoluted history lies behind Section 233, which was only enacted in 1948.[20] Prior to the twentieth century, a woman who killed her newly born child was generally charged with murder. Because so many cases of infanticide involved young women, especially those who occupied low social positions and had meagre incomes, juries and judges were often reluctant to render a guilty verdict on the charge of murder, especially since the punishment for murder at that time was death. Various legislative enactments were put in place to offer prosecutors and juries an alternative to a murder charge, including an 1803 English statute that provided that juries could substitute a verdict of guilt on the charge of concealing a pregnancy, which carried a maximum punishment of two years' imprisonment. In 1922, an Infanticide Act was passed in England, and in 1948, Canada followed suit with an amendment to the Criminal Code that created the crime of infanticide.

Within a couple of years of the respective enactments, however, a troubling issue arose that the legislation had failed to address: what exactly was a "newly-born child"? A non-lawyer reading those words might conclude that the provision was meant to address a situation where a mother killed her child within, at most, a couple of hours of the birth. That non-lawyer would be wrong. By 1954, the Criminal Code was amended again, this time to provide a definition of "newly-born child": it is "a person under the age of one year." Infanticide, then, occurs when a mother kills a child under the age of twelve months while she is suffering from a disturbed mind as a result of the effects of giving birth to the child.

In reviewing the infanticide provision in the context of the laws on homicide, the Law Reform Commission of Canada recommended in 1984 that the provision be repealed, with the intention that mothers who kill their children could be charged with manslaughter (which, unlike murder, doesn't carry a minimum sentence, allowing the judge to fashion a punishment commensurate with the circumstances of the crime).[21] The recommendation has never been implemented, partly as a consequence of the fact that as a society we maintain an aversion to formally using the phrase "murder" to describe a mother killing an infant child. In 1955, an additional provision addressing infanticide was added to the Criminal Code. Section 663 provides that, notwithstanding what Section 233 says, even where a mother has recovered from the effects of childbirth and is not of "disturbed mind," she can still be found guilty of the lesser charge of infanticide rather than murder or manslaughter. Centuries of legal precedent and social history culminate in the infanticide provisions. Though it may shock the consciences of some people that a mother can kill, say, an eight-month-old infant and only be charged with a crime carrying a maximum sentence of five years' imprisonment, it remains unlikely that modifications that are satisfactory to all those with an interest will be made to the infanticide provisions any time soon.

As we have seen, the criminal laws surrounding infants draw some very fine distinctions. This nuance extends even to the act of birth itself and its immediate aftermath. While a fetus isn't a "human being" until it emerges alive from the body of its mother (pursuant to Section 223), Section 238(1) deems it to be murder if a person causes the death *during the act of birth* of "any child that has not become a human being." So while the fetus is still in the womb (but after the birthing process has commenced) or in the birth canal, an act that would constitute murder if it was committed on a "human being" (whether a living infant who had emerged from the womb or an adult) is murder if it kills the fetus. Section 238(2) provides a saving clause for anyone who does something they believe in good faith is necessary to preserve the life of the mother. So, for example, a doctor can't be charged with murder if the doctor causes the death of the fetus during the birthing process in an attempt to save the life of the mother. The birthing process is also the subject of another provision: a crime is committed if a pregnant woman, with the intention of not allowing her soon-to-be-born child to live or with the intention of concealing the birth, fails to arrange for "reasonable assistance" in respect of the delivery of the baby and the infant either dies or is permanently injured. Similar to the punishment for infanticide, the maximum term of imprisonment for such a crime is five years.[22] It is also a crime to dispose of the body of a dead child, but only if it is done with "intent to conceal the fact that its mother has been delivered of it."[23] One is left to wonder why disposing of a dead child's body for another reason would be okay.

It Wasn't Me

It is a fundamental requirement for a finding of criminal responsibility that the accused was acting consciously when he or she committed the crime with which he or she is charged (this rationale underpins the infanticide provisions just covered: where the mother isn't fully *compos mentis* as a result of the process of delivering a baby, her culpability is deemed to be lessened). If, to take an extreme example, a person who is in a coma suffers some sort of spasm that causes the person's arm to jerk and strike an attending nurse, the comatose person can't be charged with assault — the requisite "mental state" or *mens rea* isn't present. Only voluntary acts can give rise to criminal liability.

So what happens when an accused claims he was in an altered state of consciousness that prevented his actions from being voluntary? Over the past forty or so years, Canadian criminal courts have more often been willing to at least hear an accused try to raise a defence of "automatism," which is defined as unconscious and involuntary behaviour — while the person is obviously capable of activity, that activity isn't being propelled by the conscious mind. "The mind does not go with what is being done," as one court described it.[24] A number of defendants have successfully raised a defence referred to as "non-insane automatism." The "non-insane" element of the defence is critical for the accused. If the automatism is caused by a "disease of the mind" or "mental disorder," the accused may not be found guilty of the crime, but a verdict is given of "not guilty by reason of insanity" and the accused is liable to be committed to a secure mental health facility for an indeterminate period of time.[25] Where the automatism is "non-insane," however, accused people are provided with a complete defence: they aren't guilty of the crime with which they are charged, and they can't be restrained in a mental hospital. The availability of the defence has resulted in courts grappling with, and sometimes accepting, the argument in some exceedingly peculiar cases.

In 1998, a police constable in Alberta observed a car that he thought was speeding.[26] After unsuccessfully attempting to catch the attention of the driver, the officer followed the car and observed the vehicle come to a stop. The driver, a Mr. Book, exited the car and proceeded to walk away from it. The officer confronted the driver after he walked approximately twenty-five feet and asked him what he was doing. Book replied that he was "just walking home" and at first denied the car was his or that he had been driving it. The officer described Book as having slurred speech and being unsteady on his feet. Concluding that the accused had been driving while impaired, the officer took Book to the nearest police station, where a Breathalyzer showed that the man's blood alcohol content was in excess of the legal limit of .08.

At trial, Book raised the defence of non-insane automatism on the basis that he had been hypnotized while at a bar earlier in the evening and had never come out of the state of hypnosis. Book and his friend testified that they had attended a local bar where the evening's entertainment consisted of a hypnotist who would ask volunteers from the audience to participate in his stage show. The hypnotist would then approach each volunteer and perform a "hypnotic routine" — if the volunteer's head drooped, the hypnotist would keep that person onstage. Book had volunteered and appeared to have been one of the people who was successfully hypnotized. Book then participated in the remainder of the show, performing activities (such as singing and dancing) at the command of the hypnotist.

Although the hypnotist had, at the end of his performance, done a group "de-hypnotizing," Book's friend testified that the procedure didn't seem to take with Book. He was "just kind of heavy-head kind of thing, like, rubber neck … He was just kind of slouching." Book was also able to secure an expert witness who testified that Book was "very susceptible" to hypnosis, and that a person in a hypnotic trance would be in a "state of automation, able to do some automatic activities like walking, talking and responding to questions, and possibly even driving a car, all without realizing what he or she was doing." The judge was satisfied that Book had been suffering from "non-insane automatism" and acquitted him of the charge of impaired driving.

While the Book case may seem relatively harmless (no one was hurt, after all), that certainly wasn't the situation with the most recent of the major non-insane automatism cases. During the early-morning hours of May 24, 1987, a twenty-three-year-old man named Kenneth Parks was sleeping in his living room in Pickering, Ontario.[27] At some point, the man put on his jacket and shoes, picked up his car keys, exited his house, got in his car, and drove more than twenty kilometres to the home of his in-laws in Scarborough. Once there, he parked his car, took a tire iron out of the trunk, and went into the house, where he proceeded to the kitchen to obtain a knife. From the kitchen, he entered the bedroom, where he stabbed and beat his in-laws, killing his mother-in-law and seriously wounding his father-in-law. At that point, he drove to the nearest police station and turned himself in. When charged with first-degree murder and attempted murder, he raised a somewhat unusual defence: sleepwalking.

According to Parks, he had lived through a stressful year. He had been working long hours at a job, and then run up gambling debts that prompted him to steal $30,000 from his employer, who promptly fired him and followed through with court proceedings to punish him and recover the money. In some fashion, these various stresses had culminated in his experiencing the sleepwalking episode. There was no indication that he had suffered from any similar episode prior to the attack on his in-laws or that he had suffered one subsequently. Additionally, it was introduced into evidence that Parks had always slept "very deeply" and sometimes had trouble waking up, while a number of his relatives suffered sleep-related disorders (such as bed-wetting, severe nightmares, and chronic talking in their sleep). Several expert witnesses testified on Parks's behalf that he had been "sleepwalking" throughout the entire ordeal and had been entirely unaware of his actions. They further concluded that the sleepwalking episode wasn't the result of any mental disorder from which Parks suffered. The trial judge allowed the jury to consider the defence of non-insane automatism. The jury acquitted him, and both the Court of Appeal and the Supreme Court upheld the verdict. Despite the concerns of one dissenting judge that some sort of protective measures should be crafted to ensure that nothing similar happened again, no such court order was put in place. Parks walked away completely free.

9

Of Poppies and Red Crosses

What makes up a culture? If we were going to explain to an alien from another planet what it means to be "Canadian" or what it is that makes up "Canada," we would want to go beyond the merely geographic and physical: Canada is more than a hunk of rock on a spinning globe defined by measurements of longitude and latitude. Certainly, our laws, what they are, how they have changed, and how those changes have unfolded, would form an integral component in any effort to describe the fabric of this country. Imagine how difficult it would be to accurately portray what it means to have lived as a Canadian over the past twenty-five years without ever making reference to, say, the Constitution or the Charter of Rights and Freedoms.

Matters of a much more ephemeral nature also form a significant component of our culture — from music and visual art to the traditions, pageantry, and symbols that pepper our daily experience, be it a red maple leaf gracing a building or a poppy worn for a Remembrance Day ceremony. Even such intangible images interface with the law, and on a more frequent basis than ever in today's hyperlinked world. Many of these cultural artifacts are subject to "intellectual property" laws that govern such matters as copyrights, trademarks, and patents. A most interesting dynamic unfolds around us: as technology makes it increasingly easy to infringe intellectual property rights, the more valuable and important those rights are becoming. Just ask Research In Motion, Canadian maker of the BlackBerry, which had to pay more than $600 million to settle a recent patent dispute. Even such a cutting-edge area of law and culture didn't emerge anew overnight, however, and so discussions about

Canadian culture and intellectual property inevitably involve the interface of our past and present, with implications for the future.

The Red Cross

Imagine for a moment that you have settled yourself onto your couch to play a stimulating round of your favourite Second World War video game shoot-'em-up simulation. You guide your rifle around the corner of a bullet hole–riddled building, and looming on the screen in front of you is the familiar sight of the Red Cross symbol, splayed on the side of a medical convoy. Guess what? The Red Cross isn't too happy about that. In January 2006, the Canadian Red Cross Society sent an open letter to the video game industry requesting that they cease and desist from displaying the iconic red cross (including use as "an emblem to depict 'First Aid,' 'Health' or 'Injury Recovery'") in violent video games. Such use is, the letter gently chided, a violation of international and Canadian law.[1] And so it would appear to be.

What many people might consider an innocuous, if altruistic, symbol is protected by no less than the Geneva Conventions, the Canadian Red Cross Act, and the Trade-marks Act.[2] The 1949 Geneva Conventions prohibit use of the symbol except by medical corps and the Red Cross Society. The Canadian Trade-marks Act, together with a series of obscure pieces of legislation, contain a number of provisions that seek to restrict the use of what might be considered pieces of our cultural heritage, including the Red Cross symbol. Section 9 of the Trade-marks Act, for example, prohibits using various symbols in connection with a business, including the Royal Crest, the United Nations seal, and pictorial representations of the RCMP. This provision is intended to secure from commercial abuse certain images or symbols that carry a particular cultural resonance. It is thus prohibited to use these images in a misguided attempt to "piggyback" onto the goodwill or good name of the protected marks. We don't want, say, a towel manufacturer to be able to put the Royal Crest on a line of kitchen towels — not just because such a placement of the mark might degrade the authority and dignity of the symbol, but because we don't want the manufacturer to imply that their goods have somehow obtained the approval of Her Majesty and attempt to make additional sales in light of that. (Of course, if someone has *actually* received royal assent to use the Royal Crest, that is entirely permissible.)

The federal government spends considerable time policing the use of official Canadian marks. It spends approximately a quarter of a million dollars a year putting a stop to unauthorized uses of the Canadian coat of arms, for example (one of the more interesting involved ordering the Sex Trade Workers of Canada website to cease and desist from using the coat of arms).[3] The prohibitions don't extend merely to "official" symbols of Canadian heritage, however. Also covered are the Red Cross; the Red Crescent (used in Muslim countries); the Red Lion (used in Iran); the flags, crests, and other emblems of any country that is a member of the World Trade Organization; the symbols of the United Nations; and any emblems of a university. As the Red Cross letter to the video game industry noted, the Red Cross image is being used "in videos [sic] which contain strong language and violence ... [which] directly conflict[s] with the basic humanitarian principles espoused by the Red Cross movement." While video game developers may not have given a second thought to their use of the red cross on a white background, intellectual property laws have something else again to say about the matter.

Red Poppies

Other digital and digitized uses of heritage symbols are becoming problematic as the online world presents its own challenges for trademarks and Canadian heritage. On November 4, 2005, a representative of the Royal Canadian Legion sent a stern communication to Pierre Bourque, the operator of the widely read Canadian news website *www.bourque.com*, demanding the removal of a digital image of a poppy posted on the site. The Legion asserted a right to prohibit unauthorized use of the poppy image arising from the Legion's registered trademark of the image, as well as a private act of Parliament (which can't be found in the consolidated sets of laws found in law libraries or even online). The image had been included on the website to commemorate and draw attention to Remembrance Day. An online firestorm of controversy ensued. When Bourque made note of the Legion's demand on his website (under the caption "Legion Declares War on Bourque"), the reaction was swift and furious: dozens of online pundits condemned the Legion's perceived heavy-handedness and, according to Bourque, "hundreds and hundreds of emails poured into the Legion." News coverage rapidly spread to radio, the CBC, and the Sun chain of newspapers. Many of the negative responses expressed surprise that the poppy could be the subject of a trademark registration at all, coupled with anger that well-intentioned activities on the part of a person wishing to join the Legion in remembering the sacrifices of previous generations of Canadians were giving rise to potential legal action.

Many Canadians would regard the poppy as virtually a cultural artifact. Since 1921, artificial poppies have been worn annually in Canada as a symbol of remembrance. After the First World War, inspired in particular by John McCrae's 1915 poem "In Flanders Fields," the poppy became a widespread token for commemorating war dead. Judging by the online reaction, many Canadians would be surprised to learn that the poppy image can be treated as an item of commerce, no different from a logo for a vacuum manufacturer. Troubling issues about the commodification of cultural items are raised by the episode, as well as concerns relating to the pitfall-laden nature of trademark enforcement. Do we really want the poppy to be subject to potential dilution, the vagaries of trademark law, and potentially ineffectual enforcement of their mark by the Legion? Do we want to force the Legion to be in the position of having to devote time and resources to the policing of its marks? Because of the nature of Canadian trademark laws, the Legion (and any other owner of a registered trademark) is forced into the position of protecting its marks by sending out letters of the type that Pierre Bourque received.

Broadly speaking, a trademark identifies the source of a product or service. So when you see a Coca-Cola logo on a bottle, you can be relatively sure that, somewhere along the line, the Coca-Cola Company had a hand in either making or approving the making of the contents of that bottle — you can be relatively sure, in other words, that you're getting what the trademark on the packaging tells you you're paying for. When a trademark is registered, it is registered in connection with particular goods or services. The name "Wimpy's" for example, is registered in connection with restaurant services, so if someone wanted to call their sporting goods shop "Wimpy's," the owners of the registered trademark "Wimpy's" wouldn't be able to prevent them from doing so. By means of the Trade-marks Act, the government gives trademark owners the exclusive right to use their marks — meaning that government will back up that monopoly of use with the full powers of the state to compel compliance. But in return for that, owners need to "police" the use of their marks. They can't allow unauthorized use of their marks or else they face the very real possibility of losing the exclusive rights to the mark entirely.

In the case of the poppy on the website, the Legion has trade-marked the poppy image, with the goal being that whenever you see a poppy, you can rest assured the Royal Canadian Legion is either involved in the use or has approved the use. You can imagine that the image of the poppy may have some residual value or goodwill associated with it, especially in the context of charitable endeavours. When people see the poppy on a brochure or advertisement, it may conjure associations with the Legion and the veterans it represents and may encourage people to donate. But the poppy image can be misused in other contexts, as well, for which the Legion is obliged to be on the lookout. Imagine, for example, that a toy manufacturer comes up with the idea of creating a line of military action figures that it wants to sell, and let's say some of the action figures are depictions of historic Canadian military heroes (setting aside for the moment any concerns about the personality rights of those heroes or their families). The manufacturer decides to incorporate a poppy into the logo for this range of action figures in the hope of associating the toys with the valiant sacrifices of previous generations of Canadian soldiers. Now imagine that the Legion finds out about the poppy on the packages containing the toy action figures and seeks an injunction forcing the manufacturer to desist in using the image. The toys aren't endorsed by the Legion and, in a reaction somewhat similar to the objections raised by the Red Cross in connection with the use of the red cross symbol in violent video games, the Legion doesn't take kindly to its name being associated with gaudy toy figures.

The Legion faces a danger in this action. If the toy manufacturer is able to introduce evidence into court demonstrating that the image of the poppy is being used all over the place without protest from the Legion (on, say, the Internet), the court could very well conclude that the Legion isn't doing a sufficient job of policing its mark. If so, then the mark isn't an indicator of source anymore. When people see the mark all over the place, they can't be sure that it's the Legion standing behind the mark. The Legion's exclusive rights to use and control the poppy image could therefore be lost, and the toy manufacturer (and anyone else for that matter) could then use the poppy pretty much however it sees fit. Hence, if the Legion fails to send threatening letters when it sees an unauthorized use of its trademarks, it runs the substantial risk that someone, somewhere down the line, is going to use the fact that it *didn't* send out those letters against it. This is a disastrous consequence that threatens not just the Legion but all other owners of registered trademarks, which is why you sometimes hear stories about the owners of a particularly valuable trademark (the *Star Wars* franchise, for instance) sending threatening letters to enthusiastic fans who operate websites that use registered trademarks.

The exact nature of the Legion's right to the poppy image is complex. The Legion's rights in the poppy image arise from two distinct sources: the Trade-marks Act and An Act Respecting the Royal Canadian Legion (the "Legion Act"). The poppy is the subject of seven separate registrations with the Canadian Intellectual Property

Office, which is responsible for maintaining the trademark and copyright registries. Among these registrations are an image of a poppy, various Legion logos incorporating it, and even the word *poppy* itself. The Legion Act is a private statute, first enacted in 1948. The Legion Act incorporated the Legion, and a 1981 amendment made three important additions to the statute: (1) the poppy image (together with certain other visual insignia) was made a mark of the Legion; (2) it became prohibited for any person to, without the authorization of the Legion, adopt or use, *in any circumstances* (not just in connection with a business), any mark of the Legion or any mark that is "confusing" or "likely to be mistaken" for such a mark; and (3) the poppy image was made a "registered trade-mark" for purposes of the Trade-marks Act. The poppy isn't just a trademark of the Legion, in other words, but also a kind of unimpeachable symbol. And the Legion isn't the only group that is accorded this type of property right. Others with similar rights include the Girl Guides and various charitable and professional organizations.

The foregoing two examples lead us into the crux of the current debates that revolve around cultural heritage, intellectual property laws, and digital media. Some form of protection for the poppy symbol is undoubtedly appropriate to discourage use by unscrupulous individuals or to prevent the symbols and organizations from being associated with endeavours that reflect poorly on the memory of the veterans they are meant to honour. But wouldn't it be better if the poppy were protected in some fashion such that its use in commercial activities was prohibited but that non-commercial use by people of goodwill wishing to take part in a Canadian tradition be allowed and even encouraged? Any mark that is sufficiently important to our culture should be the subject of considered rule-making in light of cultural developments and modern technology, rather than the subject of partly forgotten statutes and possibly susceptible to loss because of ineffective enforcement. Our heritage, including its symbols, deserves nothing less.

Red Ribbons

Just as the Red Cross and the Royal Canadian Legion have an interest in protecting the images associated with their endeavours, so artists too have a stake in protecting their works of art. Pursuant to the Copyright Act, artists are accorded certain rights referred to as "moral rights" — a set of prerogatives that includes the "right of attribution" (i.e., to be identified as the author of the work under the author's own name or a pseudonym, or conversely, the right to remain anonymous with respect to the work), the "right of association" (i.e., the right to control the use of a work, such as by means of advertising, in connection with a "product, services, cause or institution" if such use prejudices the author's honour or reputation), and the "right of integrity" (i.e., the right to protect a work from being "distorted, mutilated or otherwise modified" if such modification prejudices the author's honour or reputation).[4]

One of the most famous (well, to copyright lawyers at least) Canadian copyright cases involved, of all things, geese, red ribbons, and a shopping mall. If one enters Toronto's Eaton Centre from its south entrance, the mall opens into a multi-tiered panorama of shops, with an open central promenade whose ceiling rises six storeys to a glass canopy. A rather charming sculptural work is also present: a mobile of sixty geese in various poses of flight is suspended from the canopy, depicting a flock as it begins to land. The work, by the artist Michael Snow, is entitled *Flight Stop* and is as iconic a component of the centre as anything else present. (An image of a single goose in mid-flight is actually incorporated into the Eaton Centre logo itself.) As the Christmas season approached in 1982, Snow was perturbed to discover that management at the mall had done something to make the geese more, well, seasonal: they had tied a red ribbon around the neck of each goose. Outraged, Snow sought an injunction ordering the ribbons removed on the basis that his moral right of integrity in the work had been infringed; it was, in Snow's words, akin to "dangling earrings from the Venus de Milo."[5] The judge, citing the opinions of other artists and "people knowledgeable in [Snow's] field," agreed that the addition of the ribbons prejudiced Snow's honour or reputation, and the ribbons were ordered removed.

Interestingly, while tying a ribbon around the neck of a goose might infringe a Canadian artist's moral rights, simply destroying an artist's work doesn't appear to do so. In the late 1970s, a set of public sculptures in the Quebec town of Alma became the victim of vandalism. Rather than clean the sculptures up or take other steps to secure the works, the town ordered its cleanup crews to remove the pieces from public property and throw them in the river. The artist, understandably perturbed by this turn of events, launched a claim for infringement of his moral rights. The suit was dismissed by the Quebec Court of Appeal on the basis that the artist's reputation couldn't be seen to have suffered when the works were simply no longer there.[6]

Wyrd and Weirder

In the 2005 movie *Harry Potter and the Goblet of Fire*, there is a six-second appearance by a musical band of three male performers. The on-screen band isn't named in the movie, isn't listed in the credits for the film, and the on-screen "actors" portraying the band are actually members of two British rock bands, Pulp and Radiohead. Notwithstanding the foregoing, a female folk band from Manitoba sued Warner Bros., the studio behind the *Harry Potter movie*, as well as Pulp and Radiohead's record label *and* the band members themselves, seeking $40 million in damages and an injunction prohibiting the release of the film. Why? Because in the book the band is named as "The Weird Sisters," while the Manitoba group is called "The Wyrd Sisters" — a circumstance that according to the band's allegations in court would result in "irreparable harm to its reputation, goodwill in its trademark and the livelihood of its members [being] completely destroyed," evidently on the conjecture that when people around the world see that "The Wyrd Sisters" are coming to town to play a concert, they will be inevitably disappointed when the band that appears on stage is decidedly *not* the band that appeared in the *Harry Potter* film. The prospect of halting the release of the film for this court action was dismissed by the Ontario Superior Court of Justice, as the judge dryly noted that the band hadn't objected to the use of the name in the book and that any likelihood of confusion between the on-screen band and the actual live band was "highly speculative."[7] Despite being ordered to pay more than $140,000 of Warner Bros.' legal costs in connection with the dismissal, as of this writing The Wyrd Sisters continue their suit for damages.

Pretty Ladies and Other Stimulating Trademarks

Not all trademark cases are so ponderous, of course. One of the, er, crowning glories in the annals of Canadian intellectual property jurisprudence involved "culture" of a somewhat different type. The battle between the "Miss Universe" and the "Miss Nude Universe" pageants involved a trademark grudge match. The case was also a cross-border cultural battle royal. While the Miss Universe trademark was owned by an American corporation (and was later purchased by Donald Trump), Miss Nude Universe was the brainchild of a Canadian resident. In this case, while the underdog put up a valiant fight, he was destined to lose, a finding presaged by the opening words of the judgment: "The universe has not so far unfolded as beautifully as it might have for Miss Universe, Inc." But that would soon change.[8]

The saga began in 1985 when a Canadian trademark application was filed for "Miss Nude Universe." The name was anticipated for use in connection with "t-shirts, swim suits, pants, shorts, sweaters," and, perhaps surprisingly, "blouses" (the mind reels at the thought of the heretofore sensible blouse emblazoned with the Miss Nude Universe logo). Of course, those were merely sidelines to the real show — "beauty pageants." These pageants were to be held in "various public drinking establishments" and would feature contestants "who entertain in the nude." No doubt horrified by this prospect, the owners of the Miss Universe pageant and trademark filed an opposition to the attempted registration — for more than thirty years they had conducted a pageant with rather more decorum and had by 1988 nurtured the brand into a spectacle that garnered 600 million viewers and a "host fee" paid by interested cities of up to $750,000. As the Canadian Federal Court of Appeal noted, "The conditions which Miss Universe contestants must meet seem somewhat more stringent than those for Miss Nude Universe," which resulted in a "vast difference in ambiance" between the two pageants.

The trial judge had ruled in favour of the party that preferred its contestants naked, noting that it was unlikely that anyone would be confused between the two services. With respect to the competing trademarks themselves, he had further noted that the presence of the word *nude* in the Canadian version was of "arresting significance" and that therefore the marks were sufficiently distinctive. On appeal, the Federal Court of Appeal concurred that the activities in question would be easily distinguishable but disagreed that the names themselves wouldn't lend themselves to confusion. In the event, it was the perhaps overenthusiastic evidence of a witness on behalf of Miss Nude Universe that gave away the game: "The name 'Miss Nude Universe' will be a selling feature without a lot of explanations. Everyone knows the name!" As the Federal Court of Appeal dryly noted, everyone would indeed "know the name," because "Miss Nude Universe" would inevitably be associated with "Miss Universe," and the bare trademark was ordered struck from the registry.

While the Trade-marks Act contains a prohibition on using any "scandalous, obscene or immoral word or device" or any word "so nearly resembling" one of the foregoing "as to be likely to be mistaken" for one,[9] this restriction is fairly loose. The fashion house French Connection UK had little difficulty obtaining a registration for the mark "FCUK"[10] in relation to various fashion goods and accessories such as makeup products. In 2004, an eyebrow-raising application for a trademark was filed: "HEAVENLY HOOKERS."[11] Oh, get your mind out of the gutter. It was registered in connection with "printed publications namely books and magazines containing patterns and designs for knitting and crocheting." Sometimes the mark relates to exactly what you think it does: the somewhat ungrammatical "GIVE ME SEXY" is registered in connection with, among other things, "Spray-type chemical preparations for masturbation; gel-type chemical preparation for masturbation; condoms; pessary;" and "contraceptive sacks." No, I have no idea what a "contraceptive sack" is, either.[12]

Of course, a trademark need not be related to sexual matters to fall just on the far side of normal. When Normark Corporation decided to register a mark in relation to "(1) Fishing lures, fishing reels, fishing tackle, fishing tackle boxes, fishing rod and reel combinations, and fishing kits comprising of fishing rods, fishing reels, fishing lures, and fishing tackle boxes" and, somewhat oddly, "(2) Electric knives," it came up with the decidedly unique "ALWAYS THINK LIKE A FISH NO MATTER HOW WEIRD IT GETS."[13] Indeed.

Intellectual Property and Expression

It is generally underappreciated that Canadian copyright and trademark law is substantially more restrictive than its counterpart in the United States, where constitutional freedom of expression concerns mandate a somewhat less complete monopoly. As intellectual property issues pepper the pages of our newspapers (as in the case of the continuing controversy revolving around the downloading of music from the Internet), Canadians are becoming increasingly aware that over-zealous enforcement of intellectual property laws can have a significant impact on the creation and dissemination of culture. The current state of Canadian intellectual property law can thus have significantly deleterious effects on freedom of expression and, as highlighted by a somewhat disturbing recent case involving, again, *Harry Potter*, even the freedom to read.

U.S. law offers a large ambit of protected expression for "parody," which allows the re-use and re-contextualization of copyrighted material without resulting in an infringement of copyright. One of the most infamous examples involved the rap group 2 Live Crew re-appropriating the distinctive bass line and chorus from the Roy Orbison song "Oh, Pretty Woman" and turning it from a light pop music ode to a, well, pretty woman, into a somewhat risqué rumination on a hairy woman (coupled with the relieved declaration of the rapper that he's glad the aforementioned woman "was out with my boy last night," since that gives him comfort that "the baby ain't mine"). After the publisher of the Orbison composition sued the band for copyright infringement, the United States Supreme Court held that the use of the copyrighted material as a parody fell within the "fair use" exemption of United States copyright law.[14] That sort of openness to the malleability of not just the creative process but the very materials that are used in the creative process is unfortunately not quite as present in Canadian copyright and trademark law.

Two of the more prominent cases in this regard arose in the context of union disputes. In 1986, a union representing employees at the St-Hubert chain of barbecue chicken restaurants produced buttons, stickers, and pamphlets that contained copies of the stylized cartoon chicken that is embodied in the chain's logo. Eager to prevent the public from seeing their venerable mascot used on union materials that disparaged the chain, the owners of the image sought an injunction against the union on the basis that use of the image infringed on their trademarks and copyrights. The Quebec Superior Court agreed that an infringement of copyright had occurred and ordered the union to stop using the image.[15] In its efforts to garner public support for its work action, the union was henceforth limited to using the corporate name of "Rotisseries St-Hubert Ltee," rather than appealing to the public with the more familiar logo. Thus, people who level criticism of a company that employs an image or logo that is the subject of copyright protection put themselves in jeopardy of a potential infringement claim if they use the protected image.

A similar result occurred when the Canadian Auto Workers Union distributed leaflets at a Michelin plant. The leaflets bore the image of "Bibendum," the "fanciful, happy, marshmallow-like figure" that functions as the Michelin mascot. One of the leaflets depicted a large Bibendum "stomping on the head of a much smaller worker." In 1996, the Supreme Court of Canada agreed with Michelin: there was no freedom of expression defence (whether in the guise of "parody" or otherwise) available to the union, and the leaflets constituted copyright infringement and were ordered destroyed.[16]

The trend towards using intellectual property laws to stifle expression, to the extent it exists, should be the subject of careful consideration. Just as other laws discussed in this book can result in extremely serious consequences for anyone caught in the dragnet, so too can the more vigorous and more frequent enforcement of intellectual property laws. In 2005, a British Columbia court issued an injunction that prohibited Canadians, on pain of being found in contempt of court, from reading a book that was intended to be published and sold to the public.[17]

The novel *Harry Potter and the Half-Blood Prince* was due for worldwide release on July 16, 2005, and was subject to an embargo prior to that date. On July 8, 2005, it was brought to the attention of Raincoast Books, the Canadian publisher of the book, that a grocery store in Coquitlam, British Columbia, had been selling the book prior to the embargo date. It seems that when the books were shipped to the store, a notification that the books were not to be sold until July 16, 2005, had inadvertently not been included with the shipment. The publisher and the author, J.K. Rowling, upon learning of the premature sales, immediately sought an injunction that would prohibit further sales until the approved release date, compel anyone who had purchased the book to return it to the publisher, and prohibit anyone who had purchased the book from reading or discussing it. Controversy erupted as pundits, legal professionals, and fans of the *Harry Potter* series debated whether a court could or should properly prohibit someone from reading a book. Although the matter quickly became moot (people had only to wait a few days to begin reading the book without violating the court order), the incident offers a glimpse of how quickly something as seemingly arcane as "intellectual property" can impact not just daily activities we take for granted but also the manner in which our collective cultural endeavour is experienced.

NOTES

Introduction

1. See *R v Morgentaler, Smoling and Scott*, [1988] 1 S.C.R. 30.

Chapter 1: Psst, Wanna Buy a Comic Book?

1. Criminal Code of Canada, R.S.C. 1985, c. C-46. A current version of the Criminal Code can be found at the federal Department of Justice website: *http://laws.justice.gc.ca/en/C-46/index.html*.

2. See generally, D. Owen Carrigan, *Crime and Punishment in Canada: A History* (Toronto: McClelland & Stewart, 1991), 228ff.

3. K. Martin, "Sadism for Kids," *The New Statesman and Nation* 48 (September 25, 1954): 347, quoted in Janice Dickin McGinnis, "Bogeymen and the Law: Crime Comics and Pornography" (1988) 20 *Ottawa Law Review* 3, 7 (hereinafter McGinnis).

4. McGinnis, 6; see also "Canadian Golden Age of Comics, 1941–1946," *www.collectionscanada.ca/comics*.

5. See generally "Canadian Golden Age of Comics, 1941–1946," *www.collectionscanada.ca/comics*.

6. See, for example, Comment by Alan Walker (1988) 20 *Ottawa Law Review*, 59.

7. McGinnis, note 63 and accompanying text. E. Davie Fulton's personal notes reveal that the issue was garnering press coverage and even arose as a campaign issue in the 1949 federal election; see McGinnis, note 28.

8. McGinnis, note 23 and accompanying text.

9. McGinnis, note 24.

10. McGinnis, note 25.

11. McGinnis, note 30.

12. Canada, *House of Commons Debates*, vol. 5, 4th Sess., 20th Parl., June 3, 1948, 4932–33, cited in McGinnis, note 26.

13. Canada, *House of Commons Debates*, vol. 1, 1st Sess., 21st Parl., October 6, 1949, 580.

14. Canada, *House of Commons Debates*, vol. 5, 4th Sess., 20th Parl., June 3, 1948, 4932–33, cited in McGinnis, note 26.

15. Fulton read these cases into Hansard in the fall of 1949; cited in McGinnis, 15.

16. See "Crackdown on Comics, 1947–1966," *www.collectionscanada.ca/comics*.

17. At the time of passage of the Fulton Bill, the relevant provisions were numbered as Section 207; subsequent renumberings of the Criminal Code moved the clauses to section 159 before finally coming to rest at their current position.

18. G.M. Murray, in Canada, *House of Commons Debates*, vol. 2, 1st Sess., 21st Parl., October 21, 1949, 1043, cited by McGinnis, note

42 and accompanying text.

19. *R. v Roher* (1953), 107 C.C.C. 103 (Manitoba Court of Appeal) per McPherson, C.J.M.

20. See, for example, *R. v Kitchener News Co.* (1954), 108 C.C.C. 304 (Ontario Court of Appeal); *R. v Superior Publishers Ltd. and Zimmerman* (1954), 110 C.C.C. 115 (Ontario Court of Appeal).

21. *R. v Alberta News Ltd.* (1951), 101 C.C.C. 219 (Calgary Police Court).

22. *R. v Roher* (1953), 107 C.C.C. 103 (Manitoba Court of Appeal).

23. *R. v Alberta News Ltd.* (1951), 101 C.C.C. 219 (Calgary Police Court).

24. McGinnis, note 54.

25. In Canada, provinces have jurisdiction over the "administration of justice," which includes the maintenance of criminal and civil courts. Provinces also have the power to enact penal sanctions for any breaches of provincial laws, and there has been a growing tendency to permit provinces to enact quasi-criminal laws, such as careless driving and failure to remain at the scene of an accident.

26. McGinnis, note 56 and accompanying text.

27. See M. Barker, *A Haunt of Fears: The Strange History of the British Horror Comics Campaign* (London: Pluto Press, 1984).

28. The full text of the original Comics Code can be found at numerous websites, including *www.dereksantos.com/comicpage/code.html*. The code was also reprinted in Les Daniels, *Comix: A History of Comics Books in America* (New York: Outerbridge and Deinstfrey, 1971). During the period when the Comics Code was most vigorously abided by, many magazine and comic book distributors refused to

carry any comics that didn't bear a cover stamp indicating the book had been approved by the Comics Code Authority. Despite a series of revisions to the code in the ensuing decades, by the late 1990s many creators and readers viewed the code as an anachronism. In 2001, Marvel Comics, one of the industry's two largest publishers, indicated it would no longer be submitting its publications to the Comics Code Authority for approval.

29. Comment by Alan Walker, *supra* note 7, 59.

30. See R. Collins, "It Wasn't Funny: Police Seized Comic Books," *Calgary Herald*, September 24, 1987, A1; Janice Dickin McGinnis, "Police Wield Obscure Law in Comics Raid," *Calgary Herald*, September 27, 1987, C6; M. Zurowski, "Pleas Reserved in Comic Book Case," *Calgary Herald*, November 18, 1987, B3; and D. Schuler, "Police Seizure of Comics Ruled Illegal," *Calgary Herald*, December 3, 1987, B2.

31. The case prompted the creation of the Comic Legends Legal Defense Fund, which raised money for the defence and appeal. The $5,500 fine was reduced to $3,000 on appeal. More information on the Comic Legends Legal Defence Fund can be found at *http://users.uniserve.com/~lswong/CLLDF.html*.

32. Information on the CAB Violence Code and the functions of the Canadian Broadcast Standards Council, which administers the code, can be found at the council's website: *www.cbsc.ca*.

33. See, for example, Joanne Richard, "Violence Unleashed — Has Video Game Violence Finally Gone Too Far?" *Calgary Sun*, January 6, 2004.

34. See, for example, Film Classification Act, 2005 (Ontario) and Ontario Regulation 452/05.

Chapter 2: A Gun Fight at High Noon? Too Uncivilized

1. Jeffrey Miller, *Where There's Life, There's Lawsuits* (Toronto: ECW Press, 2003).

2. Hugh A. Halliday, *Murder Among Gentlemen: A History of Dueling in Canada* (Toronto: Robin Brass Studio, 1999) (hereinafter Halliday).

3. John dePencier Wright, "The Demise of Duelling," *Chitty's Law Journal* 27, 2 (1979): 53 (hereinafter dePencier Wright). John White, the first attorney general, was killed by Major John Small in January 1800; in 1812, William Warren Baldwin, treasurer of the Law Society, fought Attorney General John Macdonell. See also Halliday, 42–47.

4. See R. Douglas Francis, Richard Jones, and Donald B. Smith, *Origins: Canadian History to Confederation* (Toronto: Harcourt Brace & Company, 1992), 264.

5. See Halliday, 159–60. Halliday notes, in an odd twist, that the editor served as a pallbearer at Cartier's funeral.

6. For a comprehensive account of the duel, its precursors, and its aftermath, see Austin Seton Thompson, *Jarvis Street: A Story of Triumph and Tragedy* (Toronto: Personal Library Publishers, 1980), 65–82.

7. See Halliday, 3–4 re French duelling code and 27–29 re Irish duelling code (Halliday also reproduces the entire Irish duelling code at 177–80).

8. Honourable William Renwick Riddell, "The Duel in Upper Canada," *Canadian Law Times* 35 (1915): 726.

9. See Blackstone, Book IV, page 199, quoted in dePencier Wright, 53.

10. Halliday, 151.

11. See dePencier Wright, 54.

12. See *www.town.perth.on.ca/siteengine/ActivePage.asp?PageID=91*.

13. Halliday, 127–32.

14. Halliday, 174–76.

15. See, for example, *R v Lelievre* (1962), 132 C.C.C. 288. The court described the accused and the deceased as having challenged each other to a gun battle, at which the deceased was killed. The accused was charged with manslaughter.

16. *R v Malmo-Levine* (2003), 233 D.L.R. (4th) 415 (S.C.C.), para. 118.

17. *U.S. et al v Barrientos* (1995), 103 C.C.C. (3d) 481 (Alta. C.A.) per Harradence J.A.

18. *R v Jobidon* (1991), 66 C.C.C. (3d) 454 (S.C.C.).

19. John Barnes, "Recent Developments in Canadian Sports Law" (1991) 23 *Ottawa Law Review*, 623, 680.

20. See *R v Dix* (1972), 10 C.C.C. (2d) 324 (Ont. C.A.).

21. An Act Respecting Prize-Fights [some authorities cite this as "*an Act respecting prize fighting*"], S.C., 44 Vict. ch. 30, consolidated in R.S.C, 1886, ch. 153.

22. Criminal Code, 1892, Section 96.

23. *R v Coney* (1881), 15 Cox. C.C. 46 per Stephen J at 73.

24. Sir William Oldnall Russell, A *Treatise on Crimes and Misdemeanors*, 7th ed. (Toronto: Canada Law Book Company, 1910), 785.

25. *Steele v Maber* (1901), 6 C.C.C. 446 (Que. Magistrate's Court).

26. *The King v Wildfong and Lang* (1911), 17 C.C.C. 251.

27. *R v Orton* (1878), 14 Cox. C.C. 226.

28. *Encyclopedia of Law of England*, vol. 2, 231.

29. *R v Littlejohn*, 8 C.C.C. 212.

30. *R v Fitzgerald* (1912), 19 C.C.C. 145 (Div. Court).

31. *R v Pelkey* (1913), 21 C.C.C. 387 (Alta. S.C.).

32. *R v. M.A.F.A. Inc.*, [2000] O.J. No. 899 (Ont. C.J.). As the court noted, the Ontario Athletics Commissioner does govern kickboxing, but the sanctioned form of kickboxing is quite different from "Thai" or "Muay Thai" kickboxing. In sanctioned kickboxing, kicking below the waist is illegal, as is "striking behind the neck, spinning, grabbing, blows with elbows, or, blows with knees." Thai kickboxing has no such restrictions.

33. A website is maintained at *www.battleofthehockeyenforcers.com*.

34. See "Controversial Hockey Brawl Tourney to Go Ahead" at *www.ctv.ca/servlet/ArticleNews/story/CTVNews/1118856148400_4/?hub=CTVNews*.

35. See, for example, *Canadian Encyclopedic Digest* §75.

36. *R v McSorley* (2000), 2000 BCPC 114 (BC Prov Ct).

37. *R v Bradshaw* (1878), 14 Cox C.C. 83 (UK Assize Ct.).

38. See *Agar v Canning* (1965), 54 W.W.R. 302 (Man. QB).

39. *R v Maki* (1970), 1 C.C.C. (2d) 333 (Ont. Prov. Ct.).

40. *Re Duchesneau* (1978), 7 C.R. (3d) 70 (Que. Youth Ct.) saw a player accused of manslaughter but convicted of assault where the accused struck the victim after he knocked him unconscious.

41. *R v Smithers* (1977), 75 D.L.R. (3d) 321 (S.C.C.) involved two teenage players who were involved in a rough game where racial taunts were exchanged. Forty-five minutes after the game, Smithers confronted Cobby in the parking lot, punching him in the head and then kicking him in the stomach. Cobby died as a result of choking on his own vomit, and Smithers was convicted of manslaughter.

42. See *R v Green*, [1971] 1 O.R. 591.

43. See *R v Mayer* (1985), 41 Man. R. (2d) 73 (Prov. Ct.).

44. *R v Watson* (1975), 26 C.C.C. (2d) 150 (Ont. Prov. Ct.).

45. See generally Anna Husa and Stephen Thiele, "In the Name of the Game: Hockey Violence and the Criminal Justice System" (2001) 45 *Criminal Law Quarterly*, 509.

46. *R v Ciccarelli* (1989), 54 C.C.C. (3d) 121 (Ont. Dist. Ct.).

47. As Husa and Thiele note on page 527 of their article, "The courts are still showing a differential attitude where acts of aggression are committed inside the hockey arena. This is reflected in the lenient sentences.... While denouncing the violence verbally, the courts are sending the message that aggressive players will not be called upon to account for their actions.... Courts try to justify their non-interventionist approach by arguing that the responsibility for reform lies with the public and the [sporting] authorities that already exist to carry out disciplinary measures."

48. See, for example, Michael McCarthy, "Illegal, Violent Teen Fight Clubs Face Police Crackdown," *USA Today*, August 1, 2006 (*www.usatoday.com/news/nation/2006-07-31-violent-fight-clubs_ x.htm*).

Chapter 3: Saying Bad Things About People in Power — Crimes Against the State

1. See Joe Friesen, "The Allegations: Shocking Revelations as Terror Suspects Appear in Court," *Globe and Mail*, June 7, 2006, A1 (*www.theglobeandmail.com/servlet/story/LAC.20060607.TERROR HEARING07/TPStory/*).

2. Law Reform Commission of Canada, Working Paper 49, *Crimes Against the State* (1986), 3 (hereinafter LRCC *Crimes Against the State*).

3. LRCC *Crimes Against the State*, 8.

4. See generally Peter Hogg, *Constitutional Law of Canada* in Chapter 2 (4th ed., 1996: Carswell); and F. Murray Greenwood and Barry Wright, eds., *Canadian State Trials, Vol. 1— Law, Politics, and Security Measures, 1608–1837* (Toronto: The Osgoode Society for Canadian Legal History, University of Toronto Press, 1996), 12.

5. LRCC *Crimes Against the State*, 35.

6. S.C. 1951, c. 47.

7. LRCC *Crimes Against the State*, 12.

8. See generally, Norman Hillmer and J.L. Granatstein, *Empire to Umpire: Canada and the World to the 1990s* (Toronto: Copp Clark Longman, 1994), 211–16.

9. Section 47(2) provides that only the following forms of treason are liable to life imprisonment: using force for the purpose of overthrowing the federal or a provincial government, conspiring to commit high treason, and "forming an intention" to commit high treason or using force to overthrow a government and "manifesting that intention by an overt act." The other form

of treason (communicating information to an enemy agent or conspiring to do so) results in life imprisonment if committed during wartime — otherwise imprisonment for fourteen years is the penalty.

10. LRCC *Crimes Against the State*, 11.

11. Criminal Code, Section 46(3).

12. Criminal Code, Section 47(3).

13. Criminal Code, Section 48(1).

14. Criminal Code, Section 48(2).

15. See Will Ferguson, *Bastards & Boneheads: Canada's Glorious Leaders Past and Present* (Toronto: Douglas & McIntyre, 1999), 196–208. As of Ferguson's writing, Jacques Lanctôt, leader of the FLQ cell that kidnapped Cross, owned a publishing house; Paul Rose, involved in the murder of Pierre Laporte, was teaching at the Université du Québec à Rimouski; Serge Demers, convicted of armed robbery, planting bombs, and stealing firearms, was named chief of staff to the Quebec minister of employment in 1996; Richard Thérrien, convicted of harbouring the terrorists who murdered Pierre Laporte, was named a judge of the Quebec Court in 1996.

16. See George R.D. Goulet, *The Trial of Louis Riel: Justice and Mercy Denied* (Calgary: Tellwell Publishing, 1999), 51 (hereinafter Goulet).

17. See especially Goulet, 175–202.

18. See Goulet, 49.

19. For excellent overviews of Riel's story, see R. Douglas Francis, Richard Jones, and Donald B. Smith, *Destinies: Canadian History Since Confederation*, 3rd edition (Toronto: Harcourt Brace, 1996), 28–32 (Red River Rebellion and Manitoba Act) and 78–85

(Northwest Rebellion of 1885 and trial of Louis Riel), and also Will Ferguson, *Bastards & Boneheads: Canada's Glorious Leaders Past and Present* (Toronto: Douglas & McIntyre, 1999), 102–16.

20. See Clifford Ian Kyer, "Sedition Through the Ages: A Note on Legal Terminology" (1979) 37 *University of Toronto Faculty of Law Review*, 266–69.

21. Although the statement is glib, it isn't fanciful. The earliest cases dealing with sedition were libel cases (*De Libellis Famosis* and *John Lamb's Case*) heard in the Star Chamber in the early seventeenth century, which literally dealt with statements made by the accused that were deemed to be unflattering to persons in power. *De Libellis Famosis* concerned the publication of a crass poem about the archbishop of Canterbury. In *Pine's Case*, though he was ultimately acquitted, Pine had described King Charles I as being "as unwise a king as ever was." By the late seventeenth century, sedition trials were based on mere criticism of the government. In the *Frost* case from 1792, Frost was imprisoned for six months for declaring himself in favour of equality and abolishment of the monarchy. It wasn't until the middle of the twentieth century in Canadian law that it was definitively determined that an intention to incite violence was required to found a conviction for a sedition offence. For an excellent short summary of the early development of sedition, see Michael Head, "Sedition: Is the Star Chamber Dead?" (1979) 3 *Criminal Law Journal*, 89–99.

22. 5 Co. Rep. 125a; 77 ER 250 (Star Chamber).

23. See LRCC *Crimes Against the State*, 6–7; and see *The Case of Tutchin* (1704), 14 State Trials 1095.

24. See Gary Botting, *Fundamental Freedoms & Jehovah's Witnesses* (Calgary: University of Calgary Press, 1993), 70.

25. William E. Conklin, "The Origins of the Law of Sedition" (1972–73) 15 *Criminal Law Quarterly*, 277, 279.

26. *R v Sullivan* (1868), 11 Cox C.C. 44, at 45.

27. James Fitzjames Stephen, *History of Criminal Law*, vol. 2, 298, quoted in *R v Felton* (1915), 25 C.C.C. 207 (Alta. S.C.).

28. *Duval et al v The King* (1938), 64 R.J.Q. 270, 277.

29. See Barry Cahill, "Sedition in Nova Scotia: *R v Wilkie* (1820) and the Incontestable Illegality of Seditious Libel before *R v Howe* (1835)" (1994) 44 *Dalhousie Law Journal*, 458.

30. Barry Cahill's "Sedition in Nova Scotia: *R v Howe* and the 'Contested Legality' of Seditious Libel" (2002) 51 UNBLJ 95, is the most comprehensive and passionate recounting of Howe's saga (hereinafter Cahill).

31. Cahill, 101.

32. Cahill, 114.

33. Cahill, 127.

34. *R v Felton* (1915), 25 C.C.C. 207 (Alta. S.C., App. Div.).

35. *R v Cohen* (1916), 25 C.C.C. 302 (Alta. S.C., App. Div.).

36. *R v Manshrick* (1916), 27 C.C.C. 17 (Man. C.A.).

37. See *R v Trainor* (1917), 27 C.C.C. 232.

38. See Kenneth McNaught and David J. Bercuson, *The Winnipeg Strike: 1919* (Don Mills, ON: Longman Canada Limited, 1974), 42–43 (hereinafter McNaught and Bercuson).

39. McNaught and Bercuson, 44.

40. McNaught and Bercuson, 34ff.

41. McNaught and Bercuson, 46.

42. McNaught and Bercuson, 50–51. Three veterans associations voted in favour of a resolution expressing support of the strike.

43. McNaught and Bercuson, 62; see Peter MacKinnon, "Conspiracy and Sedition as Canadian Political Crimes" (1977) 23 *McGill Law Journal*, 622, 627 (hereinafter MacKinnon).

44. MacKinnon, 628.

45. Criminal Code Amendment Act, S.C. 1919, c. 46.

46. The eight charged were William Ivens, R.B. Russell, R.J. Johns, William Pritchard, George Armstrong, R.E. Bray, A.A. Heaps, and John Queen.

47. Taken from the January 24, 1919, edition of *Western Labor News*; quoted in Peter R. Lederman, "Sedition in Winnipeg: An Examination of the Trials for Seditious Conspiracy Arising from the General Strike of 1919" (1976–77) 3 *Queen's Law Journal*, 3, 16 (hereinafter Lederman).

48. *R v Russell* (1920–21), 33 C.C.C. 1 (Man. C.A.).

49. The cited chapters were 10:1–2 ("Woe unto them that decree unrighteous decrees, and that write grievousness which they have prescribed; to turn aside the needy from judgment, and to take away the right from the poor of my people, that widows may be their prey, and that they may rob the fatherless!") and 65:21–22 ("And they shall build houses and inhabit them; and they shall plant vineyards, and eat the fruit of them. They shall not build, and another inhabit; they shall not plant, and another eat: for as the days of a tree are the days of my people, and mine elect shall long enjoy the work of their hands.").

50. MacKinnon, 628.

51. See Lederman, note 17 and accompanying text.

52. S.C. 1919, c. 46, s. 1: "97A(1)."

53. See generally, Barry Cahill, "*Howe* (1835), *Dixon* (1920) and *McLachlan* (1923): Comparative Perspective on the Legal History of Sedition" (1996) 45 *University of New Brunswick Law Journal*, 281.

54. See MacKinnon, 631–32; *R v Buick* (1932), 57 C.C.C. 290 (Ont. C.A.).

55. Adam Mayers, "Tim Buck: Canada's Communist," *Toronto Star*, August 17, 2006.

56. Lederman, 9.

57. *Boucher v The King*, [1951] S.C.R. 265.

58. See Comment of F.A. Brewin, *Canadian Bar Review*, vol. XXIX, 193ff.

59. The judgment of the court following the first hearing (before five justices) was reported at [1950] 1 D.L.R. 657; following a motion for re-hearing, the full court of nine justices re-heard the arguments and rendered the judgment with which we are familiar.

60. See MacKinnon, 635–36.

61. See *www.varsity.utoronto.ca/archives/117/feb03/feature/oneyear.html*.

Chapter 4: Keep Your Pants On

1.   Pimping — Section 212 Criminal Code; common bawdy-house — Section 210 Criminal Code; communicating in public — Section 213 Criminal Code.

2.   *R v Pierce and Golloher* (1982), 37 O.R. (2d) 721 (O.C.A.).

3.   *Canada (Minister of National Revenue) v Eldridge*, [1965] 1 Ex. C.R. 758.

4. Deductible. Eldridge had not, however, provided sufficient evidence that the claimed expenditures had actually been incurred. The court confirmed that had she done so she would have been entitled to deduct them.

5. Deductible. Again, though, Eldridge was unable to substantiate the claimed amounts.

6. Deductible.

7. Deductible.

8. Not deductible, but only because the court wasn't satisfied that circulation of the newspaper would have been detrimental to Eldridge's business.

9. See Jeffrey Miller, *Ardour in the Court! Sex and the Law* (Toronto: ECW Press, 2002), 65–69 (hereinafter Miller, *Ardour*).

10. See *Halm v Canada (Minister of Employment and Immigration)*, [1995] 2 F.C. 331 and *R v Roy* (1998), 125 C.C.C. (3d) 442 (Quebec C. A.).

11. See *R v M(C)* (1995), 98 C.C.C. (3d) 481 (O.C.A.); *R v Roy* (1998), 125 C.C.C. (3d) 442 (Quebec C.A.); *R v Roth*, [2002] A.J. No. 159 (Alta. Q.B.).

12. See Donald G. Caswell, "Comment — Criminal Code, Section 159" (2004) 83 *Canadian Bar Review*, 217–28.

13. *R v K(CP)* (2002), 171 C.C.C. (3d) 173 (Ont. C.A.). It should be emphasized that the anal intercourse in this case was non-consensual. However, that same activity (i.e., non-consensual sodomy) is also a crime pursuant to the sexual assault provisions of the Criminal Code (pursuant to which the accused was also charged and convicted), so the section 159 charges were superfluous.

14. *Lucas v Toronto Police Services Board*, [2000] O.J. No. 4326, 51 O.R. (3d) 783 (Sup. Ct. J.), appeal by defendant attorney general

of Canada allowed (2001), 54 O.R. (3d) 715, application by plaintiff for leave to Ontario Court of Appeal dismissed, September 10, 2001, and subsequent application for leave to appeal to Supreme Court of Canada dismissed, June 13, 2002.

15. See Miller, *Ardour*, 69–74.

16. *R v Triller* (1980), 55 C.C.C. (2d) 411 (B.C. Cty. Ct.).

17. *R v Brown* (1889), 24 Q.B.D. 357 (C.C.R.).

18. 1931 S.C., c. 28, s. 2.

19. *R v Niman* (1974), 31 C.R.N.S. 51 (Ont. Prov. Ct.).

20. See, for example, *R v Peterie*, [1996] S.J. No. 35 (Sask. Prov. Ct.).

21. *R v Clark*, [2005] 1 S.C.R. 6.

22. See *R v Zikman* (1990), 56 C.C.C. (3d) 430 (Ont. C.A.).

23. See September 12, 2002, press release at *http://tntmen.abuzar.net/tnt/news/f33.html*.

24. *R v Jacob* (1996), 142 D.L.R. (4th) 411 (Ont. C.A.).

25. *R v Niman* (1974), 31 C.R.N.S. 51 (Ont. Prov. Ct.).

26. See Sopinka J. in *R v Butler* (1992), 70 C.C.C. (3d) 129 (S.C.C.).

27. *R v Labaye*, [2005] 3 S.C.R. 728.

Chapter 5: Blasphemous Pirates in Space

1. D. Stuart, "*Assault* (Review of Law Reform Commission of Canada Working Paper 38)" (1986) 64 *Canadian Bar Review*, 217, 218, quoted in 23 *Ottawa Law Review*, 680, 688.

2. Colin Campbell, "Don't Paddle Drunk," *Maclean's*, July 24, 2006, accessed at *www.macleans.ca/topstories/canada/article.jsp?content=2 0060724_130717_130717*.

3. 1541 (33 Hen. 8) C A P. VIII.

4. See, for example, *R v Milford* (1890), 20 O.R. 306 (O.C.A.).

5. See *R v Marcott* (1901), 4 C.C.C. 437 (O.C.A.).

6. *R v Stanley* (1952), 104 C.C.C. 31.

7. *R v Dazenbrook* (1975), 23 C.C.C. (2d) 252.

8. *R v Corbeil* (1981), 65 C.C.C. (2d) 570.

9. *R. v. Labrosse*, [1987] 1 S.C.R. 310

10. See Annotation, 48 C.C.C. 1 (December 1927); for some sources of blasphemy laws, see 1547, 1 Edw. VI, c.1 and 1688, 1 Wm. 3, c. 18 and The Act of 1698, 9 and 10 Wm. 3, c. 32, s. 1. See also *Taylor's Case* (1676), 1 Vent. 293, 86 E.R. 189; *R v Morton* (1841), 4 State Tr. 693; *R v Williams* (1797), 26 State Tr. 653.

11. *R v Ramsay* (1883), 15 Cox. C.C. 231.

12. See *R v Gott* (1922), 16 Cr. App. R. 87.

13. For *R v Sterry*, see *Annotation: Blasphemy*, 48 C.C.C. 1 (1927).

14. *R v Kinler* (1925), 63 Que. S.C. 483; also see generally, William Kaplan, *State and Salvation: The Jehovah's Witnesses and Their Fight for Civil Rights* (Toronto: University of Toronto Press, 1989), 10.

15. *R v Rahard* (1935), 65 C.C.C. 344.

16. *R v Palmer* (1937), 68 C.C.C. 20 (Ont. C.A.).

17. *R v Keystone Enterprises Ltd.* (1961), 133 C.C.C. 338 (Winn. Mag. Ct.).

18. See generally, Dan Ciraco, "The Money Shot: The Law Surrounding the Reproduction of Bank Note Images," Ontario Bar Association Entertainment, Media & Communications Section Newsletter, vol. 15, no. 1.

19. 1 Geo. 1, c.5.

20. *R v Allen* (1974), 17 C.C.C. (2d) 549.

21. Section 91, Constitution Act, 1867; available at *http:// laws.justice.gc.ca/en/const/index.html*.

22. National Defence Act, R.S. 1985, c. N-5; available at *http:// laws.justice.gc.ca/en/N-5/index.html*.

23. See generally, David McNairn, "A Military Justice Primer, Parts I and II," (2000) 43 *Criminal Law Quarterly*, 243–67 and 375–92.

24. See National Defence Act, s. 60(1)(*e*).

25. See National Defence Act, s. 66.

26. National Defence Act, s. 70.

27. National Defence Act, s. 130.

28. F.B. Weiner, *Civilians Under Military Justice: The British Practice Since 1689, Especially in North America* (Chicago: University of Chicago Press, 1967), 232, quoted in Janet Walker, "Military Justice: From Oxymoron to Aspiration," 32 *Osgoode Hall Law Journal*, 1, 4.

29. National Defence Act, s. 73.

30. National Defence Act, s. 74.

31. National Defence Act, s. 76.

32. See Section 6(2) Criminal Code: "Subject to this Act or any other Act of Parliament, no person shall be convicted or discharged under Section 730 of an offence committed outside Canada."

Chapter 6: Race, Religion, and the Law

1.   An Act to Further Amend "The Indian Act, 1880," S.C. 1884, c. 27.

2.   An Act to Further Amend the Indian Act, S.C. 1895, c. 35.

3.   Constance Backhouse, *Colour-Coded: A Legal History of Racism in Canada, 1900–1950* (Toronto: The Osgoode Society for Canadian Legal History, 1999), 65 (hereinafter Backhouse).

4.   Backhouse, 66ff.

5.   Backhouse. 67.

6.   It was the view of MP Frank Oliver that "ownership [and] selfishness, which is foreign to the mind of the Indian in his normal condition, is really the foundation of civilization"; *House of Commons Debates*, May 8, 1914, 3482, quoted in Backhouse, 68.

7.   Backhouse, 69 and 100.

8.   Backhouse, Chapter 3, note 148.

9.   "An Act Respecting Indians," S.C. 1951, c.29.

10. See Backhouse, Chapter 5, note 5.

11. See generally, *Destinies*, 68.

12. Backhouse, 162–63 and accompanying notes.

13. S.S. 1912, c. 17.

14. See Backhouse, 137–38.

15. See Backhouse, 139.

16. For details on all the foregoing, see Backhouse, Chapter 5, notes 59–61.

17. See Backhouse, Chapter 5, note 68, and accompanying text.

18. See Backhouse, Chapter 5, notes 126 and 127, and accompanying text.

19. See Backhouse, 253–55; see also *Loew's Montreal Theatres Ltd. v Reynolds* (1919), 30 Que. K.B. 459; *Franklin v Evans* (1924), 55 O.L.R. 349 (Ont. H.C.); *Rogers v Clarence Hotel*, [1940] 2 W.W.R. 545 (B.C.C.A.); *Christie v York Corporation*, [1940] 81 S.C.R. 139.

20. See *Johnson v Sparrow* (1899), 15 Que. S.C. 104; *Barnswell v National Amusement Company, Limited* (1914), 21 B.C.R. 453 (B.C.C.A.).

21. See generally, Simma Holt, *Terror in the Name of God* (Toronto: McClelland & Stewart, 1964) (hereinafter Holt).

22. Holt, 25.

23. John McLaren, "The Despicable Crime of Nudity: Law, the State and Civil Protest Among Canada's Doukhobors, 1899–1935," *The Advocate* (Vancouver), vol. 63, part 2, March 2005, 211–13.

24. Holt, 43–44.

25. Holt, 49–51.

26. Holt, 50.

27. See McLaren, 215; and Holt, 52.

28. Holt, 71–73.

29. Holt, 109.

30. See MacKinnon, 633–34; and Holt, 248–70.

31. Holt, 239–47.

32. Holt, 8.

33. See William Kaplan, "The Supreme Court of Canada and the Protection of Minority Dissent: The Case of the Jehovah's Witnesses" (1990) 39 *University of New Brunswick Law Journal*, 65, 67 (hereinafter Kaplan, "The Supreme Court of Canada").

34. See generally, Gary Botting, *Fundamental Freedoms & Jehovah's Witnesses* (Calgary: University of Calgary Press, 1993), 12–13 (hereinafter Botting).

35. Botting, 15–16.

36. See Botting, 19.

37. S.C. 1917, c. 19.

38. Cited at Botting, 19: *Re Cooke* (unreported) January 14, 1918 (Serial No. 548250 JC) per Duff J. (Central Appeal Court); available in M. James Penton, *Jehovah's Witnesses in Canada: Champions of Free Speech and Worship* (Toronto: Macmillan, 1976), Appendix B.

39. Botting, 21.

40. William Kaplan, *State and Salvation: The Jehovah's Witnesses and Their Fight for Civil Rights* (Toronto: University of Toronto Press, 1989), 8–9 (hereinafter Kaplan, *State and Salvation*).

41. Kaplan, *State and Salvation*, 29.

42. Kaplan, "The Supreme Court of Canada," 67.

43. *R v Kinler* (1925), 63 Que. S.C. 483; also see generally, Kaplan, *State and Salvation*, 10.

44. See, for example, *R v Brodie*, [1936] S.C.R. 188. In the *Brodie* case, the Supreme Court of Canada overturned the conviction on the count of seditious libel for failure to disclose the specific illegal act. Witnesses continued to be convicted under more tightly worded indictments. See, for example, *R v Duval* (1938), 64 Que. K.B. 270.

45. Kaplan, *State and Salvation*, 53.

46. Botting, 26.

47. *Debates*, July 16, 1940, vol. 2, 1646.

48. See Kaplan, *State and Salvation*, 127–30.

49. Botting, 27.

50. Kaplan, "The Supreme Court of Canada," 70.

51. Botting, 29.

52. Botting, 54.

53. Kaplan, *State and Salvation*, 245.

54. Kaplan, *State and Salvation*, 245–47.

55. See *Roncarelli v Duplessis*, [1959] S.C.R. 121.

56. January 28, 1959, quoted in Botting, 95.

57. Kaplan, *State and Salvation*, 258–59.

Chapter 7: It Doesn't Take a Thief —
Or, Not All the Interesting Stuff Happens in Criminal Court

1. *Wittlin v Bergman* (1994), 19 O.R. (3d) 145 (Ont. Gen. Div.), rev'd [1995] O.J. No. 3095 (Ont. C.A.).

2. Grant Robertson, "Comma Quirk Irks Rogers," *Globe and Mail*, August 6, 2006.

3. *Ruffolo v Mulroney*, [1988] O.J. No. 2670.

4. See, for example, *Haig v Bamford*, [1977] 1 S.C.R. 466.

5. S.O. 1999, c. 7, Sch. A.

6. See Interpretation Act (Ontario), R.S.O. 1980, C. 219, s. 13, which states "Every Act shall be construed as reserving to the Legislature the power of repealing or amending it, and of revoking, restricting, or modifying any power, privilege or advantage thereby vested in or granted to any person or party, whenever the repeal, amendment, revocation, restriction or modification is considered by the Legislature to be required for the public good."

7. An Act to Implement Budget Measures, 1st Sess., 38th Parl., Ontario 2004, s. 17.

8. An Act to Implement Budget Measures and Amend the Crown Forest Sustainability Act, 1994, 1st Sess., 38th Parl., Ontario 2004, Schedule B.

9. *Canadian Taxpayers Federation v. Ontario (Minister of Finance)* (2004), 73 O.R. (3d) 621.

10. The authoritative Canadian work on the law of defamation is Brown, *The Law of Defamation in Canada*, 2nd ed. (Toronto: Thomson Carswell, 1995).

11. *Lever v George*, [1950] O.R. 115 (H.C.).

12. *Stadler v Terrace Corporation (Construction) Ltd.* (1983), 41 A.R. 587 (Q.B.).

13. *Roth v Aubichon* (1998), 171 Sask. R. 271.

14. *Ralston v Fomich* (1992), 66 B.C.L.R. (2d) 166 (S.C.).

15. See generally, Michael Bennett, "The Right of the Oath" (1995) 17 *The Advocates' Quarterly*, 40.

16. *The King v Ah Wooey* (1902), 8 C.C.C. 25.

17. See *Re Patton*, [1938] O.W.N. 52 (C.A.); *Re Starr*, [1946] O.R. 252 (C.A.).

18. See Sheena Grattan and Heather Conway, "Testamentary Conditions in Restraint of Religion in the Twenty-First Century: An Anglo-Canadian Perspective" (2005) 50 *McGill Law Journal*, 511.

19. *Re Delahey* (1950), [1951] O.W.N. 143 (H.C.J.); see also D.A.L. Smout, "An Inquiry into the Law on Racial and Religious Restraints on Alienation" (1952) 30 *Canadian Bar Review*, 863.

20. *Re Noble and Wolf*, [1948] O.R. 479 (H.C.J.), aff'd [1949] O.R. 503. The condition was later deemed invalid by the Supreme Court of Canada not because it was racist, but because it was insufficiently "certain"; see *Noble v Alley*, [1951] S.C.R. 64.

21. *Re Murley Estate* (1995), 130 Nfld. & P.E.I.R. 271 (Nfld. S.C. [T.D.]).

22. *Canada Trust Co v Ontario Human Rights Commission* (1990), 74 O.R. (2d) 481 (C.A.).

Chapter 8: Most Foul

1. For current Canadian crime statistics, see *www.statcan.ca/Daily/ English/060720/d060720b.htm*; for historical and comparative rates, see D. Owen Carrigan, *Crime and Punishment in Canada: A History* (Toronto: McClelland & Stewart, 1991), 109–39.

2. Martin L. Friedland, *The Case of Valentine Shortis* (Toronto: University of Toronto Press, 1986), 7.

3. See Criminal Code, Sections 222–231.

4. Criminal Code, Section 233.

5. Criminal Code, Section 234.

6. *R v Gagnon* (1993), 84 C.C.C. (3d) 143 (Q.C.A.).

7. See, for example, *R v Murton*, 3 Foster and Finlayson, 492; *R v Towers*, 12 Cox, 530; 3 *Chitty's Criminal Law*, 726 — cited by Dorion, dissenting, in *R v Dugal*, [1878] Q.B. 350.

8. *R v Dugal*, [1878] Q.B. 350.

9. *R v Howard* (1913), 5 W.W.R. 838 (Man. P.C.).

10. *R v Powder* (1981), 29 C.R. (3d) 183 (Alta. C.A.).

11. *R v Rusland* (1992), 71 C.C.C. (3d) 574 (Ont. C.A.).

12. *R v Jordan* (1991), 4 B.C.A.C. 121.

13. See Limitations Act, 2002 (Ontario), S.O. 2002, c. 24. Limitations periods are among the more complicated areas of law, and anyone with an interest in this area or requiring further information about it is *strongly* encouraged to contact a lawyer with litigation experience.

14. Criminal Code, Section 786.

15. As noted in Chapter 3, Section 48 of the Criminal Code does provide for one other limitation period for serious crimes. Proceedings for treason must be brought within three years from the time the offence is alleged to have been committed, and proceedings for high treason "expressed or declared by open and considered speech" must be commenced within "six days after the time when the words are alleged to have been spoken."

16. For the English repeal, see Law Reform (Year and a Day Rule) Act 1996, Chapter 19 (U.K.), available at *www.opsi.gov.uk/acts/acts1996/1996019.htm*. For the Canadian repeal, see 1999, c. 5, s. 9 (Bill C-51), available at *www.canlii.org/ca/as/1999/c5/sec9%2Ehtml*.

17. See *State v Picotte*, 2003 WI 42; available at *www.wisbar.org/res/sup/2003/01-3063.htm*.

18. *R v Prince* (1988), 44 C.C.C. (3d) 510 (Man. C.A.).

19. Criminal Code, Sections 233, 237.

20. See generally, Judith A. Osborne, "The Crime of Infanticide: Throwing Out the Baby with the Bathwater" (1987) 6 *Canadian Journal of Family Law*, 47.

21. Law Reform Commission of Canada, Working Paper 33, *Homicide* (1984).

22. Criminal Code, Section 242.

23. Criminal Code, Section 243.

24. *R v K* (1971), 3 C.C.C. (3d) 84 (Ont. H.C.J.), 84.

25. See Section 16, Criminal Code, and Criminal Code Part XX.1.

26. *R v Book*, [1999] A.J. No. 1470 (Alta. Prov. Ct.).

27. *R v Parks*, [1992] 2 S.C.R. 871.

Chapter 9: Of Poppies and Red Crosses

1. The video game law group at the law firm of Davis & Company maintains a copy of the Red Cross letter here: *www.davis.ca/ community/blogs/video_games/files/red_cross_letter.pdf*.

2. The Trade-marks Act is available at *http://laws.justice.gc.ca/en/T-13/index.html*.

3. Tom Spears, "Hands Off Our Emblem, Canada Tells Illicit Users," *Ottawa Citizen*, October 30, 2006.

4. See Copyright Act, sections 14.1 and 28.2. The Copyright Act is available at *http://laws.justice.gc.ca/en/C-42/index.html*.

5. *Snow v The Eaton Centre Ltd et al* (1982), 70 C.P.R. (2d) 105 (Ont. H.C.).

6. *Gnass v Cite d'Alma* (June 3, 1977) (Que. C.A.), unreported, cited in David Vaver, *Copyright Law* (Toronto: Irwin Law, 2000), 162.

7. *Baryluk v. Warner Bros. Entertainment Inc.*, 2005 CanLII 41383 (Ont. S.C.).

8. *Miss Universe, Inc. v Bohna*, [1995] 1 F.C. 614 (F.C.A.).

9. Trade-marks Act, Section 9(1)(j).

10. "FCUK": Canadian trademark registration number TMA515878.

11. "HEAVENLY HOOKERS": see Canadian trademark application number 1041663 and registration number TMA663489. The original application was subsequently abandoned, but a different application was eventually filed and registered.

12. "GIVE ME SEXY": Canadian trademark application number 1252147.

13. "ALWAYS THINK LIKE A FISH NO MATTER HOW WEIRD IT GETS": Canadian trademark registration number TMA652864. Each of the three foregoing trademarks was brought to the author's attention at Sander Gelsing's legal blog, available at *www.gelsing.ca/blog*.

14. *Campbell v. Acuff-Rose Music* (92-1292), 510 U.S. 569 (1994).

15. *Rotisseries St-Hubert Ltee v Le Syndicat desTtravailleurs(euses) de la Rotisserie St-Hubert de Drummondville (CSN)* (1986), 17 C.P.R. (3d) 461 (Que. S.C.).

16. *Cie Generale des Etablissements Michelin-Michelin & Cie v CAW-Canada* (1996), 71 C.P.R. (3d) 348 (S.C.C.).

17. A partial copy of the court order and related commentary can be found at the website of the book's publisher: *http://raincoast.com/harrypotter/injunction.html*.

RECOMMENDED FURTHER READING

Readers interested in more detailed treatments of some of the topics discussed in this book are encouraged to consult the following sources.

The federal Department of Justice maintains a website with **current federal statutes** (including the Criminal Code and the Constitution) at *http://laws.justice.gc.ca/en/index.html*, and also provides links to similar provincial websites.

The Canadian Legal Information Institute has created an excellent resource at *www.canlii.org*, which contains an enormous (and ever-increasing) amount of **case decisions, statutes, and other legal information** — and all for free.

For **general legal history**, the work of the Osgoode Society and its various publications (a list of which can be found at *www.osgoodesociety.ca* and which are usually available at larger libraries) are indispensable. Jeffrey Miller, a Canadian lawyer and columnist, has a number of books that handsomely repay your reading investment. Some libraries maintain copies of the dozens of reports of the Law Reform Commission of Canada on numerous topics, which offer detailed historical treatments as well as recommendations for reform.

For information on **comic books**, John Bell's *Invaders from the North: How Canada Conquered the Comic Book Universe* (Toronto: The Dundurn

Group, 2006) offers a lively, fulsome, and profusely illustrated treatment of the history of the Canadian comic book industry. The work of Janice Dickin McGinnis is the most comprehensive study of the Fulton Bill available, and her article "Bogeymen and the Law: Crime Comics and Pornography" ([1988] 20 *Ottawa Law Review*, 3, 7) contains a wealth of additional references.

Hugh A. Halliday's *Murder Among Gentlemen: A History of Dueling in Canada* (Toronto: Robin Brass Studio, 1999) is the best single source for more details on **duels**.

An enormous amount of material is available on the topic of **crimes against the state**, and the Osgoode Society's *Canadian State Trials* series is as good a starting point as any. Working Paper 49 of the Law Reform Commission of Canada also offers a succinct history and critique of the current state of the law on treason, sedition, and related crimes.

For further details on the **Winnipeg General Strike**, Kenneth McNaught and David J. Bercuson's *The Winnipeg Strike: 1919* (Don Mills, ON: Longman Canada Limited, 1974) is an excellent concise primer.

Those interested in further details about the trial of **Louis Riel** are strongly encouraged to read George R.D. Goulet's *The Trial of Louis Riel: Justice and Mercy Denied* (Calgary: Tellwell Publishing, 1999), which offers some of the most in-depth research into the episode.

Simma Holt's *Terror in the Name of God* (Toronto: McClelland & Stewart, 1964) is one of the best, and certainly the most comprehensive, accounts of the **Doukhobor** confrontations with the Canadian government.

When it comes to **sex and the law**, Jeffrey Miller's *Ardour in the Court!* (Toronto: ECW Press, 2002) is a humorous and illuminating romp through legal history.

The numerous publications of Constance Backhouse, in particular *Colour-Coded: A Legal History of Racism in Canada* (Toronto: The Osgoode Society for Canadian Legal History, 1999), are highly recommended for anyone interested in further particulars about **race, religion, and the law**.

When it comes to **intellectual property** laws, David Vaver's texts *Copyright Law* (Toronto: Irwin Law, 2000) and *Intellectual Property Law: Copyright, Patents, Trade-Marks* (Toronto: Irwin Law, 1997) are among the best sources for lawyers and non-lawyers alike. Also interesting, as an entertainingly written polemic on the side of free expression, is Lawrence Lessig's *Free Culture: How Big Media Uses Technology and the Law to Lock Down Culture and Control Creativity* (New York: Penguin, 2005). And there are dozens of weblogs that provide up-to-the-minute commentary on intellectual property matters, among the best of which are *www.gelsing.ca* (which focuses on trademarks and patents) and *www.michaelgeist.ca* (which focuses primarily on copyright).